NECROPHILIA

Forensic and Medico-legal Aspects

NECROPHILIA

Forensic and Medico-legal Aspects

Anil Aggrawal

CRC Press
Taylor & Francis Group
Boca Raton London New York

CRC Press is an imprint of the
Taylor & Francis Group, an **informa** business

CRC Press
Taylor & Francis Group
6000 Broken Sound Parkway NW, Suite 300
Boca Raton, FL 33487-2742

International Standard Book Number: 978-1-4200-8912-7 (Hardback)

Library of Congress Cataloging-in-Publication Data

Aggrawal, Anil, author.
Necrophilia : forensic and medico-legal aspects / Anil Aggrawal.
p. ; cm.
Includes bibliographical references and index.
ISBN 978-1-4200-8912-7 (hardcover : alkaline paper)
1. Necrophilia. 2. Necrophilia--Law and legislation. I. Title.
[DNLM: 1. Paraphilias. 2. Forensic Medicine. WM 610]

RC560.N4A44 2011
614'.1--dc22 2010044040

Visit the Taylor & Francis Web site at
http://www.taylorandfrancis.com

and the CRC Press Web site at
http://www.crcpress.com

To my friends Bai Rufeng, Wang Yuanfeng, and Shi Meisen from the Fada Institute of Forensic Medicine and Science, Beijing, for their immense love and affection.

Table of Contents

Foreword

The first necrophile I professionally encountered was a serial sexual murderer in Chicago over 30 years ago. He would masturbate into the knife wounds of the woman he had killed. Even imagining such an act is abhorrent to most, because the largely unconscious taboo that we each carry within our internal world—one does not kill the living to sexually enjoy their corpse—becomes momentarily conscious when we read about such behavior, and engenders feelings of disgust and revulsion. It also keeps such fantasies, urges, and behaviors out of the conscious awareness of most people. But if this necrophilic act also intellectually fascinates you, welcome to the small professional circle of colleagues who are willing to journey into the darkest and arguably the most perverse of human behavior: sexual arousal to the dead.

My professional encounters with necrophiles through the ensuing years have been few and far between, but the ones I have evaluated are typically lust murderers who would fit within Dr. Aggrawal's Class IX, the Homicidal Necrophiles. The most recent case of necrophilia in which I testified to a jury, but did not examine the defendant, was a 26-year-old Oklahoma man who killed, sexually assaulted, and then partially beheaded a 10-year-old neighborhood girl. He had a detailed plan for use of her body after death. He intensified his necrophilic desires by viewing autopsy images and films on the Internet in the weeks before he carried out her abduction, and had displayed a strange and peculiar interest in *killing and tasting* people a decade earlier. I have found these individuals to be deeply disturbed and disturbing, although usually not psychotic, with multiple paraphilias other than their love of the dead. On testing, their Rorschach images are devoid of living human beings, measurably narcissistic, and convey a deep affectional hunger and sexual preoccupation. If I can set aside my own disgust—a common reaction among humans who consciously find such acts revolting, but are unconsciously drawn to necrophilic fairytales such as "Sleeping Beauty" and the currently very popular and salacious television series "True Blood," which exploits an apparent cultural hunger for the visually graphic vampiristic fusion of sex and death each week—the intellectual challenge and potential harvest are enormous. Why in God's name, or any other name, would someone actually want to have sex with the dead?

Until the publication of this remarkable book, this question has never been empirically answered, although theories abound. Etiology continues to remain elusive, even within these pages, but Dr. Aggrawal proceeds as a dispassionate scientist to unearth—I couldn't resist—both contemporary and historical cases that will amaze the reader, and also construct for the first time a classification of various kinds of necrophilia. This is the beginning step, of course, in attempting to bring typologic order to a rare naturalistic phenomenon, which hopefully then leads to further scientific investigation.

Make no mistake, this is a dark and unsettling journey. I know this book will be read by forensic psychologists, psychiatrists, pathologists, criminalists, and other forensic professionals, but it also will have an appeal to necrophiles due to its inherently lurid nature, regardless of the elegance, clarity, and scholarship that Dr. Aggawal brings to the task. I do not find this outcome appealing, but the book is purposefully devoid of necrophilic imagery, which I find reassuring.

The book instead explores in detail the epidemiology of necrophilia, ancient, historical, and contemporary case studies, the investigation of necrophilia from a psychological, medical, and forensic perspective, expert testimony concerning this rare paraphilia, and a look at the variations in legal sanctions against necrophilia in a number of countries.

Along with his previous textbook, *Forensic and Medico-legal Aspects of Sexual Crimes and Unusual Sexual Practices*, Dr. Aggrawal has once again made a very important contribution to the criminal forensic literature. Necrophilia is extreme, it is rare, and it is inexplicable to most; but until now, it has also been devoid of a systematic, scientific, and investigative textbook, diminutive in size, but large in matter.

J. Reid Meloy, Ph.D.
Clinical Professor of Psychiatry
University of California, San Diego

Preface

Necrophilia is one of the most bizarre behaviors one can think of. Thankfully it is quite uncommon. As a student of forensic psychology, I have always been interested in aberrant sexual behavior and their medico-legal aspects. This interest increased when I published *Forensic and Medico-legal Aspects of Sexual Crimes and Unusual Sexual Practices* (CRC, 2009). When I was writing this book, I realized that my chapter on necrophilia could not contain all that I had to say. The idea of a separate book on necrophilia was born then. The desire to write this book strengthened when I realized there was not even a single book that dealt with the forensic, medico-legal, and psychological aspects of necrophilia.

This book, as far as I know, is the first that deals with the scientific aspects of necrophilia from a multidisciplinary point of view. Medical, psychological, criminological, and legal standpoints have been discussed in detail. A new modern classification of necrophilia has been introduced and compared with all major existing classifications. The modern classification introduces a number of necrophilic behaviors that were previously not classified at all. This classification is based on as much empirical evidence as is currently available on this rare phenomenon. Representative necrophiles in each class and subclass have been indicated. Some classes/subclasses have been left empty, simply because no necrophile of that particular behavior has been described so far. I would like to view them much like the empty cells of Mendeleev's table, which would get filled up as more necrophiles are described in the future. It is hoped that the modern classifications will help to illustrate this bizarre phenomenon better.

Another chapter that would be of interest even to a general reader is Chapter 5, "Case Studies." Some necrophiles were not officially charged with necrophilia as a result of judicial expediency. (It was easier to prove homicide than to prove necrophilia.) In many cases, the necrophile actually denied having sex with the dead, but later admitted he had lied. The Green River Killer lied to his own lawyer, Mark Prothero, about his necrophilic acts, while he frankly admitted to police officers that he had had sex with his dead victims.*

Although laws relating to necrophilia from all major jurisdictions have been included, it is impossible to discuss all jurisdictions and many

* Prothero M, Smith C. *Defending Gary—Unraveling the Mind of the Green River Killer*, 1st ed. Jossey-Bass, California, 2006, p. 323.

readers may find laws of their own jurisdictions missing. Some laws were deliberately held back (mostly from various states of the United States) to keep the size of the book manageable. I would, however, love to hear from readers from different nations about relevant laws in their own countries as well as actual cases that have been decided based on those laws. They will all be included in the next edition of the book, with due credit and acknowledgments. Please be kind enough to respond at anil@anilaggrawal.com or anil.aggrawal@gmail.com. The author's mailing address is S-299 Greater Kailash-1, New Delhi-110048, India.

Acknowledgments

At the outset, I must express my deep gratitude to Ms. Becky McEldowney Masterman, of Taylor & Francis, who found the idea of a book on necrophilia exciting and encouraged me to go ahead with this project. She also gave me a number of valuable ideas, which I fruitfully incorporated in the book.

I am thankful to several students and colleagues in different parts of the world who spared no pains in sending me valuable material from their collections. Main among them are Venoo Kakar of the Department of Economics, University of California; Philip Lunetta from Finland; Katsuji Nishi from Japan; Ramesh Kaul from Pennsylvania; and Neeraj Gupta from New Zealand.

John Pirog from Michigan is an avid collector of material related to necrophilia, and he sent me very valuable material, much of which has found its way into this book. Many thanks to John. Shahnawaz Ibrahim made available to me many papers that I found virtually impossible to get.

I made good use of the excellent National Medical Library in New Delhi. My son Tarun and nephew Nitin, both currently in the United States, have a vast collection of papers on this subject in their collection, and they freely and ungrudgingly sent me a rare paper whenever I needed one.

Last but not least, I am thankful to my father-in-law Satya Pal Gupta ji, who helped launch my academic career in more ways than one.

Acknowledgments

Special Acknowledgment

I wish to extend a very special acknowledgment to my wife and lifelong passion, Marygold, for her patience, encouragement, understanding, and unflinching support. Needless to say, this book would never have seen the light of the day without her constant presence around me.

Author

Anil Aggrawal obtained his MD in forensic medicine and toxicology from the All India Institute of Medical Sciences, New Delhi, and then proceeded to Edinburgh—traditionally regarded as the home of forensic medicine—for higher training. He was trained further in Japan and the United States under the prestigious WHO fellowship.

Dr. Aggrawal currently teaches forensic medicine at the Maulana Azad Medical College, New Delhi, and edits a peer-reviewed Internet journal on this subject. Paraphilias, sexual crimes, and their medico-legal aspects have been his special areas of interest for the last 25 years. Earlier he wrote *Forensic and Medico-legal Aspects of Sexual Crimes and Unusual Sexual Practices* for Taylor & Francis. He lives in New Delhi with his wife and a personal library of over 20,000 books.

Necrophilia
Overview and Historical Aspects

1

Be thus when thou art dead,
And I shall kill thee,
and love thee after

—**Othello,** 5.2., 18–19

Introduction

Necrophilia, sexual gratification by having sex with the dead, is one of the weirdest, most bizarre and revolting practices of abnormal and perverse sensuality. Also known as **necrophilism, necrolagnia, necrocoitus, necrochlesis,** and **thanatophilia,** it may be seen by itself or in association with a number of other paraphilias, namely sadism, cannibalism, vampirism (the practice of drinking blood from a person or animal), necrophagia (eating the flesh of the dead), necropedophilia (sexual attraction to the corpses of children), and necrozoophilia (sexual attraction to the corpses of or killings of animals—also known as necrobestiality).[1]

The term **necrophilia** is derived from the Greek words *nekros* (corpse, dead body) and *philia* (love, friendship). Very often the corpses that are used for sexual purposes are not fresh but rather dug up from graves in a putrefied or mummified condition. Some prefer just the bones. **Necrophagists** actually feed on decaying dead bodies. (These are different from cannibals, who prefer fresh meat or who consume dead loved ones for spiritual purposes.) A vast spectrum of necrophagists is seen, from those who merely want to lick the genitals or breasts of a dead person to persons who just want to devour specific parts* to necrophiles who would eat up the whole body. Necrophilia is mostly seen in males. It is possible for a necrophile to have normal sexual relations with living beings.

The DSM-IV-TR[2] does not assign any specific or unique code to necrophilia. Instead along with several other uncommon paraphilias (seven of

* A case is known where a man merely wanted to eat the nail trimmings from a corpse. One woman, most members of whose family had died, would go into the family crypt to devour the genitals of her male relatives.

which are specifically named), necrophilia is grouped under Code 302.9 (Paraphilias Not Otherwise Specified).

Necrosadism

When seen in association with sadism, the paraphilia is termed **necrosadism.** This paraphilia involves deliberate assaults on dead bodies, subjecting them to considerable indignities and wanton mutilations. Some necrosadists may present with strange propensities. Langevin and associates[3] describe the case of one Mr. A, who murdered a woman and had intercourse with the corpse. He then removed the genitals and was contemplating eating them when he was interrupted by a third party and he ran away from the scene. He then attempted to rape and murder a second woman, but was apprehended. Upon examination, he presented as a very narcissistic individual and expressed an interest in sex reassignment surgery. He was particularly eager to have hormones so that he might grow female breasts.

Necromania is a term given to a pathological preoccupation or obsession with dead bodies.[4] The necromaniac may embalm and preserve a dead body (sometimes of a loved one) and keep it in his custody for long periods. Repeated acts of sexual intercourse may or may not be perpetrated on the body.

Necrophilia in Gravediggers and Mortuary Attendants

Gravediggers and mortuary attendants, who are the people most often found practicing necrophilia, engage in this activity perhaps because of their loneliness, coupled with easy access to corpses. It is also possible that they chose this profession in the first place because they were necrophiles. It is known that necrophiles often choose a profession that allows them free and unhindered access to dead bodies.

In ancient times, when dead bodies were transported across nations by sea for last funeral rites (as in cases of deaths of people occurring in foreign countries), sailors were often accused of necrophilia. Long transportation periods along with loneliness and lack of witnesses allowed, and even encouraged, sailors to commit acts of necrophilia with dead bodies.

In his seminal work, *Psychopathia Sexualis*, Richard von Krafft-Ebing called it a "horrible manifestation of sadism" (referring to mutilation of corpses rather than simply having sex with them).[5,6] Moll—quite rightly—objected to this view because no actual pain is caused to the corpse.[7,8] Ellis observed that infliction of pain is not necessarily a feature of necrophilia. He suggested the presence of a **strong fetishistic element** in these cases.[9]

POINT TO PONDER 1.1

During the first half of the twentieth century, the complexity and varieties of necrophilia were unknown. This is why some experts were referring to this phenomenon as a manifestation of **sadism** (referring to the mutilations caused to the dead body) and some others as having a **strong fetishistic element** (obviously referring to some cases in which portions of a dead body, such as a breast, were kept as a fetish). In actual fact, necrophilic activity—as will be seen in a later chapter—exists on a wide spectrum. **Ten classes of necrophilia,** which include both the above cases and several more, are now recognized. So obviously when Krafft-Ebing was referring to necrophilia as a "horrible manifestation of sadism," he was referring to what is now known as **class VI necrophilia** (necromutilomaniacs), and when Ellis suggested the presence of a **strong fetishistic element,** he was referring to **class V necrophiles** (fetishistic necrophiles). Both were correct in a way, and judging by the rudimentary knowledge of necrophilia that existed in those times, it was a remarkable effort on the part of both.

Early attempts at classification of necrophilia suffered from the same drawback. For instance, Hirschfeld[10] divided necrophilia into violation of a person who was already dead and sexual abuse of a person an individual had first murdered "to possess and destroy her beyond death." As is evident now, he was referring to just a few of the ten classes of necrophilia now known to exist.

Abraham A. Brill, who published one of the earliest detailed studies of necrophilia in 1941, characterized necrophiles as mentally deficient, psychotic, and incapable of obtaining a consenting partner.[11,12] Necrophilia has frequently been associated with **necrophagia** and **vampirism** (drinking blood of humans) as all are considered perversions. According to Krauss[13] necrophilia is connected with the belief in vampires in the south Slavic countries, where one occasionally finds disinterred corpses of young women and girls. The perpetrators of such acts usually violate the bodies and often mutilate the breasts.

Necrophilia may be explained—in some cases, at least—by the simple fact that the dead cannot refuse, reject, or resist; they also do not tell tales or talk back. **Necrophagia** may represent a "hangover" from our evolutionary past, where carrion eating was common.

Historical Perspectives

The term *necrophilia* seems to have been first used by the Belgian psychiatrist **Joseph Guislain** (1797–1860).[14,15,16] The passage in which Guislain coined the term *necrophilia* is found in his *Leçons Orales sur les Phrénopathies*, a lecture that was probably delivered some time during the winter of 1850:

> It is within the category of the destructive madmen [*aliénés destructeurs*] that one needs to situate certain patients to whom I would like to give the name of NECROPHILIACS [*NÉCROPHILES*]. The alienists have adopted, as a new form, the case of Sergeant Bertrand, the disinterrer of cadavers on whom all the newspapers have recently reported. However, don't think that we are dealing here with a form of phrenopathy which appears for the first time. The ancients, in speaking about lycanthropy, have cited examples to which one can more or less relate the case which has just attracted the public attention so strongly.[17]

POINT TO PONDER 1.2

A necrophile may be called the very opposite of the **legendary vampire.** While the term **vampire** generally refers to a dead person (usually referred to as the "undead") disturbing the living, the **necrophile** is a living person disturbing the dead! In this sense, a necrophile may be referred to as an **anti-vampire**.

The practice of necrophilia has a long and rich history, perhaps as old as civilization itself. Mythology abounds with instances where a queen or goddess has succeeded in getting herself impregnated by a deceased husband. The Egyptian goddess Isis was said to have conceived her son Horus after her consort Osiris had been murdered and cut to pieces—simply by using his severed member as a dildo while reciting ritual incantations.

Necrophilia in Greek Mythology

Instances of necrophilia can be seen in Greek mythology, too. One such instance is given by Parthenius of Nicaea (fl. c. first century BC), a Greek grammarian and poet and Greek tutor of the poet Virgil. His only surviving work is a collection of love stories (*Erotica Pathemata*), sourced from a variety of classical and Hellenistic Greek writers. Some are myth-themed, while others are historical or pseudohistorical tales. In this book, he mentions a curious story of Dimoetes.

Dimoetes and an Unknown Woman

Dimoetes married his brother Troezen's daughter, Euopis. Euopis, however, was besieged with love with her own brother and was even consorting with him. This enraged Dimoetes, who informed Troezen accordingly. Not able to bear the shame, Euopis hung herself, but not without having cursed her husband, who was the cause of her fate. Perhaps because of the curse, it was not long before Dimoetes came upon the dead body of a most beautiful woman thrown up by the sea, being tossed about by the waves. So beautiful was she that he immediately fell in love with her dead body and hatched a plan so he could enjoy her privately. He kept the body in his company and had sexual intercourse with her repeatedly, as long as was possible. Soon, however, the body began to decay, and became useless for intercourse. Dimoetes, who had now to give her a decent burial, built a magnificent tomb for her body. He was, however, unable to withstand the grief of losing her, whom he had come to love so much! Unable to bear the separation any longer, he committed suicide at her tomb with his sword. Curiously the grief that led to suicide in this case was not due to the loss of a living being, as is usually the case; it was the loss of a dead body that was no longer available for intercourse. Dimoetes, a true necrophile, had fallen in love with a girl whom he had never seen in life.[18,19,20]

Achilles and Penthesilea

Another famous instance of necrophilia in Greek mythology is that of **Achilles,** who had sexual intercourse with the dead body of **Penthesilea.** An Amazonian queen, Penthesilea was the daughter of Ares and Otrera. Once while hunting, she accidentally killed her sister Hippolyte, and went to Troy to seek absolution. This occurred at the time of the Trojan War, so she joined the Trojans in their fight against the Greeks. Achilles killed her in battle. However, immediately after the killing, when he removed her helmet and saw her face, he fell in love with her and had sexual intercourse with her dead body.[21] The soldier Thersites openly ridiculed Achilles and accused him of necrophilia. Achilles responded by promptly killing Thersites with a single blow.

Necrophilia in Ancient Cultures

Necrophilia was practiced in some ancient cultures as a spiritual means of communicating with the dead, while others employed it as an attempt to revive the recently departed. There is evidence that necrophilia was practiced among the Moche civilization of South America. Remains of their pottery depicts skeletal figures (presumably depicting the dead) engaged in coitus with living human beings. Androutsos and Marketos[22] have indicated that necrophilia (along with several other paraphilias) was prevalent in ancient

Egypt. Greek historian Herodotus (484–425 BC) noted that sexual interference with the dead was known and abhorred by the Egyptians. He notes,

> Wives of notable men, and women of great beauty and reputation, are not at once given to the embalmers, but only after they have been dead for three or four days; this is done to deter the embalmers from having intercourse with the women. For it is said that one was caught having intercourse with the fresh corpse of a woman, and was denounced by his fellow-workman.[23]

It has been suggested that the "curse of pharaoh's tomb" myth was deliberately created to discourage people from engaging in necrophilia. It appears that one of the reasons for burning bodies after death in some cultures (most notably Hindus) or burying them deeply or in solid granite and marble tombs was to prevent their violation by necrophiles. At one time a curious necrophilic custom prevailed in India. If a female who was engaged died before marriage, her fiancé had to deflower her before she could be cremated. This ritual had to be carried out in front of the village priest.[24]

Greco-Roman Period

Periander (625–585 BC), the second tyrant of Corinth, Greece, was a known necrophile. He learned his "savagery" from Thrasybulus, the tyrant of Miletus, who instructed Periander to get rid of anyone who could conceivably take power from him. Among his cruel acts was sending young boys from Corcyra (who were reputed to have escaped and be rescued by the Samians) to be castrated in Lydia. He also murdered his wife **Melissa** and then had sexual intercourse with her dead body. Referring to his act of necrophilia, the Greek historian Herodotus (484 BC–c. 425 BC) commented that he was "putting his loaves into a cold oven."[25] His son Lycophron discovered that Periander was the murderer, so Periander exiled him from Corinth and forbade any of his subjects to shelter him.

About the murder of Melissa, Herodotus writes,

> For after killing his own wife, Melissa, Periander suffered yet another calamity on top of what he had already suffered. He had two sons by Melissa, one 17 and one 18 years old. Their mother's father, Procles, the sovereign of Epidaurus, sent for the boys and treated them affectionately, as was natural, seeing that they were his own daughter's sons. When they left him, he said as he sent them forth, "Do you know, boys, who killed your mother?" The elder of them paid no attention to these words; but the younger, whose name was Lycophron, was struck with such horror when he heard them that when he came to Corinth he would not speak to his father, his mother's murderer, nor would he answer him when addressed nor reply to his questions. At last Periander was so angry that he drove the boy from his house.[26]

About the alleged necrophilia, he writes,

> Periander, however, understood what had been done, and perceived that Thrasybulus had counseled him to slay those of his townsmen who were outstanding in influence or ability; with that he began to deal with his citizens in an evil manner. Whatever act of slaughter or banishment Cypselus had left undone, that Periander brought to accomplishment. In a single day he stripped all the women of Corinth naked, because of his own wife Melissa. Periander had sent messengers to the Oracle of the Dead on the river Acheron in Thesprotia to enquire concerning a deposit that a friend had left, but Melissa, in an apparition, said that she would tell him nothing, nor reveal where the deposit lay, for she was cold and naked. The garments, she said, with which Periander had buried with her, had never been burnt, and were of no use to her. Then, as evidence for her husband that she spoke the truth, she added that Periander had put his loaves into a cold oven. When this message was brought back to Periander (for he had had intercourse with the dead body of Melissa and knew her token for true), immediately after the message he made a proclamation that all the Corinthian women should come out into the temple of Hera. They then came out as to a festival, wearing their most beautiful garments, and Periander set his guards there and stripped them all alike, ladies and serving-women, and heaped all the clothes in a pit, where, as he prayed to Melissa, he burnt them. When he had done this and sent a second message, the ghost of Melissa told him where the deposit of the friend had been laid. "This, then, Lacedaimonians, is the nature of tyranny, and such are its deeds. We Corinthians marveled greatly when we saw that you were sending for Hippias, and now we marvel yet more at your words to us. We entreat you earnestly in the name of the gods of Hellas not to establish tyranny in the cities, but if you do not cease from so doing and unrighteously attempt to bring Hippias back, be assured that you are proceeding without the Corinthians' consent."[27]

Death of a loved one can sometimes lead to this practice. Judaen king **Herod the Great** (c. 74–4 BC) had 10 wives, but he loved his second wife **Mariamne 1** (54–29 BC) the most. Although he had her executed on charges of adultery, so much did he love her that—according to a legend—he had her preserved in honey and had regular intercourse with her for 7 years.[28,29]

The Frankish king **Charlemagne** (742–814) is believed to have suffered from necrophilia. Many legends of the ninth century state that Charlemagne committed some "unspeakable sin," for which he was eventually pardoned directly by God without benefit of confession or priestly mediation. What that unspeakable sin was has remained largely conjectural. Most now believe that it was some kind of sexual perversion, most probably incest, but several scholars believe that it could be necrophilia.[30] **King Waldemar IV**, too, has been accused of necrophilia.[31,32]

Middle Ages

In 1533, King of England Henry VIII (1491–1547) promulgated the *Buggery Act 1533*.[33] Mainly an antisodomy law, the act also made buggery with beast punishable by hanging. Undoubted bestiality was specifically included in this act because of the widely prevalent fear in those times of hybrid births taking place consequent upon the union of man and animal. Mythical and legendary beasts such as the centaur (the body of a horse with a man's torso sprouting where the horse's head should be), satyr (an animal with the torso of a man, the legs and feet of a goat), mermaid and merman (half fish, half human), minotaur (a beast with the body of a man and the head of a bull), and manticore (a beast having the face of a man, the body of a lion, and the tail of a scorpion) were supposed to have been created out of such unions.

QUICK FACT 1.1

In the early nineteenth century, the **Catholic Church** discussed "What kind of sin it is to have carnal connection with a female corpse (*coire cum foemina mortua*)," and came to the conclusion that it should neither be considered whoring (*fornicatio*) nor bestiality, but pollution with a tendency to whoring (*Esse pollutionem et fornicationum affecitvam*).[34]

Historically, necrophilia was a frequent theme in the writings of the Marquis de Sade. Two well-known necrophiles of nineteenth century France are **Henri Blot (1860–?)** (Figure 1.1) and **Victor Ardisson (1872–?)**. On March 25, 1886, Blot exhumed and fornicated with the dead body of a

Figure 1.1 Henry Blot, a notable necrophile of the nineteenth century.

Figure 1.2 Victor Ardisson's pictures, taken at the time of his arrest.

recently buried dancer, who had died the previous day. After the sexual act, Blot lapsed into a deep sleep that was only interrupted when the cemetery's groundskeeper physically shook him awake.[35] At his trial, Blot is supposed to have commented, "Every man to his taste. Mine is for corpses."[36] He also asserted that he needed blood to live. Blot was sentenced to 2 years behind bars, but he escaped from prison and nothing further is known about him.

Victor Ardisson (Figure 1.2) was a mortician of **Le Muy,** a tiny town in France. He suffered from several other paraphilias besides necrophilia. He had a urine fetish during his younger years. He claimed to have enjoyed licking urine droplets from the toilet seats after his female classmates would use the facilities. He also insisted that episodic sexual encounters took place between him and his mother.

Victor began exhuming graves around age 19. Both prior to and after his military enlistment, he took on the job of gravedigger in his town. According to some estimates, he may have had sex with over 100 corpses, making him quite possibly history's most "busy" necrophile, at least when considering those cases that have come to light. Because he drank the blood of many corpses, he is often referred to as the **Vampire of Muy.** According to his own confessions, Victor regularly spoke to his cadaverous lovers, feeling genuine shock and hurt when they would not respond. Masters and Lea[24] (p. 117) report that Ardisson used to suck the breasts of female cadavers he exhumed and also practiced cunnilingus on them.

Once, when he was 28, the police raided his home after a tip from suspicious neighbors. They found the decaying remains of a 3-year-old girl whom Ardisson had used for oral sex. He had stolen her remains from a local graveyard sometime earlier. Until her corpse had putrefied to a dangerously contaminated state, Ardisson would perform oral sex on it with the hope that it would result in her resurrection.

Ardisson also exhumed (and retained for many years) the head of a 13-year-old girl. This girl's head served as his bedmate throughout his ownership of it, and was often referred to by him as "my little bride." He not only kissed the head from time to time, but also used it for oral sex. Von Krafft-Ebing described Ardisson as "feeble" and "devoid of all moral sense."

QUICK FACT 1.2

In an eighteenth century case, **Sir John Pryce** (c. 1698–1761) embalmed his first wife when she died and kept her in bed with him, even after he married a second time. When his second wife died, she too was embalmed and placed in the same bed. His third wife, however, wanted no part of his gruesome hobbies, and brought the facts before the world.[37]

The Legend of Jean Baptiste

While many grave robberies in the Middle Ages were connected with acquiring dead bodies for anatomical dissections, at least some were in connection with necrophilic activities. The **legend of Jean Baptiste** in nineteenth century Utah is most notable. Jean Baptiste was one of the first gravediggers ever employed in Salt Lake City in the late 1800s. He lived in a two-room house and was believed to be well off and to live comfortably. He was a quiet person and had few friends, so most people never paid much attention to him as he went about his work.

About 3 years after Baptiste came to work for the city, a man died in Salt Lake City and was buried by the gravedigger in the local cemetery. A short time later, the man's brother came to Utah from the East. He was not familiar with the Mormon religion as his brother had been, and wished to have his sibling returned to the East to be buried in the family plot. His wish was granted and the grave was uncovered. To the utter outrage of the brother, when the casket was pried open, the corpse inside was discovered to be nude and lying in the coffin face down, as though somebody had practiced sodomy on him.

Needless to say, the brother was outraged and city officials began an immediate investigation. The investigation focused on Jean Baptiste, and several men were assigned to keep him and the cemetery under surveillance. Soon after another burial, Baptiste was seen pushing a wheelbarrow from a nearby storage shed to a freshly opened grave. Authorities stopped him and found a pile of clothing hidden in the bushes. The corpse had been removed from the grave, his clothing removed, and it was now being moved from the storage shed in the wheelbarrow.

Baptiste was arrested and his home was searched. His house was filled with clothing. He had used some of it for drapes and furniture covers, and in the cellar, a large vat was placed for boiling the clothing of the dead.

The news spread and local citizens descended on the cemetery to check on their deceased loved ones. Authorities believed that he had stolen clothing and jewelry from more than 350 corpses! All of the clothing from Baptiste's home was taken to City Hall for identification by relatives. They also went to local secondhand stores, where they learned that the gravedigger had sold large amounts of stolen jewelry for cash.

Baptiste was tried and convicted of grave robbery, branded with a hot iron, and exiled to an island in the Great Salt Lake, northwest of the city. It is believed now that he may have done more than just steal clothes and jewelry from the dead bodies. He was perhaps a necrophile, as well, who used the dead bodies for his necrophilic activities.[38]

Bloch[39] describes some remarkable cases of necrophilia. In one case, a porter in a Paris morgue was arraigned in a court after being caught having intercourse with the body of a girl drowned in the Seine. The second case is more interesting. In the town of Schonau, a 30-year-old **Mrs. Maschke** was buried in the morning in a local cemetery, but the grave was not sealed. In the afternoon, a female resident visiting the cemetery observed—with considerable surprise—that Mrs. Maschke's coffin was moving. She immediately notified the caretaker, who reached the place with some local men. They were surprised to find that a poor-house inmate named Wokatsch was engaged in sexual intercourse with the dead body of Mrs. Maschke. He was immediately captured and turned over to the court in Hainspach.

Notorious French Necrophiles

Some of the most notorious cases of necrophilia have come to us from France. In 1827, a Frenchman named **Leger** mutilated the genitals of a young girl and drank her blood after necrophilia.[40] One of the most famous necrophiles was **Sergeant François Bertrand** (1824–1850), a sergeant in the French army, who during the years 1847–1849 dug up corpses from Montparnasse, a Paris cemetery, to have sex with them (Figure 1.3).

Figure 1.3 Sergeant François Bertrand, a notable necrophile of the nineteenth century.

KEY POINT 1.1

It was Bertrand's case that prompted the Belgian psychiatrist **Joseph Guislain** (1797–1860) to coin the term **necrophilia.**[17]

Widely known as the **Vampire of Montparnasse,** the sergeant showed a strange fascination with the dead early in life, when he developed a habit of dissecting dead cats and dogs (much like Jeffrey Dahmer of modern times). When he grew up, he began exhuming dead bodies to perform sexual intercourse with them. *He* also **eviscerated** and **dismembered** the bodies after intercourse. Bodies of both men and women were retrieved from graveyards. He even chewed some of the bodies, thus showing signs of necrophagia as well. (The corpses he left usually showed signs of having been gnawed upon.)

Bertrand's necrophilic impulses usually came with **headache** and palpitation of the heart. His necrophilic tendencies started unmistakably toward the end of 1846, when he first felt the desire to have sexual intercourse with human bodies. In 1847, being by accident in a graveyard, he ran across the grave of a newly buried corpse. Suddenly he got the necrophilic impulse with headache and palpitation of the heart, which became very powerful. So powerful did it become that although there were people near by, and he was in danger of detection, he started digging up the body for sexual intercourse. In the absence of a convenient instrument for cutting it up, he satisfied himself by hacking it with a shovel.

In 1847 and 1848, over the course of 2 weeks, the impulse, accompanied by violent headache, forced him to commit necrophilic intercourse about 15 times. He used to dig up the bodies with his bare hands. When he had obtained the body, he cut it up with a sword or pocket knife, tore out the entrails, and then masturbated. The sex of the bodies is said to have been a matter of indifference to him, though it was ascertained that he had dug up more female than male corpses. During these acts he declared himself to have been in an indescribable state of sexual excitement. After having cut them up, he reinterred the bodies.

In July 1848, he accidentally came across the body of a girl of 16. Then, in his own words,

> I covered it with kisses and pressed it wildly to my heart. All that one could enjoy with a living woman is nothing in comparison with the pleasure I experienced. After I had enjoyed it for about a quarter of an hour, I cut the body up, as usual, and tore out the entrails. Then I buried the cadaver again.[5] (Krafft-Ebing's case 23)

Sergeant Bertrand was eventually captured on **March 15, 1849,** as a result of being wounded by a police bullet in **Montparnasse Cemetery.**[41] Seriously wounded on his right side, he came to **Val-de-Grâce hospital,** a military hospital in Paris, for treatment. During his stay there, he not only offered no denials, but was rather unregretful of his deeds to the police investigators. He claimed he could not explain why he committed these crimes. He could only explain that he often felt compelled to exhume the recently deceased and cut into their flesh with his sword and teeth.

While still recovering from his wounds in the hospital, one of Bertrand's surgeons, the honorable **Dr. Marchal de Calvi,** obtained his full written confession, in which he stated that he had violated dozens of graves before being caught. This confession was admitted in his trial in July 1849.

Bertrand was finally convicted on 15 counts. **Dr. Lunier,** the state psychiatrist at the time, opined that the sergeant did not have all his mental faculties and should be confined and treated in a psychiatric asylum rather than be imprisoned. It was a new thought at that time. The famed McNaghten case, which had introduced the concept of insanity as a defense in criminal cases, occurred just 6 years earlier—in 1843.

Nevertheless, François Bertrand was **awarded a sentence of 1 year** and was imprisoned (the prosecution could not prove rape, as it could only be committed on live people). He proved a model prisoner, served his sentence of 1 year, and was released in 1850. He committed suicide soon afterward. Wilson[42] states that in addition to having sex with newly buried corpses, he also had mistresses who even testified to his sexual potency. **Nobus**[43] suggests that his case may not be that of a true necrophile, since what was central to his offense was **mutilation of corpses** and not sexual gratification with them. His sexual gratification was only secondary. Bertrand himself explained in a detailed response to Michéa[44] that he was principally concerned with the physical mutilation of corpses, masturbation occurring only as a secondary phenomenon in relation to his contemplation of the dismembered bodies. Bertrand—as shall be seen in Chapter 3, "Classification"—belongs to class VIIIb necrophiles. These are necrophiles who enjoy both sex with corpses and their mutilation.

Necrophilia in Wars and Battlefields

It is known that at the time of violent death, the victim suffers from **spasms of the anal sphincter.** Many potential necrophiles have sought to take advantage of this fact by engaging in anal intercourse with dying soldiers on a battlefield. Soldiers during the **Russo-Turkish War** of 1877–1878 and **Moroccan campaigns** of 1919–1926 were violated in this way on the battlefield.[24,45] The practice has been termed **warm necrophilia,** although the term is more suitably applied elsewhere. (Please see Chapter 3, "Classification.") The Chinese are known to engage in sexual intercourse with geese and to kill them intentionally at the point of ejaculation for similar reasons.[1]

During the French insurrection of 1871, many people were deported to New Caledonia as punishment. The native Kanakas were necrophiles, and when they could not get a white woman alive, they got hold of her corpse and violated it. Numerous witnesses declared that the unfortunate women and girls of the colony were first decapitated and then violated. The bodies were then erotically mutilated.[46]

Jacobus[46] mentions a specific case where a Kanaka interpreter, Louis, fell in (one-sided) love with a magnificent fair woman, the English wife of a colonist. He led the rebel Kanakas to her house while her husband and the Hebridean Kanakas were absent. The woman initially defended herself with a shotgun and killed two of her assailants. Finally Louis got the better of her and struck a heavy axe over her head, cleaving it in two halves. He then satisfied his lewd passion upon the palpitating body of his victim. Then the Kanakas dismembered her body and roasted the flesh in a Kanaka oven. Louis ate the heart, one breast, and the genital parts of the victim.

Modern Era

The *Aghoris*, a small Hindu sect in India, have been known to live in graveyards, sit on corpses, wear ash from the pyre, drink urine from skulls, use human bones from graveyards for rituals, and desecrate corpses including various acts of necrophilia. Some reputedly even eat parts of the corpse. *Aghori* means "nonterrifying" in Sanskrit, and may refer to how members of the sect view death. They are the followers of **Aghora cult.**[47]

Forced Necrophilia during "The Rape of Nanking" (1937)

During the infamous **Nanjing Massacre,** often referred to as **The Rape of Nanking,** in 1937, Japanese soldiers raped an estimated 80,000 Chinese women. Since the Japanese army had officially outlawed the rape of enemy women, Japanese soldiers found it convenient to murder Chinese women after raping them. In many cases, Chinese men were forced to commit acts of necrophilia (**forced necrophilia**) on the murdered women.[48] At least one Chinese man was murdered because he refused to commit necrophilia with the corpse of a woman in the snow.[49]

QUICK FACT 1.3

Two most notable necrophiles of modern times have been **Surendra Koli** (1970–) and **Moninder Singh Pandher** (1957–) from India, who allegedly committed several acts of necrophilia on dead bodies of young children. Their necrophilic acts came to public attention in December 2006 during Noida serial murder investigations. (Please see Chapter 5, "Case Studies," for details.)

Charles Floyd (1940s)

In 1949, **Charles Floyd,** a voyeur and a necrophile, was sentenced to life imprisonment in Texas.[50] He had a fetish for redheads. Floyd would enter homes of redheads—sometimes stalking them for months—kill them, and then have sex with the dead bodies. On July 10, 1942, he strangled the 20-year-old pregnant wife of William Brown in her Main Street apartment on Tulsa's north side. After 6 months he killed Clara Stewart and her married daughter, Georgina Green. On May 15, 1945, he bludgeoned Panta Lou Niles in her sleep, after having entered through her open bedroom window. On July 1, 1948, he broke into an apartment and clubbed its female tenant, her 12-year-old daughter, and a teenage girl who was sleeping there. He then went two blocks away and killed Ruth Norton.

In the last case, a witness came forward and offered police a description of Norton's attacker, including the piece of advice that he "looked like a truck driver." A survey of local trucking companies revealed that Charles Floyd, a driver known for his obsession with redheads, had quit his job on the morning of July 2. Police broadcast descriptions, leading to his ultimate arrest in Dallas on November 22, 1949. Floyd was able to supply detectives with substantial details of the crime known only to the killer and police. A lifelong voyeur, Floyd said that voyeurism sometimes failed to satisfy his cravings, and on those occasions he was moved to violence. Panta Niles had been a special target. She was fond of stripping down before an open window. Floyd had watched her for a period of weeks before he killed her.

All of Floyd's victims were redheads and most had been sexually violated after death. In the case of Panta Niles, he spent the entire night with the corpse, leaving after daylight. Psychiatric testing and the subject's low IQ saved Floyd from capital punishment. On confession to the string of murders and necrophilic activities, he was sent to a mental institution, where he subsequently died.

SIDEBAR 1.1 What Happened to Eva Perón's Embalmed Corpse?

Eva Perón (1919–1952), the second wife of President Juan Domingo Perón (1895–1974) and the First Lady of Argentina from 1946 until her death in 1952, was a cult figure in her country during her life. So much did her husband love her that after her death from uterine cancer on July 26, 1952, at the young age of 33, he asked Dr. Pedro Ara, a professor of anatomy, to embalm her body, so it could be preserved forever. It was decided to build a mausoleum, at the base of which the embalmed body of Eva would be kept. However, before the mausoleum could be built, a military coup occurred on September 16, 1955, forcing Perón to flee the country—without the corpse of his beloved wife.

The military dictatorship that now ruled Argentina hated the Peróns. They were also afraid that the embalmed body of Eva may become a rallying point against the regime. Colonel Moori Koenig from the military intelligence service was given the responsibility of disposing of the corpse. In order to confuse a possible future investigation into the disappearance of the corpse, Koenig, with the help of his subordinate, Arancibia, had several wax copies of the corpse made. They put them in dummy coffins and sent them to Argentine embassies in different European countries to be buried. The real corpse, it turned out, was buried in a crypt in Milan, Italy, under the name "María Maggi."

It has been alleged that Koenig fell in love with the dead body and there are subtle references to both Koenig and Arancibia sexually abusing the dead body.[51,52] Even Dr. Ara, the anatomist embalmer, has been accused of developing an intense desire for the corpse.[52] The whereabouts of the corpse remained unknown for 16 years from 1955 till 1971. In 1971, Eva's body was exhumed and flown to Spain, where Juan Perón lived with the corpse in his home. In 1973, Juan Perón came out of exile and returned to Argentina, and became president of Argentina for the third time. The embalmed body was returned to Argentina, and it now remains buried in the Duarte family tomb in La Recoleta Cemetery, Buenos Aires.

Marilyn Monroe's Case (1962)

It has been alleged that necrophilia was committed on **Marilyn Monroe's** dead body, too, after she died on August 5, 1962.[53] **Thomas Noguchi,** who performed Monroe's autopsy, found 8 mg of **chloral hydrate** in her blood and 13 mg of **pentobarbital (Nembutal)** in her liver tissue. On this basis the cause of death was given as suicidal overdose of barbiturates. However Noguchi also noted a fresh bruise spanning Monroe's lower back and hip which "might have indicated violence," but this was ignored.[53] Deputy Coroner **Lionel Grandison** signed the death certificate under protest and later resigned his position. In 1978 he disputed the suicide diagnosis, claiming his signature was "forced." He also described numerous bruises on Monroe's corpse that were not listed in Noguchi's report, suggesting a violent struggle prior to death. He claimed that one or more necrophiles employed at the county morgue had violated Monroe's corpse before it was released for burial.[53]

Jesse Timmendequas (1994)

It has been alleged by the prosecution that in the infamous 1994 Megan Kanka case, **Jesse Timmendequas** committed acts of necrophilia on 7-year-old Megan Kanka in his car, after raping and murdering her.

Chinese Case (1994)

In September 1994, Chinese police arrested a 39-year-old minivan driver from Canton, the capital of the southern province of Guangdong. He was suspected of serial necrophilia and the rape, murder, and dismemberment of 13 or 14 women since 1990. The police came to know about him by the discovery of parts of dismembered corpses in rubbish bins. All victims were prostitutes. They had been raped, murdered, and cut up. Some parts had been kept, preserved in antiseptic, "so that he could continue to use them during his fantasies." He was arrested after a prostitute from the northwestern region of Xinjiang recovered consciousness after an assault, escaped, and went to the police. There was no doubt regarding his necrophilic activities, as the police confiscated video recordings of the acts of rape, murder, and necrophilia, and a diary listing the personal details of those killed. They also found mannequins to which the skin and sexual organs of some of the victims had been glued. The suspect's wife had left him several years before he was caught because of his cruelty.[54]

Necrophilia in Folklore, Myths, and Legends

The most common folklore involving a definite necrophilic fantasy is the "Sleeping Beauty" myth, in which the corpse of a young woman is returned to life by sexual contact with Prince Charming.[31,55]

Necrophilia in the Arts and Literature

There are innumerable references to necrophilia in arts and literature, but perhaps the most notable is Hamlet's jump into Ophelia's grave at her funeral. Many interpret it as a subtle act of necrophilia.[56] His use of Yorick's skull as a *mememto mori* has also been interpreted as representing his love of necrophilia[57,58] (Figure 1.4).

In the early seventeenth century, the Jacobean theater saw plays like *The Revenger's Tragedy,* which is replete with necrophilic desire.[59,60] The play

Figure 1.4 Hamlet with Yorick's skull. This act as well as his jumping into Ophelia's grave has been taken by many as his love of necrophilia.

could quite possibly be a representation of debates between Catholicism and Protestantism, where the former defended the role of dead bodies in the form of relics and bones and the latter rejected it.[57]

In 1930, the Nobel Prize–winning American author **William Faulkner** (1897–1962) wrote *A Rose for Emily*, which has strong necrophilic overtones. The main character of the story, **Miss Emily Grierson,** kills her lover, **Homer Barron,** with arsenic, and then keeps his dead body in her room for months. When Emily dies and townspeople enter her house, they discover Homer's remains on her bed, dressed in a nightshirt.

Necrophilia in Animals

Sometimes peculiar human behaviors can be understood better by studying similar behaviors in other species. Curiously necrophilia is seen in the animal world, too. Male cane toads (*Bufo marinus*) have been documented engaging in copulation with dead toads and even inanimate objects.[61] Heterosexual necrophilia has been known in the drake mallard (*Anas platyrhynchos*).[62] Kees Moeliker of the Rotterdam Natural History Museum, The Netherlands, has described a curious case of homosexual necrophilia among drake mallards, in which a male drake engaged in copulation with a dead male drake for almost 75 minutes, with two short breaks in between.[63]

QUICK FACT 1.4 MAJOR INSTANCES OF NECROPHILIA IN THE ARTS AND LITERATURE

- Hamlet's jump into Ophelia's grave (*The Tragedy of Hamlet, Prince of Denmark* [1599–1601] by William Shakespeare).
- The lecherous Duke poisons Gloriana and then kisses her skull (*The Revenger's Tragedy* [1608] by Cyril Tourneur).
- Simone, a female necrophile, seduces Don Aminado, a young Catholic priest, and strangles him to death during his final orgasm. Her colleague, Sir Edmund, eviscerates one of the dead priest's eyes and Simone inserts it within her vagina (*Histoire de l'oeil* [Story of the Eye, 1928] by Georges Bataille).
- Emily Grierson keeps the dead body of her lover for years in her bedroom (*A Rose for Emily* [1930] by William Faulkner).
- Lester Ballard finds a dead couple in a car and carries the female corpse back to his cabin to engage in sexual acts with it. After losing her corpse in a fire, he begins murdering women to create dead female sex partners for himself (*Child of God* [1973] by Cormac McCarthy).

Variations of Necrophilia

Some variations on the theme of necrophilia are **autonecrophilia** (imagining oneself as a corpse or becoming sexually aroused by simulated corpses) and **pseudonecrophilia.** The term *pseudonecrophilia* has been used differently by different authors. Some authors take it to mean arousal from having sex with someone pretending to be dead,[64] while others use the term to describe erotic fantasies of a person to have sexual relations with a dead body and masturbation (but not actual contact).[65,66,67] Still others use it to refer to a person who has a transient attraction to a corpse, but corpses are not the main object of his sexual fantasies.[55] According to the latter definition, the preferable sexual contact in pseudonecrophiles remains a living person. Because of the multitude of meanings the term *pseudonecrophilia* has come to acquire, it is preferable to do away with this term entirely.[68] This classification is discussed in detail in Chapter 3, "Classification."

References

1. Aggrawal A. *Forensic and Medico-legal Aspects of Sexual Crimes and Unusual Sexual Practices.* CRC Press, Boca Raton, FL, 2008.
2. American Psychiatric Association. *Diagnostic and Statistical Manual of Mental Disorders*, 4th ed. Text rev. American Psychiatric Association, Washington DC, 2000.
3. Langevin R, Bain J, Wortzman G, Hucker S, Dickey R, Wright P. Sexual sadism: brain, blood, and behavior. *Ann N Y Acad Sci.* 1988;**528**:163–171.
4. Rajs J, Lundström M, Broberg M, Lidberg L, Lindquist O. Criminal mutilation of the human body in Sweden—a thirty-year medico-legal and forensic psychiatric study. *J Forensic Sci.* 1998 May;**43(3)**:563–580 at p. 564.
5. Krafft-Ebing RF. *Psychopathia Sexualis*, 1st ed. F.A. Davis, Philadelphia, 1886 [reprinted by Bloat Books, 1999].
6. Necrophilia, in *Encyclopedia of Death and Dying.* Available from http://www.deathreference.com/Me-Nu/Necrophilia.html
7. Moll A. *Handbuch Der Sexualwissenschaften.* Vogel, Leipzig, 1921.
8. Klaf FS, Brown W. Necrophilia, Brief review and case report. *Psychiatric Q.* 1958;**32(4)**:645–652.
9. Ellis H. *Studies in the Psychology of Sex* (Vol. 1). Random House, New York, 1936.
10. Hirschfeld M. *Sexual Anomalies.* Emerson, New York, 1956, p. 425.
11. Brill AA. Necrophilia—Part I. *J. Criminal Psychopathol.* 1941;**2(4)**:433–443.
12. Brill AA. Necrophilia—Part II. *J. Criminal Psychopathol.* 1941;**3**:51–73.
13. Krauss FS. *Anthropophyteia; Jahrbücher für Folkloristische Erhebungen*, Bd. II, 10 vols. Deutsche Verlagsactiengesellschaft, Leipzig, 1905, p. 381.
14. Monneret E. Traité de pathologie générale, Tôme troisième: Séméiologie—pronostic—étiologie. Béchet Jeune, Paris, 1861.
15. Nobus D. Over my dead body: on the histories and cultures of necrophilia, in *Inappropriate Relationships—The Unconventional, the Disapproved, and the Forbidden*, 1st ed. Eds., R Goodwin, D Cramer. Lawrence Erlbaum Associates, Inc., Mahwah, NJ, 2002, pp. 171–189.

16. Dubasi PM, Fosseus CG. A case of necrophilia in Medunsa. *Am J Forensic Med Pathol.* 1995 Jun;**16(2)**:162–163.
17. Guislain, J. *Leçons Orales sur les Phrénopathies, ou Traité théorique et pratique des maladies mentales. Cours donné à la clinique des établissements d'aliénés à Gand.* L. Hebbelynck, Gand, Belgium, 1852, p. 257.
18. Parthenius Longus. *Daphnis and Chloe. Love Romances and Poetical Fragments. Fragments of the Ninus Romance.* Trans. G Thornley, JM Edmonds, S Gaselee. Loeb Classical Library Volume 69. Harvard University Press, Cambridge, MA, 1916.
19. Grimal P. *The Dictionary of Classical Mythology*. Blackwell Publishing Limited, Malden, MA, 1996.
20. Hood JX. *Scientific Curiosities of Love-Sex and Marriage: A Survey of Sex Relations, Beliefs and Customs of Mankind in Different Countries and Ages.* Waverly Books, 1951, p. 24.
21. Graves R. *Greek Myths*, 2nd ed. Cassell, London, 1958, p. 675.
22. Androutsos G, Marketos S. [Sexuality in Ancient Egypt][Article in French]. *Prog Urol.* 1994 Oct;**4(5)**:715–725.
23. Herodotus. *The Histories.* Trans. A de Selincourt. Penguin, Harmondsworth, UK, 1972, p. 161.
24. Masters REL, Lea AEE. *Perverse Crimes in History: Evolving Concepts of Sadism, Lust-Murder, and Necrophilia—From Ancient to Modern Times.* The Julian Press, New York, 1963.
25. Gilman SL, King H, Porter R, Rousseau GS, and Showalter E. *Hysteria Beyond Freud.* University of California Press, Berkeley, 1993, p. 31.
26. Herodotus. *The Histories.* Ed. AD Godley. Harvard University Press, Cambridge, 1920, pp. 3.50.1–3.52.4.
27. Herodotus. *The Histories.* Ed. AD Godley. Harvard University Press, Cambridge, 1920, p. 5.92g.1–4.
28. von Huber H. Nekrophilie. *Kriminalistik.* 1962;16,564.
29. *Herod the Great: The True Story*. Available from http://www.tvthrong.co.uk/documentary/the-true-story-of-herod-the-great-tuesday-april-17
30. Hafner S. Charlemagne's unspeakable sin. *Modern Language Studies.* 2002;**32(2)**:1–14.
31. Jones E. *On the Nightmare.* International Psychoanalytic Library, No. 20. Hogarth, London, 1931, p. 111.
32. Jaffé PD, Necrophilia: love at last sight, in *Psychology and Criminal Justice: International Review of Theory and Practice* (Publications of the European Association of Psychology and Law). Eds., J Boros, I Münnich, M Szegedi. Walter de Gruyter, Berlin, 1998, pp. 242–247.
33. The Buggery Act 1533 (25 Hen. VIII c. 6).
34. de Ligorio DA, Theologia Moralis—Illustrissimi Ac Reverendissimi. È Prelo Janssens et Van Merlen, in *Platea Coriariorum*, Antverpiae, 1821.
35. *Sexual Sadism: Rape, Necrophilia, Cannibalism, Fetishism*. Available from http://faculty.ncwc.edu/TOConnor/428/428lect13.htm
36. Available at http://dahmerdame.livejournal.com/505.html
37. Hamilton D. *Best Tea Shop Walks in Mid Wales*. Sigma Leisure, UK, 2003, p. 21.
38. Taylor T. *The Ghost of the Great Salt Lake—Or, The Legend of John Baptiste, Salt Lake City, Utah.* 2003. Available from http://www.prairieghosts.com/baptiste.html

39. Bloch I. *Anthropological and Ethnological Studies in the Strangest Sex Acts in Modes of Love of All Races, Illustrated: Oriental, Occidental, Savage, Civilized*, Privately issued. Falstaff Press, New York, 1935.
40. Persaud R. Blood-lust in the clinic. *The Independent (London)*. February 2, 1993, Tuesday.
41. Dansel M. *Le Sergent Bertrand: Portrait d'un nécrophile heureux*. Albin Michel, Paris, 1991.
42. Wilson C. *A Criminal History of Mankind*, 1st ed. Granada, London, 1984.
43. Nobus D. Over my dead body: on the histories and cultures of necrophilia, in *Inappropriate Relationships: The Unconventional, the Disapproved, and the Forbidden*. Eds., R Goodwin, D Cramer. Lawrence Erlbaum Associates, Inc., Mahwah, NJ, 2002, pp. 171–189.
44. Michéa CF. Des déviations maladives de l'appétit vénérien. *Bulletin de l'Union Médicale*. 1849;**3**:338–339.
45. Ollier E. *Cassell's Illustrated History of the Russo-Turkish War*. Cassell & Company Ltd., London, 1878.
46. Dr. Jacobus, French Army surgeon, in *The Abuses, Aberrations, and Crimes of the Genital Sense*. Charles Carrington, Paris, 1900.
47. Newton M. *The Encyclopedia of Conspiracies and Conspiracy Theories*, 1st ed. Facts on File, New York, 2006, p. 4.
48. Smith MD. *Encyclopedia of Rape*. Greenwood Press, Westport, CT, 2004, p. 195.
49. Chang I. *The Rape of Nanking: The Forgotten Holocaust of World War II*. Penguin, New York, 1998.
50. Wilson C. *Origins of the Sexual Impulse*. Maurice Bassett Publishing, Richmond, CA, 2004.
51. Martínez TE. *Santa Evita*, 1st ed. Knopf, New York, 1996.
52. Davies LH. Portraits of a lady: postmodern readings of Tomás Eloy Martínez's "Santa Evita." *Modern Language Rev*. 2000 Apr;**95(2)**:415–423.
53. Newton M. *The Encyclopedia of Unsolved Crimes*, 2nd ed. Facts on File, New York, 2009, p. 249.
54. Long S. Chinese Police Hold Man for Serial Necrophilia. *The Guardian (London)*. January 5, 1995.
55. Rosman JP, Resnick PJ. Sexual attraction to corpses: a psychiatric review of necrophilia. *Bull Am Acad Psychiatry and the Law*. 1989;**17(2)**:153–163.
56. Shainess N. Hamlet—the coup that failed. *J Am. Acad Psychoanal*. 1975; **3**:383–403.
57. Howarth G, Leaman O (Eds.). *Encyclopedia of Death and Dying*. Routledge, London, 2001, p. 326.
58. Holderness G. "I covet your skull": Death and Desire in Hamlet, in *Shakespeare Survey Volume 60: Theatres for Shakespeare*. Ed. P Holland. Cambridge University Press, Cambridge, 2007.
59. Stallybrass P. Reading the body: *The Revenger's Tragedy* and the Jacobean theater of consumption. *Renaissance Drama*. 1987;**18**:129–132.
60. Coddon KS. "For show or useless property": necrophilia and *The Revenger's Tragedy*. *ELH*. 1994;**61(1)**:71–88.
61. Lewis M. (Director). *Cane Toads: An Unnatural History* (DVD-Video, NTSC, Color, running time, 65 minutes). Studio: First Run Features, New York, 2001.

62. Bagemihl B. *Biological Exuberance, Animal Homosexuality and Natural Diversity*. Profile Books, London, 1999.
63. Moeliker CW. The first case of homosexual necrophilia in the mallard *Anas platyrhynchos* (Aves: Anatidae). *Deinsea*. 2001;**8**:243–247.
64. Shaffer L, Penn J. A comprehensive paraphilia classification system, in *Sex Crimes and Paraphilia*, 1st ed. Ed. EW Hicky. Pearson Prentice Hall, Old Tappan, NJ, 2006, Chapter 8, p. 87.
65. Segal H. A necrophilic fantasy. *Int J Psychoanal*. 1953;**34**:98–101.
66. Rauch HJ. Über Nekrophilie. *Arch. Psychiat. Nervenkr*. 1947;**179**:54.
67. Lazarus AA. A case of pseudonecrophilia treated by behavior therapy. *J Clin Psychol*. 1968 Jan;**24(1)**:113–115.
68. Aggrawal A. A new classification of necrophilia. *J Forensic Leg Med*. 2009;**16(6)**:316–320.

Etiology

2

The etiology of necrophilia is not clear. One difficulty is the existence of a vast spectrum of necrophiles—from role players (Class I necrophiles) to those who can have sex *only* with the dead (Class X necrophiles). Obviously, a single definition cannot explain the behavior of all. **Etiological theories** of necrophilia can broadly be divided in two groups: **biological** and **psychoanalytical.**[1] A number of other etiological theories can all be grouped under the **miscellaneous category.** The following account discusses *all* etiological theories of necrophilia that have been proposed so far. Many of these are obviously quite dated but have been included so that the reader can critically examine each etiological theory that has been proposed so far.

Biological Theories

Genetic Basis

A **genetic basis of necrophilia** has been proposed by many authors,[2,3] without any real empirical evidence.

POINT TO PONDER 2.1

Although a **genetic basis of necrophilia** has been proposed, there is no real empirical basis behind it. No gene related to necrophilia has ever been identified. This is a potential area for future research in necrophilia.

Havelock Ellis[4] cites a case of necrophilia that he ascribes to a **congenital defect.** This case, originally described by **Belletrud** and **Mercier,**[5] describes a young man who, when assisting the gravedigger, conceived and carried out the idea of digging up the bodies of young girls to satisfy his passions with. When asked why he did this, he replied,

> I could find no young girl who would agree to yield to my desires; that is why I have done this. I should have preferred to have relations with living persons. I found it quite natural to do what I did: I saw no harm in it, and I did not think that anyone else could. As living women felt nothing but repulsion for me, it was quite natural I should turn to the dead, who have never repulsed me. I used to say tender things to them like "my beautiful, my love, I love you."

After having cited this case, Ellis remarks thus:

> But when so highly abnormal an act is felt as natural we are dealing with a person who is congenitally defective so far as the finer developments of intelligence are concerned. It was so in this case of necrophily; he was the son of a weak-minded woman of unrestrainable sexual inclinations, and was himself somewhat feebleminded; he was also, it is instructive to observe, anosmic.

The last sentence is interesting in that Ellis tries to link anosmia (inability to perceive odors) with necrophilia. There has been much speculation on the relationship between the **power of smell** and necrophilia. While **Moll**[6] thought that **some necrophiles suffer from anosmia,** Bloch on the contrary thought that stench played a large part in this paraphilia.[7]

In general, sense of smell is thought to have a strong relationship with the sexuality exhibited by human beings. **Brill**[7] mentions that the sense of smell in animals exercises the strongest attraction, particularly during the mating season. Proponents of the anosmic theory of necrophilia stress that an abnormality in perceiving smells and in expression of sexuality coexists because of a strong relationship between smells and sexuality in general.

Tsheryaskin[8] cites the role of constitution (in addition to environmental factors) in the development of necrophilia. The word *constitution* suggests that he points toward a genetic basis. He cites the case of a 19-year-old young female necrophile who was emotionally unstable and very impulsive. She always showed marked **abulia** (lack of will and initiative). Tsheryaskin thought that she became a necrophile because of her psychopathic constitution, aggravated by her harsh external environment.

Brill[7] mentions the case of a homosexual necrophile whom he calls **D.** Brill does not discuss etiological factors explicitly, but ascribes at least three different factors at different parts of his paper, that in his opinion may have contributed to D's necrophilia. (Please see Chapter 3, "Classification," under the heading "Class IV Necrophiles," for details of this case.) First he blames **heredity.** Brill writes,

> D was distinctly burdened by heredity from both the paternal and maternal sides of his family. His mother was very "nervous" and his father, though quite aggressive, was a ne'er do well of the typical "poor Southern white" variety (p. 440).[7]

Brill goes on to assert additionally that D's necrophilia represented a byproduct of his executively weak sexual constitution (p. 441). It is not clear what he means by this, but perhaps he is referring to his explicit effeminate behavior. Finally Brill mentions that his necrophilia could also be due to **oral fixation.**

Trauma

Head injury with resulting **concussion** may be a possible cause. Price[9] mentions a case of necrophilia in which the culprit—a necrophile who he refers to simply as **M**—revealed that 2 years before his necrophilic act he had been involved in a motorcycle accident. This had resulted in head injury and concussion. This may or may not have been a causative factor in his necrophilic tendencies. Certainly there are a number of similar accidents that do not result in necrophilic tendencies.

In 1983, during the trial of notorious Hong Kong necrophile **Lam Kor-wan** (1955–), sometimes referred to as the **Hong Kong Butcher,** Lam's mother, **Mrs. Lam Cheung Kim-ping,** testified that her husband (Lam's father) used to severely beat Lam when he was a child. She said that when he was about 2 years old he was slapped by his father so hard that his head banged against the wall, resulting in two black eyes and one side of his face turning red.[10]

No single etiological factor seems to account for the necrophilic behavior of **John Reginald Halliday Christie** (1898–1953). However, Christie did suffer **major head trauma** in 1934. (His necrophilic activities started from August 1943 and lasted until March 1953, when he was caught.) In that year, he was knocked down by a car that did not stop. In this collision he sustained major injuries to the head, the knee, and the collarbone.[11]

Joseph Vacher (1869–1898) started showing necrophilic tendencies after he shot himself in the head but survived. One of the bullets remained lodged in his skull. (For details of his case, please see Chapter 3, "Classification," under the heading "Class IX Necrophiles.")

Sexual Inadequacy

Sexual inadequacy may cause the necrophile to turn his attention to corpses. Some necrophiles are known to be **impotent to live women**—perhaps due to **anxiety** or some other **deep-seated psychological disorder**—but they are perfectly healthy otherwise. They are able to achieve erection and perform sexual intercourse with corpses because the fear or anxiety factor (to be able to perform or not) is not present. There is no one to chide them over their possible nonperformance. They are also able to masturbate and ejaculate. It is only in the presence of live women that they cannot perform.

Rapoport[12] describes the case of a 50-year-old necrophile, W.R. (1890–?), who had unfounded fears about his sexuality. He was adopted at the age of 4 from an orphanage, where he was placed from birth. His mother was unmarried; nothing was known of his father. In 1911 (at the age of 21), he had an appendectomy. In 1912 a hydrocele developed on the left side. W.R. became quite concerned because of this and thought that this was caused by "poison from the appendix." The fluid was removed by a tap, which left a small scar on the left underside of the scrotum. W.R. always referred to this scar as "rupture," asserting that this was from "where they let out the poison." After this operation, he was always doubtful about his sexual adequacy with live females. He did, however, enjoy kissing female dead bodies and touching their breasts. When asked why he did not attempt something similar (touching breasts) with a live woman, he replied, "I'd be afraid. A live woman would not let me do it." (For details of this case, please see Chapter 3, "Classification," under the heading "Class IV Necrophiles.")

He never tried to engage in sexual intercourse with live females. When asked why this was so, he replied,

> Never had money; never bothered; I was afraid. I had a little trouble with the testicle; they got poisoned from an operation. I was frightened to have relations after that. I had to get operation on them shortly after the operation (i.e., appendectomy). They made a hole and drained it out. I imagined it would be dangerous to go around with a woman. I felt I wasn't the way I ought to be on account of having that trouble. I felt I couldn't have relations. I'm not sure whether I could do it now or not.

It appears that his "imagined fears" about his sexual inadequacy were not the sole cause of his necrophilia. He did feel "inadequate" even before the operation, and began using this excuse only after his operation. He used other excuses for periods preceding his operation. When asked why he never went out with girls even prior to his operation, he answered—quite unconvincingly—"Folks would never let me." When pressed and asked why he did not attempt intercourse despite his feelings, he answered, "Afraid—afraid woman (sic) would find out about the testicle." When asked what was wrong with him sexually, his answer was, "Only the testicle."

W.R. was also afraid that having intercourse might result in further injury to his testis, and he might even injure his partner. He replied—rather incoherently—to a related question,

> Intercourse might cause the testicle to swell up—fill up with more water. It might have to be tapped again. Rupture (operative scar on scrotum) might prevent penis from going in too far. I wouldn't want it to go too far either. The fluid might not go in the right place. I don't think penis could go in because of the testicles. I couldn't satisfy her. I might get too rough. I'm quick-tempered. I might go too quick. It might hurt her. I might injure her insides. It might interfere with her having children.

W.R. was so sure of his sexual inadequacy that he thought he could not have a child. When asked if he wanted to have a child, he replied, "No, I couldn't; having trouble below there." When asked which is the ugliest part of his body, he replied, "where the testicles are."

Andrei Chikatilo (1936–1994) suffered from chronic impotence, worsening his social awkwardness and self-hatred. In 1963, he married a woman to whom he was introduced by his younger sister. The couple had a son and daughter. Chikatilo later claimed that his marital sex life was minimal and that he would ejaculate on his wife and push the semen inside her vagina with his fingers.

John Christie was so inadequate sexually that in his teens he was derided among his friends as "*Reggie no dick*," "*Reggie no prick*,"[13] and "*Can't do it Christie*." When he was in his teens, a girl picked him up as a friend, but realized after some intense and torrid petting that she could not arouse him. She ultimately parted ways with him, saying annoyingly to him, "You are no good to me." It is believed that it was she who told friends that Christie was impotent, and that is how his nicknames came about.

Christie married a good-looking Yorkshire girl, **Ethel Simpson Waddington,** in 1920, but the couple had no children. The marriage broke up after 3 years. Christie claimed he had no sexual relations with his wife for about 2 years, which—quite possibly true—supports the view that he could not have sexual intercourse with live women. Most of the women whose dead bodies were found in Christie's flat at 10 Rillington Place, London, were prostitutes, and semen was found in their vaginal canals. The fact that Christie needed to kill prostitutes in order to have sexual intercourse with them—a service they are meant to provide—strongly indicated he was impotent with live women and needed to kill them in order to have sexual intercourse. To kill them effectively without any mutilation (possibly so that their beauty could be preserved after death), he had invented an ingenious death jar. (Please see Sidebar 2.1.) After they were dead, Christie masturbated standing over their bodies—semen was found in the seams of his shoes, as well as on his clothes—and also violated their dead bodies—semen was found in the vaginal canal of most victims.[11]

SIDEBAR 2.1 The Death Jar of John Christie

Christie had invented an ingenious death jar with which he used to kill women and prostitutes he used to lure home. He took an ordinary square jar with two holes bored through the screw-top lid. The jar was filled with **Friar's Balsam,** a tincture having a strong smell. Two rubber tubes were passed through the holes—one through each hole. From one rubber tube, he would allow a jet of domestic gas (domestic gas in the 1940s in Britain was coal gas, having a carbon monoxide content of 15%) to enter inside the jar. The gas would emanate through the other tube, its smell having been masked by the strong smell of Friar's Balsam. Christie would then ask his gullible victims to smell the gas to cure their nasal catarrh. Some refused, but those who agreed did not know they were breathing their last. After they died, Christie would engage in necrophilic acts with their dead bodies.

Alcoholism

Many necrophiles have been known alcoholics. **Jeffrey Dahmer** (1960–1994) began drinking in his teens and was an alcoholic by the time of his high school graduation. He would often consume several beers before going to school, and friends frequently observed him swigging gin at his locker. In January 1979, he had to drop out of Ohio State University after only one term, due to alcoholism. His father suggested that he enlist in the Army. He joined the military service in January 1979 and was posted in Germany but his drinking problem persisted, which led to his discharge in March 1981. Later in the same year (1981), he was arrested for drunkenness and disorderly conduct. He tended to become belligerent while drinking alcohol, and his homicidal behavior usually took place in the context of alcohol use.[14] His stepmother, Shari Dahmer, said he was a gentle person until he got drunk, and when he was drunk it took four policemen to hold him down. When he was finally arrested on July 22, 1991, he was found to be intoxicated with alcohol. He had attempted the murder of an African-American male, Tracy Edwards, who had been able to escape and call the police.

It is noteworthy that in literature certain instances of "necrophilic rampages" have been described following **heavy alcohol intoxication.**[15,16,17,18] In August 1988, **Eli Ulayuk** (1968–), an Inuit from Igloolik, a small community in Nunavut, **Northern Canada,** killed a 23-year-old female in order to have sexual intercourse with her dead body. He confessed that he got the necrophilic urge after having consumed "home brew." (Please see Chapter 5, "Case Studies," for details.)

Drugs

Some instances of **drug use along with necrophilia** have been noticed. **Eli Ulayuk** killed twice to have sexual intercourse with the dead bodies of his victims. The first time (August 1988) he was under the influence of alcohol. He was sentenced to life imprisonment in 1992 but was released on parole in June 2004. Just 4 months after his release, on **October 6, 2004,** he killed his parole officer, **Louise Pargeter,** and had sexual intercourse with her dead body. This time he had used **crack cocaine** before the offense, and he confessed as much to the police.[19] Association of cocaine with criminal activities is well known.[20,21,22] However, this is the first time the association of cocaine with necrophilia has been reported.

Meloy[18] describes the case of a 26-year-old African-American male who killed his wife and then had sex with her dead body. (For details of this case, please see Chapter 3, "Classification.") It turned out that from early adolescence he had started using a variety of drugs including cocaine, alcohol, opiates, sedative-hypnotics, amphetamine, cannabis, hallucinogens, and phencyclidine.

Temporal Lobe Anomalies

Fugue states or severe headaches prior to or after overt necrophilic behavior have also been reported. Coupled with the fact that alcohol (one of the factors often associated with necrophilia) can induce temporal lobe abnormalities,[23] and that temporal lobe abnormalities are associated with a number of other paraphilias, it may be reasonable to deduce that **temporal lobe anomalies** may be responsible for some instances of necrophilia.

Harsh Treatment, Excessive Criticism, and Neglect during Childhood

There are reports of some cases that would make one believe that harsh treatment, excessive criticism, and so on of the patient during childhood may play a part in the patient eventually turning into a necrophile. One of the earliest cases stressing this etiological theory has been described by **Tsheryaskin.**[8] The case concerns a 19-year-old female, **TP,** who turned into a necrophile, presumably because she had been treated very harshly by her father during childhood. (For details of this case, please see Chapter 3, "Classification," under the heading "Class V Necrophiles.") Tsheryaskin traced the origin of the patient's necrophilic tendencies to her environment. She was reared in an environment of continuous friction and fights between her parents. Her father (a psychotic) was distinctly sadistic and took pleasure in maltreating animals and his family. Tsheryaskin was of the view that her necrophilia started from a particular experience. One morning her father suddenly awakened her and beat her mercilessly with a heavy rope. In confirmation of his theory, Tsheryaskin quotes Freud to the effect that anxiety plus mechanical irritation may produce a deep disturbance of the sexual mechanisms. Tsheryaskin also cites the role of constitution in the development of her necrophilia. (Please see the previous section titled "Genetic Basis.")

Klaf and **Brown**[24] report the case of a 40-year-old black male necrophile who had a very harsh family environment. (For details of this case, please see Chapter 3, "Classification," under the heading "Class IV Necrophiles.") Everybody around him—except his mother—treated him very harshly. They were harsh and critical of him. The authors speculate that ultimately their patient found solace in the dead, who never complained and who were never critical. He found that a "dead person who loves will love forever and will never be weary of giving and receiving caresses."

Sexual Abuse during Childhood

It is possible that sexual abuse during childhood may cause the victim to turn into a necrophile. **Bartholomew** and colleagues[25] describe the case of a 47-year-old single white male necrophile. His schooling was not happy. As a teenager he had been homosexually assaulted. Other etiological factors might have contributed also. He used to consume alcohol in great quantities and when under the influence of alcohol, his sexual drives became very intense. He was a known homosexual and had been convicted thrice for sodomy and once for indecent assault. His paraphilic tendencies culminated in him killing a 9-year-old boy and committing anal intercourse on his dead body. (For details of this case, please see Chapter 3, "Classification," under the heading "Anal Necrophilia.")

Erich Fromm's Theory of Personality

As mentioned previously, **Erich Fromm** (1900–1980) suggested a genetic basis of necrophilia. However, he also viewed necrophilia as a personality disorder. According to him, psychologically disturbed people are incapable of love and have failed to establish union with others. He discussed three severe personality disorders: necrophilia, malignant narcissism, and incestuous symbiosis.[26]

Fromm used necrophilia in a more generalized sense.[27,2] For him necrophilia meant any attraction to death. Normally people love life (**biophilia**), but when social conditions stunt biophilia, they may adopt a necrophilic orientation. Necrophilic persons hate humanity. They are bullies, warmongers, and racists. They prefer night to day and prefer to operate in shadow and darkness. They love terror, torture, bloodshed, and destruction. In general they delight in destroying life. They love to discuss sickness, death, and burials and are fascinated by dirt, decay, corpses, and feces. Fromm stressed that all people may behave aggressively and destructively at times, but in the case of necrophiles, their entire lifestyle revolves around death, destruction, disease, and decay.

The other two personality disorders are **malignant narcissism** and **incestuous symbiosis.** Those suffering from malignant narcissism take pleasure in destroying those they regard as inferiors. Healthy people display a **benign form of narcissism**; that is, everyone loves his own body. In case of malignant narcissism, however, the person becomes so deviant that everything belonging to him is viewed as highly valued and everything belonging to another is devalued and must be destroyed.

A third pathological orientation is **incestuous symbiosis.** These individuals possess a neurotic symbiotic relationship with their mother or mother

Table 2.1 Characteristics of Normal Individuals Contrasted with Those of Deviant Individuals

Normal Individual	Deviant Individual
Biophilia	Necrophilia
Love of others	Narcissism
Positive freedom	Incestuous freedom

substitute. They have an extreme dependence on the mother or mother surrogate. Incestuous symbiosis is viewed as an exaggerated form of the more common and more benign **mother fixation.**

All three pathological orientations have their healthy counterpart. Necrophilia is contrasted with biophilia (love of life) in healthy individuals, narcissism with love of others, and incestuous symbiosis with positive freedom (Table 2.1).

Every individual has traits that can be located somewhere on each scale (Figure 2.1). Pathologic individuals may have more deviant traits on each one. If they are maximally deviant, they are said to suffer from **syndrome of decay.** These pathological people are contrasted by normal individuals

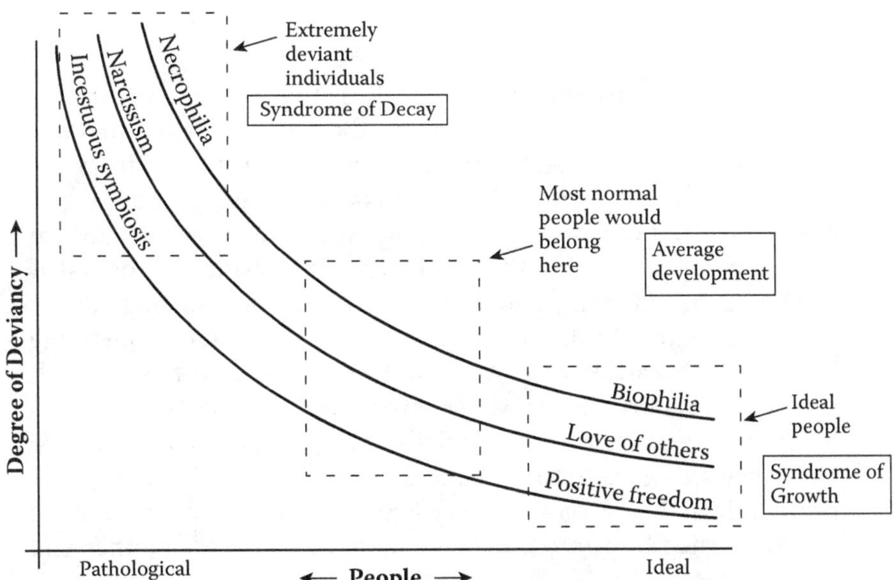

Figure 2.1 Erich Fromm's three pathological orientations. Excessive traits of necrophilia, narcissism, and incestuous symbiosis make an individual suffer from syndrome of decay. The opposite qualities result in syndrome of growth. Most individuals would fall somewhere in between.

who have all positive qualities. An ideal individual is marked by the **syndrome of growth,** where he has a maximal good trait on each scale. Fromm stressed that both the syndrome of decay and the syndrome of growth are extreme forms of development. Most people have traits midway between the two extremes. Their traits can in fact be located on a graph. As can be seen, most people have average psychological health. Fromm insisted that on this scale, **Adolf Hitler** is the best example of a person suffering from the **syndrome of decay.**

It may be an interesting exercise to locate each necrophile on these scales. **Ed Gein,** for instance, seems to have maximal deviant traits on the *incestuous symbiosis-positive freedom* scale—he was pathologically attached to his mother—and on the *necrophilia-biophilia* scale. (For more on Gein, please see Chapter 5, "Case Studies.")

Other Major Psychoanalytical Theories

German psychiatrist Albert Moll* (1862–1939) believed that **congenital degeneracy** was responsible for necrophilia.[6] Krafft-Ebing blamed it on **acquired mental weakness.**[28] After Freud, psychoanalytic interpretations of necrophilia became more "fashionable." Some common interpretations are as follows:

1. There is an **unconscious suppressed hostility** toward parental figures and sadistic impulses to explore the mother's body. In some cases, there is a deep-seated thirst for revenge displaced from the **dominating mother** onto the **dominating spouse,** resulting in a compulsive and ecstatic association between love or admiration on one hand and pain or humiliation on the other.[29] The offender takes revenge from a "female figure" (the dead female, symbolizing mother or spouse) by ravishing her. This may be one of the factors operating in **Andrei Chikatilo**'s case. As a child, Chikatilo used to sleep with his mother. A chronic bed wetter throughout his childhood, he was beaten by his mother for each offense. Other factors such as impotence may also have contributed to Chikatilo's necrophilia. Another necrophile in this category is **Jerry Brudos,** whose hatred toward his mother turned him into a necrophile. **John Christie**'s mother and

* Albert Moll was the founder of modern sexology together with Iwan Bloch and Magnus Hirschfeld.

sisters dominated him during his childhood, and one girlfriend left him, making fun of him. It is possible, every time he killed a woman, that he vicariously saw his mother, sisters, or that jeering girlfriend (who dominated and belittled him so much) dying.

2. Several psychoanalysts have emphasized the **central role of the victim's "helplessness and resistlessness."**[30,31,32] Necrophiles seem to enjoy the complete power they have over their helpless and resistless victims—the dead. Some think of the ones they kill as their possessions, to do with as they please, and enjoy the feeling of control they have over them.

Bartholomew and colleagues[25] describe a case in which a 22-year-old white married male engaged in homosexual necrophilia because he wanted a sexual relationship with a male wholly in his power—a man completely drugged or drunk, completely unconscious, or, best of all, a man who was dead. (For details of this case, please see Chapter 3, "Classification," under the heading "Anal Necrophilia.")

John Christie admitted that the only way he could attain potency was with victims he rendered helpless. When **Jon Mattsen,** a member of the Green River Task Force, asked **Gary Ridgway** why he needed to have sex with his dead victims, Ridgway replied that it could be power over his victims. The conversation went on as below:[33]

"You said that you had these urges?" [Mattsen to Ridgway referring to his necrophilic urges]
"Uh-huh."
"Explain those urges to me," Mattsen said. "Explain what's going on in your head."
"Uh . . ."
"This Gary, this is the Gary twenty years ago," Mattsen encouraged.
"Um . . . going back to have sex with them was a sexual release. Um . . . that I didn't have to pay for. Um . . . um . . . I don't remember what else, offhand. Um . . . power over them, maybe."

In fact, Ridgway did not like it when victims were found, because in such cases, he "lost" them.[34] Furthermore, he often referred to a victim as "it" (as one would refer to a possession) rather than "her." He thought he could control them by killing them.

SIDEBAR 2.2 Exercising Sexual Power over Corpses

British psychoanalyst **Hanna Segal** (1918–) writes about one of her patients, a patient who she refers to as just **M,** a man in his late 40s.[30] Once M told her about a very intriguing dream that he had had: He was lying in bed with a woman on a kind of balcony inside a room near the ceiling.

The husband of the woman was lying on the floor above; he and the woman were lying head to foot. At some point he uncovered her to make love to her, and he then realized that she was a wooden doll. He noticed especially her wooden legs.

Segal interprets that her patient was beset with fears. To the woman in bed he associated a woman of his acquaintance, old and very rich. He would like to marry her for her money, but he is terrified of how possessive and sexually demanding she would be. If he sleeps with her, she will exhaust him. On the contrary, if he attempts to sleep with some young woman, he fears either rejection or the vengeance of her husband (if she happens to be married). Driven by these fears he can enjoy an object only when it has been completely immobilized like a wooden doll—**a corpse.** Segal tentatively suggested to her patient that the wooden doll was actually a corpse, and the patient agreed to her suggestion immediately, indeed with great eagerness. He even started extolling the virtues of a corpse as a sexual object. He described with relish the **feeling of power and security** that he could enjoy in making love to a corpse: It is there when wanted; you put it away when finished with it; it makes no demands; it is never frustrating, never unfaithful, never reproachful.

It is important to remember that **M** had never had any actual sexual intercourse with a corpse. He just fantasized about having intercourse with them.

M's personality was such that he wanted to exercise power over everybody around him. Even in nonsexual relations he had to have a similar power. For instance, if he wanted his girlfriend he would simply telephone her and she would come immediately, the slightest delay giving rise sometimes to a severe attack of anxiety or depression. However, the moment he was tired of her, she must go at once. Once he even sent her home in the middle of the night when she had already fallen asleep in his bed. His relation to other people was similar: They must come and go as he wanted. He wanted absolute power over everybody around him. Such an **absolute power** in sexual matters could only be had with a corpse.

Schlesinger[35] describes the case of K.M., a 16-year-old high school sophomore, who had been forced by his mother into having incestuous relations with her (her husband presumably had sexual problems) since he was 7 years old. He and his mother had sexual relations about twice a week. Most of the time his mother would masturbate him and perform oral sex. K.M. also performed oral sex upon her at her instruction. K.M. did not like to engage in sexual relations with his mother, but he was helpless, as his mother dominated him. He could not tell his father about it, as he feared it would result in all of them splitting up. Two days after his 16th birthday, when his mother was yelling at him, anger suddenly welled up within him. He pulled her out of the bathroom (where she was at the time of yelling) and shoved her upstairs. He did not speak a word, although his mother kept asking him to let her go. He took her to her bedroom, choked her to death, and then committed vaginal and anal necrophilia with her dead body. A clinical interview revealed that when he was having sexual relationship with his mother's dead body he felt that at last he was in a position of power after having been dominated by his mother for so long.

> I felt like I was out of control. My body was responding to the anger, all the anger that was bursting out from me. I shoved her in her bedroom; I put my hands around her neck and I got really excited. I choked her; I didn't say a word. After she was dead, I tore off her clothes. I was still angry. I had sex with her after she was dead. At the time I thought maybe she was just unconscious.

> I had an erection. I was aroused by her. It went through my mind that she was dead, since she was not moving. I felt in control of her now. She was in control of me all of the time. I was like a play toy. I felt I was getting her back by doing this. I did it to her.[35]

3. **Castration anxiety,** feelings of **male inadequacy,** and **fear of women** may be at work in some cases. As a result of these factors, the offender feels a need to prove his strength by inflicting humiliation on a totally subservient victim.
4. **Brill**[7] believes that in some cases, necrophilia could be as a result of **oral fixation.** He mentions the case of his necrophile patient **D.** (For details of this case, please see Chapter 3, "Classification," under the heading "Class IV Necrophiles.") His psychoanalysis revealed that D's love of corpses may be based on **grandmother** and **mother fixations.** The **corpses represented his dead mother** whose breast he still craved. By fellating the corpses, he was trying to suckle the breast of his long dead mother. Brill states that he had encountered many women during the course of his career who expressed a similar desire (of performing fellatio). This desire was always traceable to the suckling age, when the nipple from the mother's breast afforded both satiation and pleasure. In classical psychoanalytical theory, if the child is weaned too early from the mother's nipple, the child may become orally fixated and may resort to fellatio in a later part of life. According to Brill, his patient D was orally fixated and performed fellatio initially on living men, whenever such an opportunity arose. Once when he tried to perform fellatio on a sleeping person, the man woke up and gave him a severe beating. Thereafter, D resorted to performing fellatio on people who couldn't possibly beat him—corpses.
5. It is theorized by some psychoanalysts that a necrophile's concept of sexuality is somewhat infantile. Psychologically healthy people participate in human relationships by receiving and giving pleasure. With a corpse, one only gets pleasure, with no need to give, indicating an **immature** and **narcissistic ego** of the necrophile.

KEY POINT 2.1

Both **biological** and **psychoanalytic** factors may be at work **together** in a necrophile.

6. Unconscious internalization of the **parental attitude that sex is dirty and unnatural.** This may lead to a compulsion to have sex with the dead. Since sex with the dead is not true sex, it cannot be dirty. A relevant example is **Ed Gein,** whose mother, a fervent Lutheran and the absolute matriarch of the Gein household, convinced him that sex was dirty.
7. Dalmau[36] has tried to explain necrophilia by modifying Freud's theory to some extent. He asserts that the concept of **Oedipus complex** (as explained by Freud) was formulated at a time when the patriarchal family structure made the father the primary source of authority. More recent sociological trends brought the woman into a better and more adequate perspective. Dalmau asserts that in the male, the original drive does view the father as a rival, but eventually the mother is seen as the frustrating figure. Phallic sadistic drives emerge with murderous and rape feelings toward her. This is the nuclear pathologic core in **necrophilia,** male homosexuality, and impotence. To illustrate his theory, he gives an example of one of his patients who unofficially reported to having committed between 15 and 20 rapes, including one of a woman in labor, and a necrophilic attempt that was frustrated by the unexpected appearance of the owner of the funeral home where he worked. This patient supposedly had unresolved conflicts toward his mother, which he expressed by sexually attacking women—living and dead.
8. Bonaparte[37] points to probable quantitative constitutional factors and to qualitative factors determined by events in infancy, especially the witnessing of the **primal scene,** which the child interprets as a sadistic act. Later identification with the father may impel the potential necrophile to commit lust murder. Later empirical studies have found that such pervasive beliefs in the harmfulness of primal scenes have been exaggerated.[38]

QUICK FACT 2.1

In psychoanalysis, the **primal scene** is the initial witnessing by a child of adult nudity or a sex act, usually between the parents, which traumatizes the psychosexual development of that child.

Miscellaneous Causes

There could be a number of other causes why the dead are ravished. According to Stekel,[3] Hellwig reports that a mother, in order **to cure her hermaphroditic son,** opened the grave of a virgin. The son had to follow the counsel of his mother and lie naked upon the corpse "in order to bring his sex in order." It must, however, be remembered that acts like this, although simulating necrophilia, **are not true necrophilic acts.** According to DSM-IV-TR, the "essential features of a paraphilia are recurrent, intense sexually arousing fantasies, sexual urges, or behaviors."[1] A single act of lying naked upon the corpse, especially as a superstitious belief, is *not* necrophilia in the true sense.

In some cases necrophilia may be an attempt to overcome the loss of a love object. This seemed to be the factor in Rapoport's case.[12] Although from the description of this case, sexual inadequacy seems to be the most likely etiological factor (as mentioned earlier), Rapoport himself thought otherwise. He thought that the etiological factor was a reaction to the patient's period of mourning for his foster mother (p. 287). He describes this period of mourning for his foster mother as one of **melancholia** in which feelings concerned with his original loss of his own mother were reactivated. In other words, necrophilia, like the process of **mania,** was an attempt to overcome the loss of the object rather than to succumb to its loss.

QUICK FACT 2.2

Miscellaneous causes of necrophilia:

- Necrophilia may be a means of aiding the patient in overcoming the loss of a love object, dynamically similar to the manic defense
- Superstitions (such cases may not be true cases of necrophilia, though)
- Rejection by living partners

In the case of **Eli Ulayuk,** the criminogenic factors were identified as **substance abuse, education/employment,** and **emotional stability.** (Please see Chapter 5, "Case Studies," for details of his case.) **Burg**[39] (p. 243) states that according to Krafft-Ebing, **congenital feeblemindedness** and early **masturbation** caused the preference for the dead in Bertrand's case, and Havelock Ellis agreed with him in part. But Ellis also made it clear there were other reasons for necrophilic actions. He reported the case of a gravedigger who turned to corpses **after having no success with living women.**

Table 2.2 depicts deviations from the normal lifestyles of some necrophiles as reported in the literature. It may give some valuable insights into why a person may end up being a necrophile.

Table 2.2 Deviations from the Normal Lifestyle of Some Necrophiles

Necrophile	Major Deviations from a Normal Lifestyle
Jerry Brudos	Brudos's mother had wanted a girl and would dress Brudos in girl's clothing. She would also constantly belittle him and treat him with disdain, as well as abuse him. At 16, when Brudos was going through natural pubertal changes, his mother again showed her disgust for anything sexual in nature. She chided him for having a natural wet dream and forced him to wash his stained sheets by hand after his nighttime "indiscretion[s]." Later, in a psychiatric ward at Oregon State Hospital, it was found that his sexual fantasies revolved around his hatred and revenge against his mother and women in general.
Ted Bundy	Brought up to believe that his mother was his sister, and his maternal grandparents, his parents.
Andrei Chikatilo	As the young Chikatilo grew up, his mother kept him in constant fear of cannibals—she said they had eaten his older brother shortly before he was born—and during the war he saw his mother and possibly his sister raped by Nazi soldiers.[40] He grew up to become a cannibal necrophile.
John Christie	Fifth child in a family of seven children. Had a troubled relationship with his father, carpet designer Ernest John Christie, who was an austere and uncommunicative man and displayed little emotional warmth toward his children. Christie was dominated by his five sisters and his mother, Mary Hannah Halliday. His family experiences tended to undermine his self-confidence. At the age of 8, he saw the open coffin of his maternal grandfather, who always used to frighten him. Seeing his dead body lying in a coffin was a profoundly traumatic experience for Christie. In later life, Christie's childhood peers described him as "a queer lad" who "kept to himself" and "was not very popular."
	Impotent from his teens. Hypochondriacal. Always whining about his real or imaginary illnesses. While serving in the infantry during World War I, injured in a gas attack (1918) that he claimed blinded him for 5 months and rendered him mute for 3 1/2 years. Quite possibly he was merely feigning those symptoms.
Jeffrey Dahmer	Dahmer was the product of a pregnancy complicated by the fact that his mother suffered from disabling and protracted nausea, anxiety, and dysphoria. She also used tranquilizers during her pregnancy.[41] Dahmer was sexually molested by a neighbor boy at the age of 8 and was witness to ferocious arguments between his parents, who had a troubled relationship. Both parents were underinvolved with Dahmer as child, with the father having frequent absences from the home to work late or take trips in connection with his work. The mother had been hospitalized for psychiatric reasons during Dahmer's first years of life.[42] Parents divorced in 1977. These incidents may have had a role to play in his subsequent psychopathology.[43]
Ed Gein	Alcoholic father; overbearing, demanding, and abusive mother. Tried to convince her children that all women were prostitutes and instruments of the devil. Gradual death of all family members left him completely alone.

Table 2.2 Deviations from the Normal Lifestyle of Some Necrophiles (Continued)

Necrophile	Major Deviations from a Normal Lifestyle
Winston Moseley	Wife-beating father. His mother's infidelity to his father early in his life. Father stalking his wife (Moseley's mother) with a gun.
Eli Ulayuk	
16-year-old high school sophomore described by Schlesinger[35]	Parents had a very troubled marriage for years. K.M., the necrophile child, had been forced by his mother into having incestuous relations with her. He did not like this, but could not resist since his mother was in a position of power. Substance abuse (used to consume "home brew"); lack of education and employment; emotional stability. After the commission of his first crime, when he was sent to a correctional facility in 1992, these were identified as criminogenic factors in his case.
26-year-old African-American male described by Meloy[18]	Multiple separations between the parents throughout offender's childhood and latency years. Corporal punishment given. Assaulted and battered by mother, stepfather, and her mother's boyfriends. Witnessed mother's physical victimization. Childhood sexual abuse by an uncle (fondling), a friend of the mother (vaginal intercourse), and a female cousin (masturbation). Witnessed and participated in gang violence. Used alcohol and a variety of drugs. Legal employment intermittent. Extensive use of visual pornography, usually video, to facilitate sexual arousal. Fulfilled diagnostic criteria for antisocial personality disorder, polysubstance dependence, and major depressive disorder, single episode (DSM-IV). Use of nortryptiline, a tricyclic antidepressant.

Conclusion

Many theories of necrophilia have been proposed so far, but none seems entirely satisfactory. Maybe a number of factors together operate on a person to turn him into a necrophile. Many authors have directly pondered the theories of necrophilia, while many others[17] have not directly dwelled upon the question, but their writings do indicate possible etiological factors. For instance, Lancaster[16] does not dwell upon the etiological factors at all. However, from the case study that he describes, one can extrapolate that heavy alcohol intoxication may be either an etiological or contributory factor. Before all three known acts of necrophilia, the subject of his paper got very heavily drunk. Similarly Rosman and Resnick[17] do not dwell upon the etiological factors at all. However their epidemiological analysis makes it clear that alcohol may be a possible etiological factor. The writings of these authors indirectly point toward a possible etiological factor.

Table 2.3 summarizes the key theories that have been proposed (directly or indirectly) so far.

The debate regarding the etiology of necrophilia is far from over. Clearly more research is needed to settle this issue.

Table 2.3 Major Etiological Theories of Necrophilia

Theory	Proposed by
Genetic abnormality	Stekel, 1929;[3] Fromm, 1973[2]
Heavy alcohol intoxication	Gromska, 1969;[15] Lancaster, 1978;[16] Rosman and Resnick, 1989[17]
Congenital degeneracy	Moll, 1912[6]
Acquired mental weakness	Krafft-Ebing, 1886[28]
Being able to exercise unlimited power over their sexual partners	Segal, 1953[30]

References

1. Aggrawal A. *Forensic and Medico-legal Aspects of Sexual Crimes and Unusual Sexual Practices.* CRC Press, Boca Raton, FL, 2008.
2. Fromm E. *The Anatomy of Human Destructiveness.* Holt, Rinehart, and Winston, New York, 1973.
3. Stekel W. *Sadism and Masochism: The Psychology of Hatred and Cruelty.* Grove Press, New York, 1929.
4. Ellis HH. *Studies in the Psychology of Sex, Volume V: Erotic Symbolism, The Mechanism of Detumescence, The Psychic State in Pregnancy.* FA Davis, Philadelphia, 1923.
5. Belletrud M, Mercier E. Perversion de l'instinct Génésique. *Annales d'hygiène publique et de médecine légale.* 1903;**49(6)**:481–490.
6. Moll A. *Handbuch der Sexualwissenschaften mit besonderer Berücksichtigung der kulturgeschichtlichen Beziehungen.* FCW Vogel, Leipzig, 1912.
7. Brill AA. Necrophilia—Part I. *J. Criminal Psychopathol.* 1941;**2(4)**:433–443.
8. Tsheryaskin WG. Zur Frage der Nekrophilie (The Question of Necrophilia). *Zeitschrift für sexual wissenschaft-wiss.* 1929;**16**:386–392.
9. Price DE. Necrophilia complicating a case of homicide. *Med Sci Law.* 1963 Apr;**3**:121–131.
10. Lowe S. Slice of life; From the South China Morning Post this week in: 1983. *South China Morning Post*, March 18, 2008 (Tuesday), p. 2.
11. Wilson C, Pitman P. *Encyclopedia of Murder.* Pan Books, London, 1984, pp. 165–171.
12. Rapoport J. A case of necrophilia. *J Criminal Psychopathol.* 1942;**4**:277–289.
13. Jackson R. *Francis Camps—Famous Case Histories of the Celebrated Pathologist.* Panther Books, London, 1983, pp. 70–97.
14. Silva JA, Ferrari MM, Leong GB. The case of Jeffrey Dahmer: sexual serial homicide from a neuropsychiatric developmental perspective. *J Forensic Sci.* 2002 Nov;**47(6)**:1347–1359.
15. Gromska J, Smoczyński S, Bardzik S. [A case of necrophilia committed in a state of pathological alcoholic intoxication][Article in Polish]. *Psychiatr Pol.* 1969;**3(2)**:207–209.
16. Lancaster NP. Necrophilia, murder and high intelligence: a case report. *Br J Psychiatry.* 1978 Jun;**132**:605–608.

17. Rosman JP, Resnick PJ. Sexual attraction to corpses: a psychiatric review of necrophilia. *Bull Am Acad Psychiatry Law*. 1989;**17(2)**:153–163.
18. Meloy JR. Pseudonecrophilia following spousal homicide. *J Forensic Sci*. 1996 Jul;**41(4)**:706–708.
19. *R. v. Ulayuk*, 2006 NWTSC 10.
20. Pottieger AE, Tressell PA. Social relationships of crime-involved women cocaine users. *J Psychoactive Drugs*. 2000 Oct-Dec;**32(4)**:445–460.
21. Kasarabada ND, Anglin MD, Stark E, Paredes A. Cocaine, crime, family history of deviance—are psychosocial correlates related to these phenomena in male cocaine abusers? *Subst Abuse*. 2000 Jun;**21(2)**:67–78.
22. Hunt D, Spunt B, Lipton D, Goldsmith D, Strug D. The costly bonus: cocaine related crime among methadone treatment clients. *Adv Alcohol Subst Abuse*. 1986 Winter;**6(2)**:107–122.
23. Simon R, DeVito H. Alcohol activation of EEG abnormalities in persons with a history of violence precipitated by drinking alcoholic beverages. *Clin Electroencephalogr*. 1976;**7**:145–148.
24. Klaf FS, Brown W. Necrophilia, brief review and case report. *Psychiatric Q*. 1958;**32(4)**:645–652.
25. Bartholomew AA, Milte KL, Galbally F. Homosexual necrophilia. *Med Sci Law*. 1978 Jan;**18(1)**:29–35.
26. Feist J, Feist GJ (Eds.). *Theories of Personality*, 6th ed. McGraw-Hill, New York, 2006, pp. 198–200.
27. Fromm E. *The Heart of Man*. Harper & Row, New York, 1964.
28. Krafft-Ebing RF. *Psychopathia Sexualis*, 1st ed. F.A. Davis, Philadelphia, 1886 [reprinted by Bloat Books, 1999].
29. Hucker S. Necrophilia and other unusual philias, in *Principles and Practice of Forensic Psychiatry*, 1st ed. Eds., R Bluglass, P Bowden. Churchill Livingstone, Edinburgh, 1990, chap. VIII.9.
30. Segal H. A necrophilic fantasy. *Int J Psychoanal*. 1953;**34**:98–101.
31. Jones E. *On the Nightmare*. Hogarth Press and Institute of Psycho-Analysis, London, 1931.
32. Calef V, Weinshel EM. On certain neurotic equivalents of necrophilia. *Int J Psychoanal*. 1972;**53(1)**:67–75.
33. Prothero M, Smith C. *Defending Gary—Unraveling the Mind of the Green River Killer*, 1st ed. Jossey-Bass, San Francisco, CA, 2006, pp. 317–318.
34. Ramsland K. *Inside the Minds of Serial Killers—Why They Kill*, 1st ed. Praeger, Connecticut, 2006, p. 30.
35. Schlesinger LB. Adolescent sexual matricide following repetitive mother-son incest. *J Forensic Sci*. 1999 Jul;**44(4)**:746–749.
36. Dalmau CJ. Post-oedipal psychodynamics. *Psychoanal. Rev*. 1957;**44**:1–9.
37. Bonaparte M. Deuil, nécrophilie et sadisme. *Revue Française de Psychoanalyst*. 1931;**4**:716–734.
38. Okami P, Olmstead R, Abramson PR, Pendleton L. Early childhood exposure to parental nudity and scenes of parental sexuality ("primal scenes"): an 18-year longitudinal study of outcome. *Arch Sex Behav*. 1998 Aug;**27(4)**:361–384.
39. Burg BR. The sick and the dead: the development of psychological theory on necrophilia from Krafft-Ebing to the present. *J Hist Behav Sci*. 1982 Jul;**18(3)**:242–254.

40. Newsome B. Friday—Pay TV. *The Age (Melbourne, Australia)*, September 13, 2007, Thursday, First Edition, Section: Green Guide; Preview; p. 42.
41. Dahmer L. *A Father's Story*. William Morrow and Company, New York, 1994.
42. Davis JA. Profile of a sexual predator: a psychological autopsy of an American serial killer. *Forensic Examiner*. 1998 Jan-Feb;7:28–33.
43. Newton M. *The Encyclopedia of Serial Killers*, 2nd ed. Facts on File, New York, 2006.

Classification 3

Introduction

A disorder like necrophilia, which has many nuances, cannot be studied properly without first classifying it into its logical component parts. It is well known that necrophilic behavior spans a wide range of behaviors ranging from simply wanting to cohabit with a living partner pretending to be dead, to actually killing human beings to be able to cohabit with a corpse. Many attempts have previously been made to classify necrophilia.

Existing Classifications

Krafft-Ebing's Classification

In 1886, **Krafft-Ebing**[1] proposed one of the first classifications of necrophilia. He distinguished between necrophiles seeking only sexual contact with the dead, as sex objects that can be subjugated absolutely, and necrophilia accompanied by murder and mutilation. He reportedly made his nosological proposals based only on two cases of necrophilia.[2] For ease of reference, we will refer to these two classes as **Class I-KE** and **Class II-KE.**

Wulffen's Classification

Erich Wulffen[3] divided necrophilia into three types: lust murder or necrosadism, necrostuprum, and necrophagy. In **lust murder,** the offender kills first and then goes ahead with sexual intercourse with the corpse; in **necrostuprum,** he steals the corpse in order to have sexual intercourse with it; and in **necrophagy,** he mutilates and eats parts of the corpse.

Jones's Classification

Jones,[4] who was influenced by Freud's paper on mourning and melancholia, described two varieties of necrophilia: that committed with the dead body of a loved one and that committed with any other corpse. The first type, called **inhibited necrophilia,** "is little more than an extension of the part played by love in mourning, the frantic aversion against accepting the event and parting for ever from the loved being." Examples are cited of husbands who could not bring themselves to believe that their wives had died and continued to perform sexual intercourse with their dead bodies (Periander, King Herod, King Waldemar IV, and Charlemagne). It has been suggested that American writer **Edgar Allan Poe** (1809–1849) had this type of necrophilic love for his mother. It developed when his mother died at the young age of 24, when Poe was only 3 years old. His necrophilia was manifested in his great literary concern with horror, death, and love of the dead.[5,6,7] Burdened by his sadonecrophilic fixation to his mother, Poe was never able to attain to normal love.

The other, more gruesome, form of necrophilia was called **overt necrophilia.** It was supposed to rank as perhaps the most extreme imaginable perversion of the love instinct. In it, the person obtains gratification with any corpse, not that of a loved object, and he does so either by performing some kind of sexual act on the corpse or, more characteristically, by biting, tearing, and devouring its decaying flesh. Jones thought that it signified a reversion to the most primitive aspects of sadism, both of the oral and anal kind.

Hirschfeld's Classification

Hirschfeld[8] divided necrophilia into violation of a person who was already dead and sexual abuse of a person an individual had first murdered, "to possess and destroy her beyond death." For ease of reference, we will refer to these two classes as **Class I-Hf** and **Class II-Hf.**

Rosman and Resnick's Classification

Rosman and Resnick[9] classify all necrophiles in two groups: **genuine necrophilia** and **pseudonecrophilia.** Genuine necrophilia (which the authors frequently refer to as **true necrophilia**) involves cases that have a persistent sexual attraction to corpses. This class is further subdivided into three subgroups: **necrophilic homicide,** offenders who commit murder to obtain a corpse for sexual purposes (equivalent to Wulffen's lust murderer); **regular necrophilia,** offenders who use already dead bodies for sexual pleasure (equivalent to Wulffen's necrostuprum); and **necrophilic fantasy,** offenders who fantasize about sexual activity with a corpse without carrying out any necrophilic acts. The name of this class sounds very similar to modern classification's Class III necrophile, but what they describe under this class is more akin to **Class VI necrophilia.**

Pseudonecrophiles are offenders who have only a transient attraction to a corpse, but corpses are *not* the object of his sexual fantasies. These prefer sexual contact with living partners. The authors state that this group is subdivided into **sadistic, opportunistic,** and **transitory** cases, but do not explain further what is meant by these different terms. However, they do describe in detail one case of pseudonecrophilia that suggests that the pseudonecrophilia described by them belongs to Class VII of modern classification. In a personal communication, Rosman agreed that no definitions of these three terms were given in their paper, because they were meant to be interpreted "by their ordinary English-language meanings."[10]

Conclusion

Table 3.1 gives a bird's eye view of some major earlier classifications of necrophilia. Considering the limited amount of literature on necrophilia in those times, these classifications were good attempts. However, with more literature pouring in since these early suggestions, a newer classification is more appropriate.

Table 3.1 Earlier Classifications of Necrophilia

Krafft-Ebing's Classification (1886)

- Necrophiles seeking only sexual contact with the dead, as sex objects that can be subjugated absolutely (Class I-KE)
- Necrophilia accompanied by murder and mutilation (Class II-KE)

Wulffen's Classification (1910)

- Necrosadism (lust murder)
- Necrostuprum
- Necrophagy

Jones's Classification (1931)

- Inhibited necrophilia
- Overt necrophilia

Hirschfeld's Classification (1956)

- Violation of a person who was already dead
- Sexual abuse of a person an individual had first murdered, "to possess and destroy her beyond death"

Rosman and Resnick's Classification (1989)

- Genuine (or true) necrophilia
  - Necrophilic homicide
  - Regular necrophilia
  - Necrophilic fantasy
- Pseudonecrophilia
  - Sadistic
  - Opportunistic
- Transitory

Need for a New Classification

A new classification is also desirable, because with current classifications, there is an enormous amount of confusion centering around some subjective terms related to necrophilia. One such term is **pseudonecrophilia.** According to some authors it refers to an arousal from having sex with someone pretending to be dead,[11] according to others[12,13,14] it refers to people who find sexual stimulation in the presence of the dead, and according to yet others[9] it refers to those persons who are normally content with having sex with the living, but given an opportunity, would have sex with the dead, too.

Prins[15] has used a classification of **vampirism** (sexual arousal attained through blood extraction), in which he uses terms such as necrophilia and necrosadism to define various shades of vampirism. He describes four types of vampirism: **complete vampirism** (necrosadism, ingestion of blood, and necrophilic activity); **vampirism without ingestion of blood** ("necrophilia"); **vampirism without death being involved;** and **autovampirism** (ingestion of one's own blood).

Such classifications and terminologies—while having great merit in themselves—seem to have generated considerable confusion among scientists trying to communicate with one another.

Some general classifications of diseases, especially DSM-IV-TR[16] and ICD-10,[17] have been devised precisely to prevent such confusion occurring among scientists. This is achieved by assigning mathematical codes to diseases, instead of subjective names. Mathematical codes also enable easy computerization and communication, but neither DSM-IV-TR nor ICD-10 assigns any specific or unique code to necrophilia, let alone to its subclasses. **DSM-IV-TR** assigns code **302.9** (Paraphilias Not Otherwise Specified) to necrophilia along with several other uncommon paraphilias. **ICD-10** classifies necrophilia under the code **F65.8** (Other Disorders of Sexual Preference) along with several other paraphilias such as telephone scatologia and frotteurism. A classification system—preferably mathematical for easy computerization and communication—for all subclasses of necrophilia is thus highly desirable.

Aggrawal[18] proposed a 10-tier classification—from class I to class X—in order to address this issue. As can be seen, the three different definitions of pseudonecrophilia mentioned earlier would now fall in three different classes according to the new proposed system: classes I, III, and VII. Thus there is no scope for any confusion over terminologies. Instead of talking about subjective terms such as *pseudonecrophilia*, one would refer to objective mathematical classes.

The classification is based on severity of psychosexual disorder present among the necrophiles. This classification appears to have an intuitive appeal. From the least innocuous to the most, all necrophiles have been categorized in the following 10 categories.

Class I Necrophiles: Role Players

Role players do not engage in sexual activity with the dead, but with living people pretending to be dead. These comprise two groups of people:

1. The first group seems to be unable to get an erection in the presence of a conscious woman. Thus, they need to ask their partners to pretend to be dead, so they can get an erection.
2. The second group enjoys a kind of role playing with their live partners. They can perhaps get an erection in the presence of the living, but would get a more intense sexual orgasm if their partner pretended to be dead. It is a kind of *sexual role-play.*

Since this activity does not involve sexual activity with the dead, some authors have called this practice **pseudonecrophilia.**[11] Some others have used the terms **simulated necrophilia** and **symbolic necrophilia.**[19] A more appropriate term appears to be **necrobiophilia** (from Greek *nekros* ["dead"] and *bios* ["living"]).

German psychiatrist **Arthur Kronfeld** (1886–1941) mentions one case from this category. The patient was a compulsive neurotic, suffering from many obsessive disturbances. He was able to have sexual relations only with girls who acted as if they were dead or fast asleep.[20]

The Austrian sex offender **Josef Fritzl** (1935–), who is more commonly known for having imprisoned his daughter Elisabeth Fritzl for 24 years in a concealed part of the basement of his home and fathering seven children with her, was also a **class I necrophile.** He used to visit brothels where he ordered frightened prostitutes to pretend to be dead before having deviant sex with them.[21]

Holmes and Holmes[22] describe two cases from their files that belong to this class. According to them, a prostitute stated that she had two clients, both professionals, one a lawyer and the other a dean of a local university, who would belong to the modern classification of class I necrophiles. They were her frequent customers. The attorney wanted only to look at her while she lay on the bed, whereas the dean had intercourse with her as she lay like a corpse.

Certain brothels cater to this perversion; the prostitute is made up like a corpse with a pallid appearance and **dressed in a shroud,** and lies in a coffin (often known as **casket sex**).[23] A person may want his sexual partner to cover her body with a whitish cosmetic to simulate the blood-drained skin of a corpse, cover her in a plastic sheet, and even add a toe tag before starting sexual intercourse. Some may utilize a resurrection fantasy where the lover brings the "dead" partner to life through sexual activity. The lover who pretends to be brought back to life may turn the tables on the other, dominating him, and even acting out a **zombie fantasy.**

Sometimes a **vampire fantasy** is involved where the lover simulates a killing by biting the neck. **Masters and Lea**[24] (pp. 229–230) describe the case of a 28-year-old white female, **M,** who is highly imaginative and well versed in psychological literature. During **mescaline intoxication,** she "experimented" by fantasizing that her husband was dead and his penis was in rigor mortis. To make his penis stiff, as in rigor mortis, she performed fellatio on him while requesting him to lie still like a cadaver. When it got stiff, she would pretend that the stiffness was due to rigor mortis, and this would give her erotic pleasure. She would then squat above him and introduce the penis in her vagina, and then twist her body around it. She also imagined herself to be a vampire, and used to nibble at her husband's body. She had a strong impulse to actually draw blood, but she would restrain herself.

Class II Necrophiles: Romantic Necrophiles

These people show only very mild necrophilic tendencies. These include normal bereaved people who cannot bear separation from their loved ones. They do not seem to agree that their loved ones have died. They mummify their loved one's dead body (or parts of them) and may continue to relate to them much as they did in life. They may prefer to eat dinner in their company, sit as companions while watching television, or dance with them.[25] The behavior has also been called **necromania.**[26] **Sir John Pryce** (c. 1698–1761) is known to have embalmed his two wives after death and kept them with him in his bed. (Please see Chapter 1, "Necrophilia: Overview and Historical Aspects," for details.)

Masters and Lea[24] (p. 222) describe the case of an eccentric necrophile, **Giuseppe Alessandro,** who lived in a small, isolated house near Caserta. (Masters and Lea ascribe this case to **Wulffen.**) His eccentricities attracted the attention of neighboring peasants, who climbed a tree near his house and peeped into his window. To their utter surprise, they saw him passionately kissing the female corpse of his fiancée, **Elvira Skarlingi,** from a neighboring village. He had dressed the corpse in an elaborate silken gown with a strand of pearls about its neck. The peasants broke into the house and confronted him, but Allesandro produced a revolver and succeeded in making his escape. It was discovered that after Elvira died and was buried in the cemetery, Alessandro had disinterred her body and transported her coffin over the mountains. From the diary that Alessandro left, it was clear that he was a psychotic individual.

Martin Schurig (1656–1733), in his *Spermatologia,* describes the case of a Belgian lady who secretly cut off the penis of her husband when he died and treasured it as a sacred relic in a silver casket.[27] She eventually made it into a powder which she found to be an efficacious medicine for herself and others. Havelock Ellis[28] cites an earlier example, another lady at the French

Figure 3.1 Joanna of Castile.

court who embalmed and perfumed the genital organs of her dead husband, always preserving them in a gold casket.

A classic example belonging to this class is that of **Joanna of Castile** (1479–1555) (Figure 3.1). When her husband, **Philip the Handsome,** died on September 25, 1506, at the young age of 28, she refused to abandon her dead husband's corpse and kept his dead body with her for 12 months. She pretended he was dozing and would soon wake up. She paid him compliments and made her servants treat him as a king.[29] She would periodically have Philip's casket opened so that she might embrace his decaying body. She would not let any woman near her husband's body—even if they were nuns. At one time, she ordered the coffin be taken from the monastery and out to the open fields, where she slept beside it all night.

A similar example is of Italian princess **Christina Trivulzio Belgiojoso** (1808–1871) (Figure 3.2). She was a patriot revolutionary who participated actively in the *Risorgimento.* Her lover, **Gaetano Stelzi,** died on June 16, 1848 (at the age of 27), and was laid to rest in the presence of numerous witnesses on June 19. Italy in those times was at war with Austria. As Austrian armies advanced toward Milan, Christina left for the Orient on August 3, 1848. Later, the Austrian authorities searched her villa trying to find incriminating papers related to her revolutionary activities. During the search they found the carefully embalmed and perfectly preserved, clothed body of **Stelzi** in one of her wardrobes! An investigation of his grave revealed only a heavy log of wood. The mystery of the secret transfer of Stelzi's corpse to a cupboard in her villa, and to the sham funeral services held over a bit of timber, has never been solved.[30,31,32]

Figure 3.2 Christina Trivulzio Belgiojoso (by Francesco Hayez).

A number of such cases have come to notice in recent times. In August 2007, a woman in Mexico City, **Mercedes Velarde,** was caught with the body of her dead husband, **Edmundo,** aged about 60, by her bedside when neighbors, disturbed by the smell, called the police. He had died a year earlier. The police broke down her door and found the putrefied body of her husband on the floor of her bedroom.[33]

More recently, in June 2009, in Pasadena, a demented woman in her mid-70s was discovered to be living with the dead body of her elderly husband, who had been dead for 2 to 4 months. The body was in an advanced stage of decomposition. The police found the body of the husband seated upright in a couch near the front door.[34] In September 2009, in Tirunelveli, South India, a 67-year-old woman, **Lakshmi Ammal,** was found to have kept the body of her dead husband, 75-year-old **Krishnamoorthy,** in their house for 3 days before neighbors noticed the foul smells and informed the police. The matter did not come to anybody's notice as the couple lived by themselves.[35] Table 3.2 gives a list of people who embalmed their loved ones or their body parts after their death and kept them in their bed with them.

Table 3.2 People Who Embalmed Their Loved Ones (Whole or Body Parts) (Class II Necrophiles)

Name	Act
Sir John Pryce (c. 1698–1761)	Embalmed his two wives
Belgian lady (unidentified, described by Martin Schurig[27])	Embalmed the penis of her husband
French lady (unidentified, described by Havelock Ellis[28])	Embalmed and perfumed the genital organs of her husband
Christina Trivulzio Belgiojoso (1808–1871)	Embalmed the body of her lover **Gaetano Stelzi**
Mercedes Velarde (2007)	Kept the body of her husband with her
Pasadena lady (2009, unidentified)	Kept the body of her husband with her
Lakshmi Ammal (2009)	Kept the body of her husband, Krishnamoorthy, with her

SIDEBAR 3.1 Sleeping with Wife's Dead Body

Browne[29] mentions the case of a landed proprietor who, although on bad terms with his wife during life, was so aggrieved at her death that he carried her body with him and placed her coffin under his bed. There is no mention, however, of the length of the period for which he kept her there.

More recently a Vietnamese man, **Le Van,** 55, from **Ha Lam,** a small town in the central province of **Quang Nam,** was found sleeping with the dead body of his wife. She had died in 2003. Initially he used to sleep on top of her grave, but rain, wind, and cold often disturbed him. About 20 months later, he decided to dig a tunnel into the grave "to sleep with her." His children found out, though, and prevented him from going to the grave. So one night in November 2004, he dug up his wife's remains and brought them home. He then molded clay around the remains to make the figure of a woman, put clothes on her, and then placed her in his bed. He slept with her for 5 years.[36] Le Van lived at home with his three children. He was described by neighbors as a normal and well-behaved man.

The psychopathology of class II necrophiles may be only transient in nature, and they would normally recover as time passes. From a legal standpoint, class I and II necrophiles are quite innocuous. There are no cases on record in which they have been prosecuted; class II necrophiles may be in need of psychiatric help, though.

Class III Necrophiles: People Having a Necrophilic Fantasy (Necrophilic Fantasizers)

Class III necrophiles are somewhat less innocuous from a legal standpoint. Psychosocially they do show an aberrant behavior and are thus abnormal. These necrophiles do not engage in sexual intercourse with the dead. They are content simply with fantasizing about sexual intercourse with the dead or perhaps fantasizing about sexual involvement with the dead in any other manner. British psychoanalyst **Hanna Segal** (1918–) mentions a patient (whom she just refers to as **M,** a man in his late 40s), who fantasized about having intercourse with corpses, but never actually had intercourse with one.[12] (For details on this patient, please refer to Chapter 2, "Etiology.") Brill[37] mentions the case of a **blind necrophile** (Sidebar 3.2) who fantasized about getting a dead body that he could mutilate, wallow in, and perhaps also eat. He even thought of killing in order to get a dead body to carry out his fantasies, but he never put his fantasies in practice, perhaps because of his blindness.

SIDEBAR 3.2 The Case of a Blind Necrophilic Fantasizer

Brill[37] describes perhaps the only case of a **blind necrophile.** Brill calls him **H** (1897–?), and saw him for the first time in May 1929, after he had been seen by Dr. Leonard Rothschild. **H** was an American, and when seen by Brill, 32 years old, single, and unmarried. He was almost blind from birth, and completely so after the age of 4, when his eyes had to be enucleated (because of some congenital defect, which Brill does not dwell upon).

H was eighth of 13 children, five of whom died in early infancy. There were three brothers and four sisters besides the patient. **H** received only high school training and appeared to be a well-educated person. He read everything that he could get in Braille, and seemed well versed in the arts and literature. He loved music and was supposedly a good violinist.

H consulted Dr. Brill because he had a morbid desire to kill in order to get a dead body (typical of **class IX necrophiles,** but he never carried out this morbid desire and remained a fantasizer). As his blindness precluded the possibility of murdering someone to obtain a human corpse, he was willing to substitute a dead horse, or any other big animal, for it. (He even thought of getting a dead elephant or dead whale, which he could mutilate, but he could go only as far as getting a dead chicken, which he mutilated to his heart's content.) Screams of women gave him mixed feelings of fear and pleasure: fear because of possible interference by somebody hearing that scream and pleasure because of the hope that the cry was out of pain and perhaps approaching death. His immediate impulse on hearing such a cry was to rush at her, strike, or in some other way crush out whatever life may remain. (As Brill states, these characteristics, if actually carried out are typical of *lust murderers.* In the modern classification, this would signify characteristics of **class IX necrophilia.**) So strong was his desire to kill women that when asked if he would not fear detection, he replied, "I must be prepared for such an emergency."

Brill mentions that in his entire career, he dealt with just one other case who harbored similar fantasies (of killing a woman in order to get a dead body). This other person eventually became a member of a "sadist circle" and sublimated his murderous thoughts and fantasies by writing and acting out sadistic stories. **H** ultimately gave up the idea of killing a woman and substituted it with the fantasies of killing a horse instead. He explained, "Kill a woman and it is murder; kill a horse, and as long as the act is committed far from human haunts, nobody will interfere."

Besides being a necrophile, **H** displayed many other paraphilic tendencies; he was a **masochist, sexual vampire** (drinking blood for sexual excitement), **coprophile,** and **urophile,** too. He also suffered from **osmolagnia** (arousal caused by bodily odors, such as sweat) and **salirophilia** (arousal from ingesting sweat). He also had a **breast fetish.** He frequently had thoughts about a dead woman and a baby on her breast. The fantasy would sometimes end by the breast bursting open and the child falling into it. Furthermore in many of his dreams when he had fantasies of eating women, he always began by sucking at the breasts, and consuming the rest of the body later. He often dreamt of sucking cream directly from a woman's breast. He thought that human breasts offered only a small amount of milk and biting them open would cause unlimited flow of creamy milk. One of his fantasies was to make a hole between the breasts of a woman, stick his penis into it, and dance around carrying her in this way! Both Dr. Rothschild and Brill thought that this was because he did not get enough milk from his mother.

Brill thinks that his sexuality concentrated toward other senses (such as smells and odors) because of the absence of his eyesight. Because of this disability, his other senses became highly enhanced, and his sexuality came to depend much on these. He liked putrid odors—odors associated with death and decay. In conversation with girls **H** always brought up the subject of perfume, and usually remarked, "A sweet girl like you needs no perfumes." What he really meant was, "I wish you were dead and in a putrid condition." He claimed that this craving was heightened when he heard a girl or woman speak softly or in a whisper. At the age of about 8, he started fantasizing about a fat, tall woman either in a dying condition or already dead. He then took her to some deserted place, kept her warm, filled her with water, and covered her naked body with water in order to bring about as quickly as possible a condition of rapid decay.

Besides necrophilia, **sexual vampirism** was one of his chief paraphilias. Before he was totally blind, once he heard that a young girl with whom he used to play was sick and dying. He asked her older sister if he could drink the little girl's blood, since she did not need it any more. He repeatedly tried to sneak in to see the corpse, but was turned away. This paraphilia was intimately intertwined with his love of the dead. When she finally died and the hearse was bearing the body away, he yelled to the driver to take him along. He wanted to be buried with the body. In this case **taphephilia** (sexual stimulation from being buried alive) appeared to coexist with necrophilia.

When he was 11, his grandmother fell sick. **H** used to hug her during her illness, and every time he hugged her, he thought what fun it would be to be sinking into her dying remains. On one occasion, when she said that she felt she was dying, **H** said, "Grandma, I wish you would do me a favor. If you die, I wish you would let me have your dead body." Quite expectedly, she began to cry at this outlandish suggestion. At this, **H** kissed her and said, "What difference would it make to you? If you are buried, the worms will eat you, so you may as well leave your body to me to let me enjoy it." His grandmother burst out in a louder fit of crying. At this juncture, **H**'s sister came along and discovered what had happened. She loved him a great deal, and advised him to keep it a secret and say nothing about it any further to anyone.

She was also the one who loved **H** so much that she virtually did everything to treat **H** for his necrophilia. At one stage, she came to believe that her brother wanted a dead body for intercourse perhaps because, being blind, he could not get a live woman for intercourse, which he needed. She even offered herself to **H,** so he could have intercourse with her, and at least be cured of his necrophilia. However, despite his repeated efforts, and despite help from his sister, he could never perform intercourse with her. Even when he got a slight erection, after much effort, it always dwindled in the first attempt at penetration. His sister finally was convinced that her brother wanted **nothing but a dead body.** Significantly, **class X** necrophiles have precisely this trait—they can have sexual intercourse only with the dead to the complete exclusion of the living. Quite possibly, if **H** had had full vision, he would be a **class X necrophile.** We do know that he was **unsuccessful in having sexual intercourse with a living person,** but we do not know if he would have successfully had sexual intercourse with the dead. Perhaps he would have, but he never had a chance to have intercourse (successful or unsuccessful) with a dead body, because of his disability. When **H**'s sister discovered that her brother wanted a dead body for intercourse, with the complete inability to have intercourse with the living, she suggested that it would be better for him to commit suicide than to disgrace everybody.

Once again, when he was 27, an attempt was made to cure him of his necrophilia by allowing him to have **intercourse with a prostitute.** (The presumption, once again, was that **H** needed sexual intercourse, but since he was not able to get a live partner, because of his blindness, his interests came to lean toward the dead.) However, he was not interested in sex with her. Instead of looking forward to sexual intercourse with her, he thought of taking along a pocketknife, so he could cut one of her arteries and drink her blood. He forgot the knife, though. Brill states that "the whole experiment turned into a fiasco." The intended sexual intercourse presumably never took place.

Once when **H** was asked how he came to desire dead bodies, he replied,

> When I was a child, I preferred to play with girls. I was especially fond of kissing and hugging girls taller and stouter than myself. But as they usually resisted my advances, I reasoned that if they were dead, they could not object to my company. When I used to hug and kiss my sisters or my mother more than they liked to be caressed, I would say bitterly, "If you were dead, I could kiss and hug you as much as I like and you could not refuse." In such cases my sister would sometimes ask, "Then you want me to die?" I would naturally say "No," but often I thought that if I found a sick or dying girl or woman, I probably would not call a doctor or give relief, but would try to cause her death in some painless way.

H had a particularly violent method of kissing. He would hold the girl tight, standing face to face, and would put his lips against hers, his nose against hers, and would breathe in when she breathed out and vice versa. Girls objected most to the last procedure; but the more resistance he encountered, the greater was his wish that they should be dead, or absolutely passive. **H,** in fact, desired for a dead female through which he could gratify all his necrophilic cravings.

As was common in Brill's times, he tries to analyze **H**'s necrophilia psychoanalytically. According to Brill, **H** remained on a pregenital level and never attained genitality and object-finding in the normal sense.

Necrophilic fantasizers may visit cemeteries and funeral parlors often for this purpose, and merely the sight of dead bodies may give them erotic pleasure.[38] Although Rosman and Resnick[9] describe a similar-sounding category (**necrophilic fantasy**), the case they describe to illustrate this class is more akin to **class VI necrophilia.** Browne[29] describes the case of two females from the Western Isles who frequented their respective parochial graveyards, scaring the superstitious population around, who at first thought that they must be the ghosts of the departed. One lay upon the earth beneath a flat stone, supported on short pillars, which marked the place of interment of clansmen. The other woman used to sit upon mounds under which dead bodies had been interred. Repeated efforts and even force were required to stop them from doing so.

Bauer and colleagues[39] describe the case of a 40-year-old married civil engineer who used to **compulsively study obituaries and then visit cemeteries**. His interest was not limited to merely visiting cemeteries, however. He was on the lookout for a body that he could steal for sex and mutilation. (His behavior was more characteristic of a class VIIIb necrophile, with some class III and V characteristics.)

SIDEBAR 3.3 Pietro Pacciani—Sexual Intercourse in the Presence of a Corpse

Pietro Pacciani (1925–1998) was a farmer of Mercatale, San Casciano in Val di Pesa, Italy, who was arrested on January 17, 1993 (at the age of 68), on suspicion of being the infamous serial killer who came to be known as the **Monster of Florence** (*Il mostro di Firenze*). The Monster of Florence was a **class IXa necrophile** who killed 16 people—mostly couples—between 1968 and 1985 and mutilated many of his victims.

After the first trial **Pacciani** was convicted for seven of the double murders (allegedly committed by the Monster of Florence) and sentenced to life in prison. Later, however, he was cleared of all charges due to lack of evidence. The Italian Supreme Court ordered a fresh trial, but Pacciani died in February 1998—after a fatal combination of drugs caused him a cardiac arrest—and the trial did not take place.

It will perhaps never be clear if Pacciani was indeed the Monster of Florence, but his past record shows some activities similar to, although not exactly the same as, class III necrophilia. Pacciani was a semiliterate farmhand and amateur taxidermist who had been convicted in 1951 of murdering a traveling salesman caught "in an affectionate embrace" with Pacciani's girlfriend. Following the murder, Pacciani had made the woman lie beside the corpse and had intercourse with her.[40] It is possible that Pacciani increased his orgasmic intensity by this behavior. This makes **Pacciani**'s behavior very similar to a class III necrophile.

Some would like to have **sexual intercourse in the presence of a coffin**, or a corpse, because it increases their orgasmic intensity. Some would masturbate or have sexual intercourse (with a living partner) inside a coffin. While doing so, sometimes they would cover themselves with a shroud.

Some others would like merely to view a person having sexual intercourse with a corpse (not engaging in intercourse themselves).

Thoinot[41] (p. 402) describes two cases that belong to this category: one from his own experience and one from Dr. Brouardel. His case concerned a person who could get an erection only by having a funeral scene enacted at a bordello. He had the room hung in black, candles lighted, prayers said; without this artificial representation of funeral pomp, he remained absolutely impotent. Thoinot, however, considers it a case of **fetishism,** and ends the case by asking the reader, "Is not this a case of perfectly characterized fetichism (sic), but under a very broad definition?"

He then goes on to describe an almost analogous case from Dr. Brouardel in which the subject could not meet a funeral or be present at a death mass without experiencing terrible erections, which drove him to despair. So great and uncontrollable was his paraphilia that at the death of his father, he had to abstain from being present at the ceremony, lest he would get erections (p. 403).

Some **may be seen masturbating during funeral sermons** or dirges as they sit in a crowd of mourners. These kinds of incidents occurred at the Paris morgue several years ago, whereby a certain number of individuals were discovered, on different occasions, in the act of masturbating in front of the glass case where the cadavers were exposed. These incidents ultimately necessitated a well-directed surveillance system to prevent repetitions (p. 448).[41]

Some necrophiles would **see pictures of the dead** and would masturbate. A typical case has been described by **Bauer and colleagues**[39] where the necrophile had collected and stored in his computer more than 5000 digital images of a stolen corpse in various stages of dissection. The authors feel that this allowed him to have an unlimited and fast access to pictures with a necrophilic content. According to the authors, the offender could thus engage in "**virtual necrophilic acts**" whenever feasible without a need to have physical contact with the dead body or its parts.

Rauch[13] describes the case of a 24-year-old epileptic who used to have fantasies of naked women. He wanted sex relations with a corpse but was fearful of catching contagious diseases from corpses, so he devised a way to achieve orgasm without ever having to touch the dead bodies. He would enter cemetery chapels seeking female corpses. Finding one, he would put it on the ground and then masturbate, so he would have no sexual contact with the body. On one occasion, he did insert his finger in the vagina of a corpse.

Most paraphiliacs in the first three classes **never touch a dead body.** Those who never touch the dead but find sexual gratification merely from looking at them have been labeled *platonic necrophilists*, or *platonic necrophiles.* All these cases may be termed as cases of **latent necrophilia** or **fantasy necrophilia,** with the subjects known as **latent necrophiles** or **fantasy necrophiles.** As seen earlier, many authors have called this pseudonecrophilia.[12,13,14] **Taphophilia** is the name given to people who get arousal from funerals.

Class IV Necrophiles: Tactile Necrophiles

These necrophiles go one step further than class III necrophiles and need to touch a dead body in some erotic way in order to get an orgasm. They enjoy touching, stroking, or licking parts of the dead body, such as genitalia or breasts. Some may even take jobs as mortuary attendants, or some other job dealing with the dead, because they want to be near dead bodies. They feel that authorities in funeral homes, and even relatives of the dead, should encourage attendance of anyone at funeral homes, so that these tactile necrophiles may get an outlet for their fantasies. They would be able to touch dead bodies and get their orgasms. They feel that since this practice does not harm anyone in particular, this practice is acceptable and should be encouraged. Medical students who get an erection while dissecting cadavers also fall in this group. **Stekel** mentions the case of a student who, when dissecting a corpse during anatomy classes, would have a sudden erection.[42] Legally, in most jurisdictions, these necrophiles may be sued for disturbing the dead.

Rapoport[43] describes a typical case belonging to this class. The offender, to whom the author refers simply as **W.R.** (1890–?), was 50 years old when he was arrested for kissing the lips and touching the breasts of a female corpse in a funeral parlor. After his arrest he was admitted to the **prison ward** of **Bellevue Hospital** on August 9, 1940. He was an old, pale, emaciated man, who simply liked to **kiss the lips of corpses** or **touch their breasts.** If any of these were not possible, he would **just look at the body** to get an erection. After having done any of these actions (looking at the body, kissing or touching breasts), he would go to a lavatory or return home to masturbate. Dead relatives, including females, never excited him, save for two instances, when his maternal aunts died. In 1930, when his aunt died (third oldest, and next to the youngest), she was laid out in a casket. Simply looking at her dead body gave W.R. an erection. Rapoport reports the offender's account of his experience thus: "I went inside the bathroom, I spit on it (penis) and rubbed it with my right hand. Nothing went through my mind, just relief afterwards. I felt it was something I shouldn't be doing." In 1932 or 1933 (the offender is not sure), another of his maternal aunts died. He just looked at her and had an erection. He went home and masturbated.

After 1930, when he masturbated after seeing the dead body of his maternal aunt, W.R. developed a habit of visiting funeral parlors. He would cut out death notices from the daily newspapers, dress up, and visit the bodies (about twice or thrice a week). Both his landlady and the aunt with whom he lived reported seeing a large collection of such newspaper clippings in his room. He preferred visiting the funeral parlors early in the morning (about 9 AM) in order to avoid the relatives of the deceased. In 1935, when an actress whom he used to see in movies died, he went out to see her dead body and got such a strong erection that "I had to masturbate—it wouldn't go down otherwise." In 1936, he masturbated at the death of another actress.

W.R. did get an erection on seeing **male corpses,** but he never kissed them. He kissed only female corpses. He also never visited the corpses of children. He also claimed that he masturbated only when he saw a corpse, or if he had a vision of a (dead) body just before going to sleep.

Apart from the erections achieved at seeing dead bodies of his two maternal aunts, W.R. never had an erection seeing the dead bodies of any of his other relatives. He reported no erection at the death of his grandmother (1895), his adoptive father (1919), or his adoptive mother (1924). It is significant that his mother's dead body did not give him an erection, although he could clearly see an erotic portion of her anatomy—upper part of her breasts. In fact, this was the first time he ever saw the body of a woman. According to him, "Hers was the only dead body I didn't admire. The one I thought would be good looking turned out to be worst." At one time W.R. expressed the wish to be a morgue attendant, because he felt that this job would sufficiently satisfy his craving for visiting dead bodies.

Significantly, W.R. never wanted to have anything more to do with the corpses than touching their breasts or kissing them. In fact, when asked if he ever felt like inserting his penis into corpses, he replied, "No, because it is wrong." This answer suggests that W.R. was a typical **tactile necrophile.** When he was asked why he was attracted to the corpses of middle-aged or elderly females, he replied, "Because (their) breasts are more developed." Since tactile necrophilia involves getting pleasure only from touching, this answer suggests further that he truly belonged to this class. Fuller breasts are likely to be more stimulating on touching. In reply to the question, "What attracts you most in the bodies of corpses?" he replied, "upper part." Some other questions and answers are illustrative:

Q: What do you think of breasts?
A: I like them. I like to touch them. Touch them on bodies if I get a chance [i.e., if no one is looking].
Q: Why do you touch the breast?
A: Breast is soft. I like the touch.

During an interview W.R. expressed the view that if he were prevented from seeing corpses, he might resort to killing. He never killed, though. Upon being asked how he would kill, he replied, "I might hit him. I wouldn't use a knife. I don't like the sight of blood. If I see my own blood, it weakens me." Killing *per se* does not seem to give any pleasure to W.R. When asked if he would kill an animal, he replied, "No, it would only be someone who would interfere with my seeing bodies." It is interesting that unlike a class IX necrophile, he does not want to kill in order to get a dead body for necrophilic activities. Instead he would kill if he were not allowed to see (and touch) a dead body, indicating how strong a tactile necrophile he is.

SIDEBAR 3.4 Performing Fellatio on Corpses—A Class IV Activity

There are reports of necrophiles who go no further than performing fellatio on corpses. Such necrophiles would belong to **class IV,** as their involvement with corpses is mainly tactile in nature. **Brill**[44] presents the case of **D** (1880–?), a 30-year-old, single, male clerk. He was fourth of eight children, two of whom died in infancy. Out of the five remaining siblings, only the eldest was a boy (six years older than D). The rest were girls, so D basically grew up in the company of girls. He grew up to be a very effeminate person, so much so that he was always timid and awkward in the company of boys. He had many girlfriends who treated him as one of themselves.

For several years during his childhood, D lived with his parents on his maternal uncle's farm. (His parents were impoverished, and it was his uncle—a prosperous farmer—who was supporting them.) Once during this period—when D was between 3 and 4 years old—his cousin, four years older than him, initiated him into playing "cow and calf," where D played the role of calf, and supposedly performed fellatio on him. For several years thereafter, he performed this activity without complaining to anyone. Eventually the families separated, but D liked performing fellatio so much that he never gave up this habit. He practiced it with older men whenever the opportunity arose. Once he attempted fellatio on a farmhand who was deep asleep, but the man immediately woke up and gave him a sound thrashing. D felt so terribly disgraced that he had to leave the village.

D's homosexual activities were not confined to performing fellatio. He also acted as a passive partner (**catamite**) in homosexual acts and lent himself to *coitus inter femora* (allowing the thrusting of the partner's penis between his upper thighs).

Besides homosexuality, he also showed necrophilic tendencies. In fact, because of the concurrent occurrence of these two behaviors, Brill designates him as a **homosexual necrophile** (as shall be seen later, he is actually **homosexual necrophile Type I**). Interestingly, during the early period of his life, D had a **morbid fear of dead people.** Someone told him he could be cured of this fear by touching a dead person. He mustered enough courage to request a local undertaker to allow him to do so. He was allowed, and seemingly as soon as he touched a corpse, his phobia of dead bodies actually turned into the opposite—a **strong attraction for corpses!**

The undertaker seemed pleased to have him around, and D became a regular frequenter of his establishment. He was so fascinated by his freedom from his dread of corpses that he began playing tricks on those who were known to be afraid of corpses. He would fix himself up like a corpse and get into a coffin. An accomplice then brought in a timid acquaintance. As soon as the somewhat hesitant newcomer came near the coffin, D would suddenly sit up in the coffin, experiencing great pleasure at the fright of the victim. His pranks came to an end after he played this trick on a woman who became so hysterical that she required medical attention.

As his fascination for corpses increased, he became the undertaker's paid assistant. D finally got involved with the law, as he was convicted for sending love letters to a man, who turned them over to the post office authorities. He was sentenced to 3 years of imprisonment. During his interviews with Brill, D confessed that during his work at the undertaker's place, he had repeatedly **committed fellatio on corpses.** One would expect this kind of activity from a female necrophile, but coming from a male, this sounds exceptional. D was involved in no other sexual activity with the corpses.

Klaf and **Brown**[45] present the report of a 40-year-old black male who presents many features of a class IV necrophile (no name has been given; we would call him **KBP**, after **K**laf and **B**rown's **P**atient). From the description, he appears to have been born in 1918 (in their 1958 paper, the authors report that he is a 40-year-old male). KBP was born in New York City and was the youngest of five children. A father of five children himself, he was discharged from the army in 1943 because of acute schizophrenia, auditory hallucinations, depression, emotional instability, and multiple phobias, the most troublesome of which was the fear that pigeons would attack him. He found peace and quiet only in funeral parlors. His interest in the dead began when he was 9 years old. At that time he used to assist in a local funeral parlor. He enjoyed a number of activities involving touching of dead bodies. Even though he never got paid for it, he helped with the embalming process, drew blood from the bodies, made restorations where death was caused by a disfiguring accident or disease—once he stitched back the decapitated head of a beautiful girl and derived great pleasure from it—and even hugged the dead bodies. Some of his other thoughts and activities displaying necrophilic tendencies were running home to masturbate after seeing dead bodies, and substituting a corpse for his wife in his imagination during sexual intercourse with her. Interestingly, while he denied erotic interest in the dead, the above information was derived during **sodium amytal interviews.** During such interviews, he revealed that the onset and progress of **rigor mortis** had a peculiar fascination for him. He thought that the postures and expressions assumed by the corpse as rigor mortis progressed was evidence that the dead had the personality of a live person. He thought that the best part of a funeral was when dirt was thrown on the coffin. He liked the hollow sound that it made. Repeatedly he would seek permission to assist in the hospital morgue. The authors consider this as an example of **inhibited necrophilia** as described by Jones.

During his childhood, he was a sickly infant and a frail, undernourished child who had to be placed in special health classes at school. He had the habit of eating ashes. He did not receive love from anyone except his mother, who died when he was very young. His father was a feared and stern figure who beat his children on their wet skin to make the blows more painful. His grandmother and sister were very critical of him. His intelligence was above average (IQ 115). He was hospitalized, where he received insulin coma therapy and psychotherapy. Gradually his anxiety and phobias decreased, but he remained fearful of pigeons. He also retained an interest in the dead, hoping to find a job in a mortuary.

Class V Necrophiles: People Having a Fetishistic Necrophilia (Fetishistic Necrophiles)

These necrophiles are a bit more abnormal than class III and IV necrophiles, but they still do not engage in any copulatory activity with the dead. Instead, if they come across a dead body and if chance arose, they would cut up some portion of the body—perhaps a **breast**—for later fetishistic activities. They may even keep some portion of the dead body—**pubic hair** or a **finger** perhaps—in the pocket for continuous erotic stimulation, or sometimes may wear it as an amulet for similar pleasure. Bauer and colleagues[39] describe the case of a 40-year-old, married civil engineer who once removed the breasts and eyeballs of the dead body of a 20-year-old woman, and took them away for fetishistic activities.

Some remove clothes, especially panties or even tampons, from corpses to keep as fetish objects. These necrophiles are **necrofetishists,** and their paraphilia is known as **necrofetishism.** At first glance, they may appear to be similar to class II necrophiles, as the latter engage in similar activities. However, class II necrophiles preserve parts of their recently dead loved ones in order to fill up a psychosexual vacuum that their death has caused. They would not do so with the dead body of a stranger, as do necrophiles of class V.

KEY POINT 3.1

Although activities of class V necrophiles may result in mutilation of the dead body, their primary motive is to acquire a fetish, and never to mutilate the dead body, as would a class VI necrophile. While class VI necrophiles get an orgasm simply by mutilating the dead body, class V necrophiles would not get an orgasm from mutilation. It would come from the fetish they have acquired.

Tsheryaskin[46] has described a rare case of a female necrophile from this category whom he treated at the psychiatric clinic of the **University of Saratov, Russia.** The case describes a 19-year-old female (no name has been given; we would call her **TP,** after Tsheryaskin's Patient), whose parents and two siblings (a sister and a brother) were psychotic. Intellectually she was quite normal. She was a **zoosadist** as well as a **sadomasochist.** At the age of 5–6 years, she took pleasure in sticking needles into dogs and in torturing cats. As she grew older, she behaved in the same way toward her companions. Her masochistic tendencies expressed in the form of torturing, pinching, beating, and sticking needles into herself. She also used to cut herself with a razor. From the age of 14, she began to lead a **loose sexual life** without, however, attaining any gratification.

During her youth, her psychotic mother took her along on her frequent visits to cemeteries. This seemed to have developed in TP a morbid desire to see dead people and to read about murders and suicides. One of her pleasant fantasies was to commit suicide by cutting her throat. At the age of 16, she tried to poison herself by taking **mercury,** but she recovered after many months in a hospital. Her desire to see corpses kept on increasing. So intense did the desire become of remaining near corpses that she took a course in anatomy, hoping thereby to obtain some fetishistic object from them, such as some **skin with hair,** or a **finger from a corpse.** She also had a strong desire to talk to corpses and to embrace them and to weep. So much did the thoughts of corpses torment her that she presumably prayed to them to leave her in peace.

The paper does not inform us whether TP ever put her desires into practice, but presumably she did. Tsheryaskin tried to treat her with hypnotism and persuasion, and though his treatment gave some relief to the patient, it was not of lasting benefit.

Ehrlich and colleagues[47] describe the case of a young necrophile (exact age not stated) who continued committing necrophilic acts for 15 years. A total of 12 necrophilic acts committed by him during this period are described that place him predominantly in class V, but at times he also displayed characteristics of other classes, most notably classes III and VI. He also holds the distinction of having been legally convicted twice on charges of defiling the dead.

His paraphilic tendencies started at the age of 13, when he first started gratifying himself sexually with underwear stolen from his adoptive mother (fetishism). Later he started stealing shrouds from coffins and clothes from dead bodies for fetishistic purposes (class V necrophilia). His initial necrophilic activities consisted of breaking into mortuaries, from where he stole shrouds and burial clothes twice for fetishistic purposes. Three times he severed the breasts of female corpses. (Once he used a scalpel stolen from a mortuary for this purpose, and a jackknife at all other times.) Of these three cases, in one case, he fastened the severed breasts to his naked chest using a bra, and then masturbated in front of a mirror (much in the fashion of Ed Gein). In one case, in addition to severing the breasts, he cut off the right arm of the corpse, inflicted a deep cut wound to the neck and a stab wound on the abdomen (displaying predominantly class VI characteristics). After this activity, he was arrested and put in a penitentiary clinic on charges of defiling the dead. He was discharged 3 years later and received outpatient psychotherapy.

However, his necrophilic activities did not end. He continued stealing shrouds and burial clothes from coffins. Once he opened a 3-week-old grave of an 8-year-old boy and removed his corpse. However, the corpse failed to arouse him sexually and once he realized that, he threw the body into a nearby vault without any further manipulations. On one occasion, he broke into a cemetery chapel, opened two coffins, removed the corpse from one of them, and put it together with the other body in the other coffin. He thus effectively emptied one coffin so that he could enter it and then covered himself with a shroud and gratified himself sexually (displaying class III characteristics). Once he opened a relatively fresh grave and groped for the genitals to determine the sex of the corpse. On finding that it was a male corpse, he left it alone. On three occasions, he "skinned" the trunks of female corpses, removing large flaps of skin much in the shape of a shirt. He would then "wear the shirt" on his naked body and masturbate. In one of these cases, after mutilation, he slept for the whole night in the vault in company of the mutilated corpse. After this last act he was arrested by the police. He refused an examination by a psychiatrist. The District Court of Berlin convicted him again on a charge of defiling the dead and committed him to a closed psychiatric institution.

Significantly, nearly all his acts were done in a cemetery situated halfway between his apartment and the psychiatrist's practice he regularly consulted following the court order (after his first conviction). During interrogation, he admitted that after his therapy sessions, he would have an overpowering state of arousal that compelled him to visit the cemetery. The authors do not dwell on the possible etiological factors.

QUICK FACT 3.1

When the home of **John Reginald Halliday Christie** (1898–1953) was raided after some dead bodies were recovered from his cupboards and backyard, a curious object that was recovered was a tobacco tin containing four lots of pubic hair. Its presence can be explained only by the fact that Christie displayed some characteristics of class V necrophilia. It is inconceivable that women allowed him to clip their pubic hair during life. He also had a fetish for female knickers. None of the dead bodies recovered from his house was wearing knickers.

An interesting instance of fetishistic necrophilia is possession of books bound in women's skin, **preferably from the bosom**, with nipples forming very characteristic protuberances on the outer part of the back and front covers. The practice of binding books in human skin—**anthropodermic bibliopegy**—dates back to the seventeenth century, and it was an acceptable practice in those times. Usually medical books, especially anatomy texts, were bound in human skin, especially as medical men had unrivalled opportunities for obtaining human skin. Sometimes judicial proceedings were bound in the skin of the murderer convicted in those proceedings. Necrofetishists, or **class V necrophiles,** carried this practice to the extreme, where books were bound with the skin of women's breasts so they could have a feeling of holding breasts as they read the book! The publisher of obscene books, **Isidore Liseux,** claimed to have bound one edition (1793) of *Justine et Juliette* by the Marquis de Sade in female breasts.[48] Naturally for such books, skin from the female bosom had to be procured from cadavers. It is said that some interns in the Clamart were dismissed because they used to deliver skin of the breasts of deceased female patients to a binder of obscene books in the Faubourg Saint-Germain.[48] Coin purses made of male scrotum and carried by females have also been reported.[48]

Sometimes **cremated remains** may be used as a **necrofetish.** An interesting case came to light in 2009, when a 41-year-old man, identified only as **Park,** was arrested for stealing an urn containing the ashes of the late South Korean actress **Choi Jin-sil** (1968–2008). Choi was one of the most beloved actresses in South Korea, often referred to as **Korea's sweetheart.** The urn containing her ashes was discovered missing from her grave around 8:10 AM on **August 15,** 2009.[49] Ten days later, on **August 25, Park,** a kitchen appliance installer, was arrested, and on interrogation he confessed to the crime. According to surveillance camera images, the suspect first visited Choi's tomb on **August 2,** and two days later broke the tomb's lower part, which was encircled with marble plates, with a hammer and took out the urn.[50] Criminal psychologists have raised the possibility that the suspect is a necrophile.[50] This is an interesting case of **class V necrophilia,** where ashes of a dead person were stolen for necrophilic activity.

SIDEBAR 3.5 The Curious Case of Park—Cremation Urn Thief

South Korean actress **Choi Jin-sil** (1968–2008), popularly known as Korea's sweetheart, was depressed after her marriage to baseball player **Jo Seong-min** went sour and ended in a divorce in 2004. She committed suicide on **October 2, 2008,** by **hanging** herself in the bathroom of her Seoul home. No suicide note was ever found. However, Choi sent an assistant two cell phone text messages on October 1 asking her to "take care of my children no matter what happens" and telling her that "I'm sorry." She was duly cremated and her ashes preserved in an urn, which was buried at Kapsan Park in Yangpyeong, according to prevailing customs.

Almost a year later, on **August 15, 2009,** her tombstone was found vandalized and the urn containing her ashes was missing. A closed circuit camera was located about 17.5 meters from the burial site. Examination of film footage revealed that the crime took place on **August 4, 2009,** sometime between 9:55 PM and 10:58 PM.

In the film, a man who looks around 35–50 years old appeared near Choi's burial site around 9:56 PM. He had short hair and wore a jacket and gloves. He appeared to wander around the site, making sure he was alone, before removing a hammer from a sack, smashing the back of Choi's headstone several times, taking out the urn containing her ashes, and then driving off in a car. The suspect—later identified as **Park**—returned to the location the next morning at 3:36 AM with a bucket and a cloth and cleaned up the tombstone, presumably to hide his tracks. He took special care to brush off any signs of damage, cleaning his fingerprints and placing a bouquet of flowers to mask the broken tiles. Park was arrested on **August 25, 2009,** and is currently on trial.

Class VI Necrophiles: People Having a Necromutilomania (Necromutilomaniacs)

These are more severe cases than earlier classes. Wulffen[51] describes this class under the type **necrophagy.** These individuals normally do not engage in sexual intercourse with the dead. Their erotic pleasure comes primarily from mutilating an already dead body and masturbating simultaneously. An important point to note is that these necrophiles do not kill; they merely get sexual satisfaction from mutilating an already dead body. It is possible that mutilations such as stab wounds represent a kind of "penetration" for these offenders. Indeed, many mutilations are found to be concentrated around victims' genitals and breasts.[52]

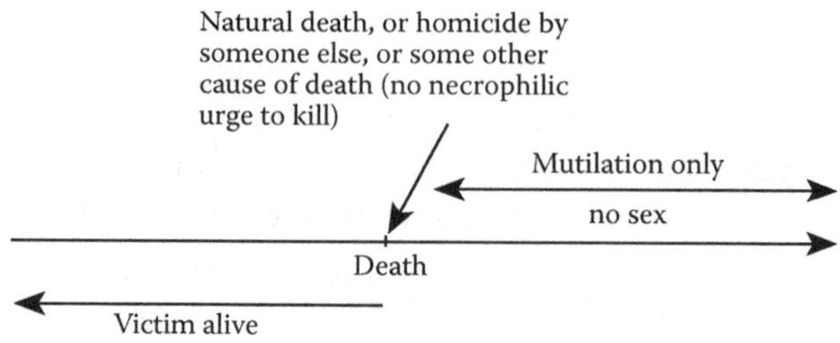

Figure 3.3 Class IV mutilators as described by Rajs and colleagues.[26] No sexual activity and/or mutilation occurs in the living. The victim is *not* killed by the offender. The offender merely happens to find a dead body and carries out mutilation on it. No sexual activity is carried out on the dead body. This category is congruent with class VI necrophiles. Except in the last category, where the cause of death was natural, all deaths in the first three groups were homicidal, or homicide was strongly suspected.

It is illustrative to compare and contrast this class with classes mentioned by Rajs and colleagues,[26] who studied **mutilations of corpses** in Sweden from 1961 to 1990. They recorded a total of 22 deaths with criminal mutilation or dismemberment of the human body. Four types of mutilations were identified: defensive mutilation (Type I), which is done in order to get rid of the corpse or make its identity more difficult (10 cases); aggressive mutilation (Type II) following rage killing, in which the killer mutilates the face and genitals following death due to rage (overkill) (four cases); offensive mutilation (Type III), also known as **lust murder** or **necrosadistic murder,** where the offender may have necrophilic urges for postmortem sexual activity with the victim, which may involve pre- or postmutilation (seven cases); and finally necromanic mutilation (Type IV), where the offender mutilates the already dead body (he does not kill) in order to use body parts as trophies or to use as fetishes (one case) (Figure 3.3). In the last category, there was only one case. This case involved an unnamed 63-year-old male who worked as a sailor and car driver. He was born in Russia (for ease of reference he will be referred to as **R**) shortly before the revolution. The family lived near a graveyard, where he witnessed executions and mutilations of bodies. He witnessed victims digging their own graves before execution. R came to Sweden with his mother at school age. He had psychiatric problems as a child and teenager, with thoughts about death, corpses, graves, and violence, and problems with nervousness and stuttering. R was also afraid of the police. His mother took him to psychiatrists because of his lack of interest in women. R had no known drug problems. In 1941, after 2 years of friendship he murdered a waitress and shot himself in the chest. He was diagnosed with schizophrenia (DSM-IV 295.90), described as psychoinfantile, and sentenced to psychiatric care.

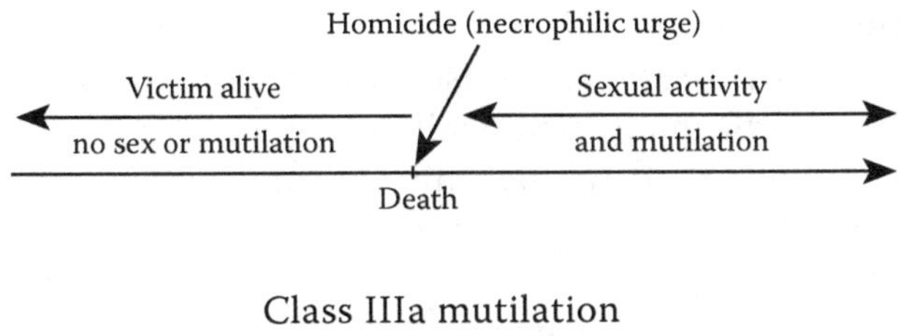

Figure 3.4 Class IIIa mutilators as described by Rajs and colleagues.[26] No sexual activity or mutilation occurs in the living. The victim is killed due to a necrophilic urge. Sexual activity and mutilation are then carried out on the dead.

In February 1979, R mutilated the dead body of his own mother, who had died of myocardial infarction in the hospital at the age of 85. Her body was embalmed and buried. R opened the graveyard, decapitated her, and also sawed off both hands and little toes. He used to walk about with her head in a plastic bag. The removed body parts were found in R's house. No mention is made in the paper of any sexual activity with the dead body. It is this last category of Rajs ([Type IV] necromanic mutilation) that is congruent with class VI necrophiles (people having a necromutilomania—necromutilomaniacs).

The authors **subdivide type III mutilations into two further types**: those motivated by a necrophilic urge to kill and then carry out sexual activities with the dead body and those who begin mutilating a living person before killing and continuing sexual activity. **No activity (sex or mutilation) occurs during the life of the victim.** On the dead body, mutilation may occur prior or subsequent to sexual activity, or perhaps simultaneously **(class IIIa)** (Figure 3.4), and in those cases where the mutilations are initiated in a living person—conscious or unconscious—sexual activity and mutilation continue on the dead victim (**class IIIb**) (Figure 3.5).

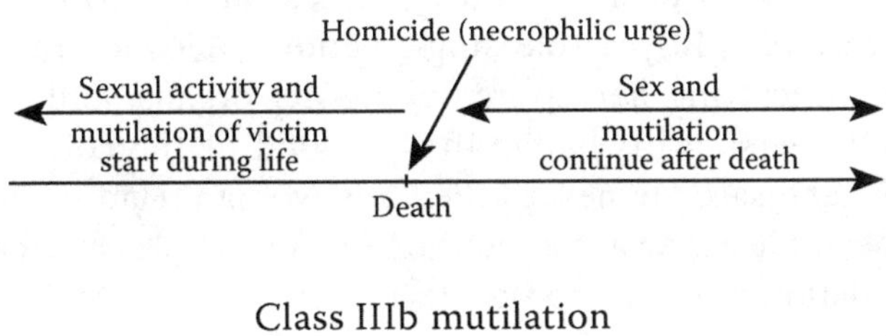

Figure 3.5 Class IIIb mutilators as described by Rajs and colleagues.[26] Sexual activity and/or mutilation initiates in the living. The victim is killed due to a necrophilic urge. Sexual activity and mutilation are then continued on the dead body.

In the latter type, the offender seems to have combined sexual sadistic and necrophilic needs. The sexual sadistic need compels the offender to carry out sexual activities or intercourse while inflicting pain or injuries on the living. The necrophilic need compels him to carry out sexual activity once the victim is dead. Both these types (class IIIa and IIIb) may include **eating of human flesh.**

In some cases, the offender may eat parts of a corpse as part of sexual gratification (**necrophagia**). Necrophagic tendency starts from this class onward, and may be seen with increasing frequency as we go higher up in the classification.

QUICK FACT 3.2

Anthropophagy (Greek *anthropos* ["man"] and *phagein* ["to eat"]) refers to the eating of human flesh (also known as **cannibalism**). It is more or less a culturally sanctioned practice in some primitive communities, and is *not* associated with sexual arousal. When eating of human flesh *is* associated with sexual arousal, it is referred to as *necrophagia*. *Parthenophagy* refers to eating dead bodies of young girls in order to achieve sexual arousal. **Albert Fish** used to practice parthenophagy. Necrophiles who also indulge in cannibalism are more appropriately referred to as **cannibal necrophiles. Andrei Chikatilo** is a prototype of a cannibal necrophile.

Eating of virtually any part of a corpse may cause sexual arousal. **Masters and Lea**[24] (p. 117) report the case of a man who derived sexual gratification from eating the nail trimmings of corpses. They also describe the case of another necrophile who was attracted to the hair of cadavers. (What exactly he did with the hair is not mentioned.)

Class VI is akin to Rosman and Resnick's[9] **necrophilic fantasy.** They describe the case of a 40-year-old single white male who fantasized about killing a woman, cutting her up, removing her organs, and then masturbating while immersing his hands in the blood of the corpse. (He never did act on his fantasies. He never killed any woman. Had he done that, he would have been a class IXa necrophile.) His erotic pleasure came mainly from the mutilation of warm bodies. In his late 20s, he obtained a job in a morgue for the sole purpose of being near dead bodies and being able to cut them up. Although he denied any actual sexual contact with the corpses, he became sexually excited by cutting them up. His case represents a typical class VI necrophile. Many mortuary attendants and technicians belong to this category.

Class VII Necrophiles: Opportunistic Necrophiles

Rosman and Resnick[9] describe this category under the term *pseudonecrophilia*. Normally they are quite content having intercourse with the living and would not think of engaging in sexual intercourse with the dead. However, if an opportunity arose, they would. Rosman and Resnick[9] describe an interesting case under this category. A 37-year-old single white male was dating a 49-year-old woman, and was having normal sexual relations with her. One day he accidentally shot her while under the influence of alcohol. He panicked and tried to hide the dead body. When he was hiding her body, he became sexually excited and had anal intercourse (**anal necrophilia**) with the corpse, and then disposed of it. He was aware of necrophilia and necrophiles as he had earlier read about them in pornography magazines.

POINT TO PONDER 3.1

It might appear at first glance that the offender described here by Rosman and Resnick[9] belongs to class IX, because he actually murdered his girlfriend and then had anal intercourse with her, which is what class IX necrophiles are known to do. However, he did not murder her for the specific purpose of sexual intercourse, which is the hallmark of class IX necrophiles. The murder was accidental; it was only when he was hiding the body that he got aroused and had sexual intercourse with her. Thus, this offender belongs more appropriately to class VII, an opportunistic necrophile.

Meloy[53] describes a very similar case. In this case, a 24-year-old female victim was found dead at 3 AM in the living room of her apartment where she resided with her two children, ages 1 and 3, and her common-law husband, an African-American, aged 26. She was in the lithotomy position with her hips extended and her knees flexed. Her body was nude except for clothing pulled above her breasts. It was obvious that sexual intercourse had been performed on her—quite possibly after death. She had been stabbed 61 times with a 14.5-inch switchblade knife, which was found in a kitchen drawer. Blood stains indicated that she had been dragged from the kitchen approximately 7 feet onto the living room carpet. The children were asleep in the bedroom. Vaginal smears showed semen, but oral and anal smears did not. There was no evidence of trauma to the vagina or anus. Toxicology detected methamphetamine with blood and urine screens, which was confirmed with GC/MS screen.

Witnesses testified that her husband had been drinking alcohol that evening with friends. He returned to the apartment and the couple were heard arguing. At 2:15 AM "violent screaming and struggling" began. At 2:25 AM (the moment she was killed) the noise suddenly stopped. At 2:28 AM he ordered by telephone a pornographic film to be shown through his cable television service in the apartment. His subsequent interactions with his neighbors aroused their suspicions, and they called the police. By the time the police arrived, he had fled through the bedroom window. However, he was apprehended one hour later.

His interrogation revealed that he killed his wife because during the verbal encounter she had provoked him with a knife. He described his intense anger toward her for "'doggin' me out." He admitted that he had been drinking alcohol, and 8 hours after the homicide his blood alcohol level was .04%. He tested negative for all other illicit drugs. In a subsequent clinical interview he stated that he had sex with her dead body, "because I wanted to make love to her one last time. 'Cause she was gone." His description of sex with his wife's dead body was consistent with depersonalization (a feeling of watching oneself act, while having no control over a situation). He said, "somebody over her . . . , they was fucking her . . . I do remember looking down, like I wasn't, like somebody else was making love to her, but I know it was me. No one else was there. I'm not stupid."

Mortuary attendants and **funeral workers** who resort to sexual intercourse with the dead because they have an easy access to them fall under this category. **Kenneth Douglas** (1953–), a mortuary attendant at Hamilton County morgue, Ohio, from 1976 to 1992, who had sex with the dead body of murder victim **Karen Range,** 19, in 1982, and possibly with several other dead bodies during his tenure, is a classic necrophile belonging to this class.

Karpman[54] describes several cases of necrophilia that he has taken from the literature. His case #137 belongs to this class. **D.W.** was a 21-year-old unmarried white male who worked as a morgue attendant. He was a confirmed masturbator but denied homosexual acts. At the age of 18, he performed one act of heterosexual intercourse with his girlfriend, who died several months later. He wished to be buried with her (**taphephilia**). D.W. wanted to enter medical school but was financially unable to do so. Ultimately he was admitted to a school of undertaking and embalming. Here he encountered dead bodies of many females on a regular basis. Initially he fought off a desire for intercourse with the corpses, but finally yielded and performed **cunnilingus on a corpse,** which resulted in emission. Gradually he undertook all kinds of sexual activities on female cadavers of all ages, from infants to elderly women. He sucked their breasts, performed cunnilingus on them, and had sexual intercourse both vaginally and anally. This occurred as many as four to five times weekly. On one occasion he drank blood and urine from the corpse, and bit its flesh. He was sent to a hospital for the criminally insane.

Sometimes a person may murder his consort for other reasons (say jealousy) and then have sexual intercourse with the dead body. **Setia and Tabin**[55] describe a rare case where the accused killed his wife and then had sexual intercourse with her. The reason he gave in his testimony was that she had not consented to intercourse with him for the last few years, as she was having an extramarital affair with someone else. Sometimes she would have physical relations with her boyfriend even in the presence of her husband, which frustrated him very much. There was no previous history of any psychiatric illness in the accused. The authors see the behavior of the accused as being a result of both jealousy resulting from his wife having extramarital affair and frustration for not getting sexual gratification. The reason these people are not classified among class IX (homicidal necrophiles) is that their primary intention for killing is never to acquire a dead body for sexual intercourse. In class VII necrophilia, sex is generally carried out without mutilation of the dead body. No case seems to have been reported so far in which a class VII necrophile has also mutilated a dead body.

Class VIII Necrophiles: Regular Necrophiles

Class VIII necrophiles would not enjoy sexual intercourse with the living, even if this choice were available to them. Instead they would seek out a dead body to have sexual intercourse with, because they get more pleasure in having sex with a dead body. They would thus resort to **stealing dead bodies from mortuaries or graveyards** for this purpose. Sometimes they may **furtively enter funeral parlors** to perform sexual intercourse with the dead. And for this they may travel far and wide. Some would **bribe mortuary attendants** to let them have access to dead bodies. **Brierre de Boismont**[56] has described one such case. (For details, please see Chapter 4, "Epidemiology of Necrophilia," under the heading "Occupation.")

QUICK FACT 3.3

To have sexual intercourse with the dead, **class VIII** necrophiles would

- Furtively enter funeral places, often posing as mourners
- Bribe mortuary attendants to let them have access to dead bodies
- Steal dead bodies from mortuary or graveyards

However, they **would not resort to killing**, as would be done by **class IX** necrophiles.

A typical case of class VIII necrophilia has been described by **Torre and Varetto.**[57] A 15-year-old girl died on July 10, 1984, of cranial trauma suffered in a road accident. In the same accident, her left lower limb suffered a fracture and a plaster cast was applied over it. The body was buried, presumably without a postmortem,* in the cemetery of a small town near Turin, Italy, on the following day, July 11.

Two days later, on the morning of July 13, when an old lady was visiting the graves of relatives, she noticed that the grave of the young girl had been dug up. There were heaps of removed earth all around the grave and two shovels lying along the two longer sides of the grave. Two shovels indicated that at least two persons may have been involved in digging. The cover of the nonmetal-lined coffin had been removed. One of its sides showed deep indentations caused by a lever.

The corpse, still wearing the plaster cast on its left lower limb, was lying on its right side. It was dressed in white funeral clothes. The funeral cloth, however, had been lifted up over the hips. The pants had been pulled down, exposing the buttocks.

When the surroundings were searched for additional clues, the lavatory of the cemetery showed a few pages of pornographic cartoons. One such page, curled up, showed some semitransparent, shiny, dried stains. A laboratory examination revealed spermatozoa on this page.

Examination of the dead body did not show much of note. Rigor mortis was in a passing phase but had not passed off completely. It was clearly noticeable in the unplastered right knee. There were no postmortem lesions on the body, including genitals and breasts. The hymen was intact and barely permitted passage of a gloved little finger. There were no lesions around the anal area. The anal orifice was wide open allowing easy entry of two gloved fingers. A mass of solid stool was present about 4–5 cm from the anus. Swabs taken from vaginal and anal canals were negative for spermatozoa.

Although the body did not reveal any sign of sexual activity, the digging of grave and the position of the body within the grave make it very likely that the grave had been dug up by some necrophile, perhaps with an associate, who may or may not have been a necrophile, too. The sexual motive of the digging was very obvious.

The authors conclude by stating that the body had likely been anally penetrated, perhaps by a stiff male organ that did not complete ejaculation, by one or more fingers, or perhaps by some inanimate object with a rather smooth surface. They assert that this anal penetration was the reason for its dilation.

A remote possibility that the authors have mentioned is possible masturbation using the pornographic cartoon strip while viewing the naked dead

* The paper does not mention this. Also, one would expect the plaster cast to have been removed had the postmortem been done.

body. It that were indeed the case, that would make the case very unique, because then the necrophile would be a class III necrophile, a necrophilic fantasizer who likes masturbating in the presence of a corpse. The peculiar aspect in this case then would be that the necrophile needed to unearth a body, expose its sexual parts, and then masturbate. No such case of a class III necrophile has been reported so far.

Rosman has indicated that many **genuine necrophiles** whom he studied consciously chose their occupations (as mortuary attendants, for example) in order to provide them with an opportunity to have sex with corpses.[10] These would be class VIII necrophiles, because they make specific efforts to acquire a dead body in order to have sex with it. However, a mortuary attendant who never took up the job with the specific motive of having an easy supply of corpses for sex, but fell prey to a wish to have sex with a corpse simply because it was easily available, would be a class VII necrophile (opportunistic necrophile). Thus not all necrophilic mortuary attendants fall into one class.

Some necrophilic mortuary attendants outwardly may appear to belong to class VII necrophiles, but they actually belong to class VIII. **De River**[52] describes the case of a mortuary attendant, **N.C.,** belonging to this specific category. A 43-year-old white male with a fifth grade education, he came to the United States from Italy as a young man. When he was only 11, in Milan, Italy, he had a job as a gravedigger. He was stimulated by the cadavers of attractive young women, and would masturbate while fondling them. Later, he began inserting his penis into the vagina. Upon arriving in America, he soon obtained work washing dead bodies in a mortuary. During the course of his duties, he not only copulated with female cadavers, but also resorted to **sucking their breasts** and performing cunnilingus (**necrocunnilingus**). In fact, when he was caught, he was performing cunnilingus with a female cadaver. He confessed that he had had sexual intercourse with hundreds of female corpses.

From this description, it would appear that he was a class VII necrophile (an opportunist necrophile who would have sexual intercourse with cadavers merely because they were easily available), but this was not the case. He **actively sought cadavers** by going to funeral parlors and posing as a mourner. When he ascertained that the body would remain at the funeral parlor overnight, he returned, managed to gain entrance, and had sexual intercourse with the cadaver. He was sent to a state mental institution as a sexual psychopath.

Two subcategories seem to exist within this class: **VIIIa** and **VIIIb. Class VIIIa necrophiles** would acquire a dead body (from a grave perhaps) and would be content to just have sexual intercourse with it. **Class VIIIb necrophiles** need to mutilate the body in addition to having sexual intercourse with it (Table 3.3).

Table 3.3 Various Subclasses within Class VIII Necrophiles

Class	Sex	Mutilation	Major Protagonists (Examples)
VIIIa	Yes	No	**Nicholas** and **Alexander Grunke** and their friend **Dustin Radke**
VIIIb	Yes	Yes	**Sergeant François Bertrand**

Class VIIIa necrophiles are the "classic" necrophiles, as one normally understands them. Wulffen[51] describes this class under type **necrostuprum,** and Rosman and Resnick[9] under their subclass **regular necrophilia.** Twins **Nicholas** and **Alexander Grunke** and their friend **Dustin Radke,** who exhumed the body of motorbike accident victim **Laura Tennesen** for sexual intercourse, are classical examples of **class VIII necrophiles.** (For details, please see Chapter 5, "Case Studies.")

As seen above, a mortuary attendant who has intercourse with the dead *only* because a dead body was easily available to him would not fall under this category. (He does not go out of his way to get a dead body.) However if he preferred a dead body to living partners for sexual intercourse, he would fall under this category. Regular necrophiles may have sexual intercourse with the living from time to time, but their preference remains sex with the dead.

Necrophiles in all categories are mostly males, but **Rosman and Resnick**[9] describe the case of a female under this category (**class VIIIa**). A 21-year-old, separated white woman was employed as an apprentice embalmer for 4 months. She had been sexually molested at the age of 8 and raped by a teacher at the age of 14. At the age of 20—perhaps as a result of repeated childhood trauma—she came to regard herself as having "died in spirit," started drinking heavily, avoided living beings, and enjoyed the company of the dead only. She had very low self-esteem. During the short period she was employed as an apprentice embalmer, she had sexual intercourse with as many as 20–40 male corpses. Her case is typical of **class VIIIa necrophilia.**

Camille Allaman[58] describes the case of a **class VIIIb** necrophile. (For details, please see Chapter 4, "Epidemiology of Necrophila," under the heading "Intelligence.") Another case typical of **class VIIIb necrophilia** is that of **Sergeant François Bertrand.** One of the most notorious and well-known necrophiles, he robbed bodies from graveyards and not only had sex with them, but mutilated them. (Please see Chapter 1, "Necrophilia: Overview and Historical Aspects," for details.) Another typical case has been described by **Bauer and colleagues.**[39] The offender in this case tried vaginal intercourse with the dead body of a 14-year-old girl, but could not achieve an erection. He then manipulated the breasts and genitals of the dead body and masturbated. In all, the offender stole three dead bodies and mutilated them. About 18 years before, he had stolen the corpse of an 18-year-old woman who had been killed in a traffic accident. He amputated the legs and left them in the casket, perhaps to make the body easier to carry. At home, he dissected the abdomen, and then buried the body. The authors do not mention anything about him engaging in sexual intercourse with this body. The disappearance of the corpse was never detected. Five years later he exhumed the remaining bones and stored the spinal column in his house, replacing the sacroiliac joint surfaces with Velcro fastenings and fixing the vertebrae together with wires, creating a compound anatomical specimen. An exhumation of the remains was required to confirm his statements, but it was not considered necessary.

He stole the next body 14 years earlier, when he entered another mortuary close to his residence and opened a casket containing the body of a 20-year-old woman. After slashing the abdomen with a knife he removed both breasts and eyeballs and took them away (fetishistic necrophilia). Some days later he disposed of the tissues somewhere along a road. This mutilation of the corpse was detected and an autopsy was performed prior to the funeral, but the case remained unsolved. (Please see Chapter 6, "Medicolegal Investigation," for other relevant details.) This case is that of a **typical class VIIIb necrophile**, but with some additional characteristics of **class III** and **class V** necrophilia, also.

Within **class VIIIb necrophiles,** there seem to exist **three** distinct types: those whose **primary motivation is mutilation,** with sex occurring only as a secondary activity (Sergeant Bertrand); those whose **primary motivation is sex,** with mutilation occurring as a secondary activity; and finally those who are motivated by **both sex and mutilation equally.**

Class IX Necrophiles: Homicidal Necrophiles

This is the most dangerous category of necrophiles. They need to have sex with a dead body to the extent that they resort to killing (**a necrophilic urge to kill**). They are also known as **violent necrophiles** or **lagnonectors** (persons who kill in order to have sex with the corpse), and the practice is often known as **homicidophilia.** The term **warm necrophilia** may be applied to these cases, since intercourse is attempted on fresh bodies, which are recently dead. In many cases, the necrophilic urge to kill is so strong and repetitious that it compels the necrophile to become a **serial killer.**[59]

At least six **distinct subclasses** within this class seem to exist depending on how the necrophile treated the victim during life and death (Table 3.4). In all six classes, the necrophile kills the victim due to a necrophilic urge (an urge to kill because a dead body is required for necrophilic activities). However, his behavior with the victim during life and after death would put him in different classes.

Offenders belonging to **class IXa** would be content to just kill a victim and then mutilate the body to have sexual orgasm. On August 24, 1867, at about 1:30 PM, **Frederick Baker** (1838–1867), a clerk of a local

Table 3.4 Various Subclasses within Class IX Necrophiles

	Victim Living		Victim Dead		
Class	Torture/Mutilation	Sex	Mutilation	Sex	Major Protagonists (Examples)
IXa	No	No	Yes	No	Jack the Ripper, Ed Gein, Monster of Florence (*Il mostro di Firenze*), Frederick Baker
IXb	No	No	No	Yes	John Christie (1898–1953), Eli Ulayuk (1968–)
IXc	No	No	Yes	Yes	Joseph Vacher (1869–1898)
IXd	Sex (nonconsensual) *or* torture/mutilation		Sex *or* mutilation		Surendra Koli (1970–), Gruyo
IXe	Sex (nonconsensual) *and/or* torture/mutilation		Sex *and/or* mutilation (Note: This subclass would include those combinations that do not fall in subclass IXd and IXf.)		Jerry Brudos (sex during life; sex *and* mutilation after death—most typical behavior)
IXf	Yes	Yes	Yes	Yes	Ted Bundy, Jeffrey Dahmer

solicitor in Alton, Hampshire, tried to lure 8-year-old **Fanny Adams** to accompany him to a lonely road by giving her a halfpenny. When she refused, he picked her up forcibly and carried her into a nearby hop field. There he killed her by hitting her head with a stone, and badly mutilated her body.

At 7 PM, the neighbors formed a search party and discovered the mutilated remains of Fanny's body. Her severed head was found laid on two poles, deeply slashed from mouth to ear and across the left temple. Her right ear had been cut off. Both her eyes were missing; they were later found in the River Wey. A leg and thigh had been removed from the body. Her torso had been dismembered, and the entire contents of her chest and pelvis had been torn out and scattered. Some internal organs were even further slashed or mutilated. So savage was the mutilation that other parts of her body were recovered only after extensive searches over several days. Baker was arrested later the same night.

Baker represents typical **class IXa** necrophilia. There is no evidence that Fanny was sexually assaulted. The postmortem report did not mention sexual assault. Even a diary that Baker maintained, which was discovered by the detective in charge of the case, Superintendent William Cheyney, on August 26 (it was more or less an admission of guilt), did not mention sexual assault. Written shortly before his arrest, it simply noted, "24th August, Saturday—killed a young girl. It was fine and hot." This is not Rajs's Type I or Type II murder, either, as there is no apparent motive.

Another representative case of class IXa necrophilia occurred on February 11, 1987. On this day 37-year-old Peggy Hettrick was stabbed in the back and then mutilated in a field in southern Fort Collins, Colorado. No semen was found on the body (ruling out sexual assault), but her left nipple and areola had been removed with precision.

SIDEBAR 3.6 Jack the Ripper—A Typical Class IXa Necrophile

During a span of 71 days from August 31, 1888 (Friday) until November 9, 1888 (Friday), **Jack the Ripper** killed and mutilated five prostitutes (the canonical victims): **Mary Ann "Polly" Nichols** (August 31), **Annie Chapman** (September 8), **Elizabeth Stride** (September 30), **Catherine Eddowes** (September 30)—since Stride and Eddowes were murdered the same day, the murders are often referred to as the **double event**—and **Mary Jane Kelly** (November 9) (Figure 3.6).

All bodies were badly mutilated. The mutilations surely did not start when the victims were alive, because of the absence of their cries. Contemporary medical examinations on the Ripper's canonical victims reported that there was **no evidence of "recent connexion"** (a Victorian euphemism for sexual intercourse). Thus Ripper only murdered and mutilated his victims, making him a **class IXa necrophile.** It has been counter-argued by some that in those times prostitutes commonly practiced extravaginal sex as a means of birth control, and the Ripper might have engaged in this kind of sex. However, no semen was found at any of the crime scenes. Complicating the matter further is the fact that the nineteenth century forensic pathologists may not have looked for evidence of extravaginal sexual activity. So although one cannot be absolutely certain that no sex of any kind took place, there is absolutely no evidence to show that it did. What can be said with certainty is that the available evidence indicates that the **Ripper did not have sexual relations with his victims.** He seems to have derived sexual pleasure merely from killing the victims and then mutilating their bodies. Thus Jack the Ripper represents a **typical class IXa** necrophile.

Figure 3.6 The *Illustrated London News* for October 13, 1888, carried this image showing the members of the Vigilance Committee shadowing a shady character suspected to be Jack the Ripper. The Ripper had committed four of his five canonical murders by this time.

Some would kill the victim and have intercourse with the dead body (**class IXb**) without causing any mutilation. Rosman and Resnick[9] include this in their subclass **necrophilic homicide.** They describe the case of a 25-year-old, single white male who had a very high sex drive. He masturbated at least seven times a day, had a large collection of pornography, and had committed acts of bestiality, urophilia, coprophilia, and necrophilia with animals (necrozoophilia) and dead bodies in the morgue of the hospital where he worked as an orderly. He murdered an 8-year-old neighborhood girl in order to carry out his sexual fantasy.

Moreau[60] describes the case of a 23-year-old man who could be categorized as a class **IXb necrophile.** He attempted to rape a 53-year-old woman. Struggling, he killed her, and then violated her, threw her in the water, and fished her out again for renewed violation. The murderer was executed. In a rare report of an autopsy on a necrophile, Moreau reports that the meninges of the anterior lobes were thickened and adherent to the cortex.

A more severely pathologic subclass is **class IXc,** where the necrophile, in addition to sexual activity with the dead, also needs to mutilate the body, especially the breasts, sexual organs, and genitals. This class (**class IXc**) corresponds closely with Wulffen's[51] **lust murderers** or **necrosadists,** and **class IIIa** of Rajs and colleagues.[26] (Please see under the previous heading "Class VI Necrophiles.")

Moreau[61] describes the case of a 24-year-old man who belongs to **class IXc.** He was involved in sexually violating children for 9 years. His last act involved killing a child in a marsh. He pierced her abdomen with a branch of tamarisk, ripped out her earrings, and then satisfied his bestiality on the mutilated corpse. He was sentenced to death (*Cour d'assises de la Charente-Inférieure,* November 24, 1876).

SIDEBAR 3.7 Joseph Vacher—A Typical Class IXc Necrophile

Joseph Vacher (1869–1898) was a French necrophile, sometimes known as "The French Ripper" or "*L'éventreur du Sud-Est*" ("The South-East Ripper"), due to comparisons to the more famous Jack the Ripper (Figure 3.7). His scarred face, accordion, and plain, white, handmade rabbit-fur hat became his trademark appearance.

In 1893, while in military conscription, he fell in love with a young maidservant, **Louise,** who did not reciprocate his feelings. When she mocked him once, he became enraged and shot her four times, injuring her badly. (She survived, however.) Vacher tried to commit suicide afterward, shooting himself twice in the head. He too survived, but one bullet remained lodged in his skull and it paralyzed one side of his face. He also began to show mental symptoms after this incident and had to be put in a mental institution in Dole, Jura. He was released one year later as completely cured.

Shortly after his release, at the age of 25, he began his necrophilic murder spree. During a 3-year period beginning in 1894, Vacher murdered at least 11 people (one woman, five teenage girls, and five teenage boys), and then mutilated and committed sexual intercourse with their dead bodies. Many of them were shepherds watching their flocks in isolated fields. The victims were stabbed repeatedly, often disemboweled, and after death raped and sodomized.

In 1897, Vacher tried to assault a woman in a field in Ardèche. She fought back and her screams soon alerted her husband and son, both of whom came rushing to her aid. The men overpowered Vacher and took him to the police. Vacher confessed to his crime, but claimed he was insane because

Figure 3.7 Joseph Vacher.

of a quack cure given to him as a child when a rabid dog bit him. He kept changing his story, and in the end was judged sane by the *Cour d'Assises* of Ain and sentenced to death on October 28, 1898. Vacher was executed by guillotine 2 months later, at dawn on December 31, 1898.

In subclasses **IXd** and **IXe** the offender engages in various combinations of sex or torture/mutilation before and after killing.

Krafft-Ebing[62] (p. 99, case 22) describes a case from **class IXd** that he ascribes in turn to Lombroso. The case concerns a person named **Gruyo,** 41, from Vittoria, Spain. He had been married three times and led what appeared to be a normal life. He strangled six women in the course of ten years. Almost all of his victims were public prostitutes and quite old. After strangling he tore out their intestines and kidneys per vaginum. Some of his victims he violated before killing; others, because of the occurrence of impotence, he did not. He set about his horrible deeds with such care that he remained undetected for 10 years.

Finally, in subclass **IXf,** the offender seems to have combined sexual sadistic and necrophilic tendencies. Mutilation (picquerism) and sex start in the living victim. The victim is then killed because of sadistic and necrophilic needs, and finally the sexual activity and mutilation continue over the dead body. This is **class IIIb** of Rajs and colleagues.[26]

Unlike class IXd, IXe, and IXf necrophiles (who interact with the victim both during life and after death), class IXa, IXb, and IXc necrophiles interact with the dead body only. Their fascination is with bodies that do not resist, reject, or pose a threat. Class IXa, IXb, and IXc necrophiles thus kill their victims very quickly. Class **IXd, IXe,** and **IXf** necrophiles, however, may take a sadistic pleasure in torturing living victims (and perhaps having sex with them as well), so they may take a while before killing their victims. After the killing, they continue with the mutilation of the dead body and/or further sexual activity with it.

A reappraisal of the term **lust murder** (sometimes called **sexual homicide**) may be appropriate here, inasmuch as it overlaps with some variations of necrophilia. This is a term that has resisted precise definition so far. Various authors have defined it differently. In fact, a major shortcoming in the study of sexual homicide is the lack of a standardized definition.[63] Table 3.5 lists some major definitions proposed so far.

What is clear from perusal of the previous definitions is that **lust murder** involves sex, mutilation, and death in various permutations and combinations. In order to avoid the prevailing confusion, it may be more appropriate to avoid the use of terms such as *lust murder* and *sexual homicide* altogether, and use a neologism, **necromutilosexuality,** instead. It may be defined as "Homicide accompanied by sexual activity on the victim and/or mutilation of

Table 3.5 Lust Murder (Sexual Homicide) as Defined by Different Authors

Author	Definition of Lust Murder (Sexual Homicide)
Bartholomew, Milte, and Galbally[64]	Homicide in which the killer **derives sexual pleasure from the act of killing** is termed **erotophonophilia,** or **lust murder.**
Burgess and colleagues[65,66]	Sexual homicides "result from one person killing another in the context of power, control, sexuality, and aggressive brutality."
Geberth[67,68,69]	A **homicide is classified as "sex-related"** when there is evidence of sexual activity observed in the crime scene or upon the body of the victim.[68] **Lust murders** are homicides in which the offender stabs, cuts, pierces, or mutilates the sexual regions or organs of the victim's body. The sexual mutilation of the victim may include evisceration, piquerism, displacement of the genitalia in both males and females, and the removal of the breasts in a female victim (defeminization). It also includes activities such as "posing" and "propping" of the body, the insertion of objects into the body cavities, anthropophagy (consumption of blood and/or flesh), and necrophilia.[69]
Holmes and Holmes[70]	Sexual murder involves a combination of lethal violence with a sexual element.
Meloy, Gacono, and Kenney[71]	Sexual homicide is the intentional killing of another human being during which there is evidence of sexual activity by the perpetrator
Ressler, Burgess, and Douglas[72]	For a **murder** to be considered **sexual**, the homicide must include at least one of the following: (1) victim's attire or lack of attire, (2) exposure of the sexual parts of the victim's body, (3) sexual positioning of the victim's body, (4) insertion of foreign objects into the victim's body cavities, (5) evidence of sexual intercourse (oral, anal), and (6) evidence of substitute sexual activity, interest, or sadistic fantasy such as mutilations of the genitals.

the body. Sex may consist of oral, anal, or vaginal sexual intercourse with the dead body, vaginal fisting, insertion of foreign objects into the victim's body cavities, acts of frotteurism with the dead body, or masturbating over the dead body. Sex and/or mutilation (1) may start during the life of the victim and continue after death, (2) may stop at death, or (3) may initiate after the death of the victim. In some cases, the offender engages in activities such as 'posing' and 'propping' of the body. Necromutilosexuals often have a compulsive need to act out their fantasies with their victims and their victims' bodies."

Based on this definition, 13 classes of **necromutilosexuals** can be identified. Table 3.6 describes these classes briefly in increasing amount of psychopathology.

Many murders of the American serial killer **Jeffrey Dahmer** (1960–1994) are typical of class IX necrophilia. He was believed to be aroused by just pieces of the bodies of his victims (he was also aroused by dead animals). **Mark Dixie** also murdered women in order to have sex with their dead bodies. His murder of **Sally Anne Bowman** and sex with her dead body ultimately led to his capture. (Please see Chapter 5, "Case Studies.")

Another offender who could be listed among this category is **Gary Leon Ridgway** (1949–), also known as the Green River Killer. He claimed an addiction to prostitutes, and most of his victims were either prostitutes or female teenage runaways. He would return to places where he had dumped his victims' bodies and have sexual intercourse with their corpses. It has been suggested that on one instance he left his son in the vehicle while he went into the woods and undertook sexual activities with the dead body of one of his victims. Other offenders belonging to this class are **Ted Bundy, Albert Fish, Ed Gein, Serhiy Tkach** (Pologovsky Maniac), and **Edmund Emil Kemper.**

SIDEBAR 3.8 Notable Classifications of Killers Compared and Contrasted with Modern Classification of Necrophilia

Several classifications of killers exist already, and it may be instructive to compare and contrast those classifications with the modern classification of necrophilia. (Please see Table 3.6, "Various Shades of Death/Homicide Accompanied by Sex and/or Mutilation.") The classification by Rajs and colleagues[26] has already been dealt with.

Other major classifications of killers include the following:

1. **FBI's classification:** FBI classifies all homicides in **four broad classes** on a motivation model,[73] and assigns a numeral to each class.
    - **Criminal enterprise homicide** (100) entails murder committed for material gain. This material gain takes many forms (for example, money, goods, territory, or favors). It is further subdivided into eight categories.
    - **Personal cause homicide** (120) is homicide motivated by personal cause. It is an act ensuing from interpersonal aggression. It is further subdivided into 11 categories.
    - **Sexual homicide** (130) involves a sexual element (activity) as the basis in the sequence of acts leading to death. Performance and meaning of this sexual element vary with offender. The act may range from actual rape involving penetration

Table 3.6 Various Shades of Death/Homicide Accompanied by Sex and/or Mutilation (Necromutilosexuality)*

Class	Behavior of Offender with Live Victim	Death of the Victim (How Caused)	Behavior of Offender with Dead Victim	Class/Typology of Offender	Chief Protagonist
I	No activity	Death caused by unrelated factors. Offender *not* involved in causing death. He happens to find the dead body, either deliberately or by chance.	Mutilation only. Mutilation *is* associated with sexual satisfaction or orgasm. No actual sexual activity with the dead.	Class VI necrophile. Rajs' type IV (Necromanic Mutilation).[26]	Unnamed 63-year-old male (**R**) described by Rajs and colleagues.[26]
II	No activity	As above	Sex only. No mutilation.	Class VII and VIII necrophile.	**Kenneth Douglas** (1953–).
III	No activity	As above	Both sex and mutilation of the victim.	Class VI traits (mutilation of dead) overlapping with Class VII and VIII traits (sex with dead).	**Sergeant François Bertrand** (1824–1850).
IV	No activity	Killed by offender (no necrophilic urge)	Mutilation only. No sex. Mutilation *not* associated with any sexual satisfaction or orgasm. Motive is merely to get rid of the body (Defensive Mutilation), or may be outrage (Aggressive Mutilation).	Rajs's type I (Defensive Mutilation) and type II (Aggressive Mutilation).[26]	
V	Torture/ mutilation of victim. No sexual activity	Killed by the offender (no necrophilic urge)	No further mutilation. No sexual activity.	Sadism.	

VI	Sex with the victim. No mutilation	Killed by the offender (no necrophilic urge)	No further sexual activity. No mutilation.	Rape and murder.	**Clifford Robert Olson, Jr.** (1940–); **Albert DeSalvo** (Boston Strangler, 1931–1973).
VII	Torture/ mutilation *and* sex	Killed by the offender (no necrophilic urge). May derive sadistic pleasure from the plight of their victims. Thus, may not kill their victims very quickly.	No further sex or mutilation.	Sexual sadism. Somewhat similar to FBI's "Organized sexual offender."[73]	**Charles Chi-Tat Ng (1960–)** and **Leonard Lake (1945–1985)**. Close behind is **Larry Gene Bell** (1949–1996) (not an exact protagonist, as he did not mutilate his victims, but did torture them).
VIII	No activity	Killed by the offender (Necrophilic urge)	Mutilation only. No sexual activity with the dead body.	Class IXa necrophile.	**Jack the Ripper**, **Ed Gein.**
IX	No activity	Killed by the offender (Necrophilic urge)	Sexual activity with the corpse. No mutilation.	Class IXb necrophile.	Eli Ulayuk (1968–).
X	No activity	Killed by the offender (Necrophilic urge)	Sexual activity *and* mutilation occurs on the dead body.	Class IXc necrophile. Rajs's Type IIIa mutilation.[26] FBI's "Disorganized Sexual offender."[73] Holmes and DeBurger's[74] Hedonistic type serial killer.	Joseph Vacher (1869–1898).
XI	Sex (nonconsensual) *or* torture/ mutilation	Killed by the offender (Necrophilic urge)	Sex *or* mutilation.	Class IXd necrophile.	

(*continued*)

Table 3.6 Various Shades of Death/Homicide Accompanied by Sex and/or Mutilation (Necromutilosexuality)* (Continued)

Class	Behavior of Offender with Live Victim	Death of the Victim (How Caused)	Behavior of Offender with Dead Victim	Class/Typology of Offender	Chief Protagonist
XII	Sex (nonconsensual) *and/or* torture/ mutilation	Killed by the offender (Necrophilic urge)	Sex *and/or* mutilation. (Note: This subclass would include those combinations that do not fall under subclass IXd and IXf.)	Class IXe necrophile.	Jerry Brudos.
XIII	Sex (nonconsensual) *and* torture/ mutilation initiated in the living	Killed by the offender (Necrophilic urge)	Sexual activity *and* mutilation continue on the dead body.	Class IXf necrophile. Rajs's type IIIb mutilation.[26]	Jeffrey Dahmer.

*Necrophilic activities/offenders are shaded in gray. When a death is caused due to necrophilic urge, it means that the offender commits murder *in order to use the dead body for his necrophilic activities*. When death is not caused by necrophilic urge, it refers to a killing with other motives.

(either pre- or postmortem) to a symbolic sexual assault such as insertion of foreign objects into a victim's body orifices. It is further subdivided into five categories.

- **Organized** (131): The organized offender possesses higher intelligence (mean IQ 123) and is more socially and sexually competent. He plans his murders, targets his victims, and displays control at the crime scene. Victims are typically strangers; they are chosen because they share common characteristics such as age, appearance, occupation, hair style, or lifestyle. Restraints are used. *Aggressive* as well as *sexual acts* usually take place *prior to death.* For organized offenders, who are also sexual sadists, necrophilia represents the total and complete domination of another person's being.[75] **Ted Bundy** was an archetypical organized killer. **Jeffrey Dahmer** was a typical organized, nonsocial lust murderer.[76]
- **Disorganized** (132): The disorganized offender has a below-average intelligence (mean IQ <90). He is socially immature and sexually incompetent. He may even be mentally deficient The killing is spontaneous and unplanned. Other typical characteristics in his crime are lack of criminal sophistication, minimal use of restraints, and the use of drugs and alcohol. Victims are known. While for the organized offender, necrophilia represents domination of the other person, the disorganized offender engages in necrophilia because the activity sexually arouses him. The dead body becomes his "date."[75] *Sexual acts* are obviously *postmortem* and often involve insertion of foreign objects into body orifices (**insertional necrophilia**). This is often combined with acts of mutilation, for example, slashing, stabbing, and biting of the buttocks and breasts. Since these acts often do not coincide with completed acts of sexual penetration, evidence of semen may be found in the victim's clothing or (less frequently) wounds. Meloy[77] and Schlesinger[78] have devised their own typologies of sexual homicides, in which organized and disorganized sexual homicides roughly correspond with **compulsive** and **catathymic homicides,** respectively. **Organized/disorganized typology** has recently been challenged.[79]
- **Mixed** (133): In mixed sexual homicide, the crime scene reflects aspects of both organized and disorganized characteristics. This could be due to several reasons; for example, the attack may begin as a well-ordered, planned assault, but it deteriorates into disorganized homicide as unanticipated events occur (such as inability to control the victim).
- **Sadistic murder** (134): Sexual gratification is obtained from torture involving excessive mental and physical means. Greatest satisfaction is derived from the victim's response to torture. Sexual acts are paired with domination, degradation, and violence, which ultimately result in death. Since an unconscious or dead victim does not afford the offender the gratification he seeks, great care is taken not to prematurely end her or his life. In fact, offenders take special measures to keep their victims conscious and sometimes even revive near-dead victims in order to cause additional suffering. The most common cause of death is by an asphyxial modality in the form of ligature strangulation, manual strangulation, hanging, and suffocation, because this death is slower and is accompanied by more pain and writhing. Gunshot wounds, cutting and stabbing wounds, and blunt-force trauma, which would cause quick and relatively painless death, are less frequently used to kill.
- **Elder female sexual homicide** (135): The victim is typically a woman 60 years of age or older. The average age of the offender is 27. Most activity engaged in by the offender, including the sexual interaction, occurs postmortem.[80] Despite the sexual interaction, there is often the absence of semen. Many offenders engage in other sexual acts to include foreign object insertion and oral copulation. Nearly 60 percent of offenders live within six blocks of the victim. Only a fifth of the offenders have a criminal history involving sexual offenses. Most are unskilled and unemployed and have less than a high school education.

• **Group cause homicide** (140) pertains to two or more people with a common ideology that sanctions an act, committed by one or more of its members, that results in death.

2. **Holmes and DeBurger's classification:** Holmes and Deburger[74] classify serial murderers into four types, to which a fifth type—the predator—was added by Holmes later. The types are as follows:
   - **Visionary type**—These murderers suffer from some kind of psychosis and kill in response to the commands of imaginary voices or visions.
   - **Mission-oriented type**—These murderers believe that it is their mission in life to rid society of certain people, for example, prostitutes.
   - **Hedonistic type**—The hedonistic serial killer gets a thrill out of murder. Lust murderer is a subcategory within this class. He is involved in anthropophagy, postmortem mutilations, dismemberment, and necrophilia.
   - **Power/control-oriented type**—Primary source of pleasure is *not* sexual but the killer's ability to control and exert power over his helpless victim.
   - **Predator**—This sexual killer has the mind-set of a predator and is on the hunt constantly. It is his style of living and perhaps a form of recreation.

A variation within this class seems to be that of **incestuous homicidal necrophilia,** whereby the necrophile kills a close relative and then has sex with his or her body. On July 13, 2007, **Sergei Isaac Carlson,** a 15-year-old North Dakota boy, asphyxiated his 16-year-old sister **Whitney Carlson** with pillows and then had sex with her body. Their mother found Whitney Carlson's body in the family's Fargo home.[81] Sergei and Whitney were not biological siblings, though. Sergei was adopted from Russia when he was 7 years old. He moved with his father, the Rev. Scott Carlson, to Wisconsin in 2002. Whitney Carlson lived with her mother in Fargo.

Schlesinger[82] describes the case of a 16-year-old high school sophomore (referred to as K.M. in the paper) who killed his mother and committed vaginal and anal necrophilia on her dead body. (For details, please see Chapter 2, "Etiology.")

Table 3.7 lists some major instances of incestuous homicidal necrophilia as reported in the literature so far.

Class X Necrophiles: Exclusive Necrophiles

This group, which is perhaps the rarest of all, is not necessarily the most dangerous. However, this is still listed in the last class because these offenders need *only* dead bodies for intercourse. They are **unable to perform intercourse with the living,** or, in other words, the necrophile is impotent as far as the living are concerned. Interestingly, a similar phenomenon is not unknown in normal people, whereby a person is impotent with respect to one woman only (e.g., one's wife) but is perfectly virile with respect to others.

Table 3.7 Instances of Incestuous Homicidal Necrophilia

Necrophile	Victim/Act
Sergei Isaac Carlson, 15 years	16-year-old sister; vaginal intercourse
K.M., 16 years	Mother; vaginal and anal intercourse

This is known as *impotence quoad hoc* (Latin for "impotence with respect to"), and has even led to many successful divorce suits.

Since dead bodies are an absolute necessity for class X necrophiles for sex, they may go to any length to acquire them. Thus they may be more dangerous than the rest. If a given necrophile is able to perform sex with a living person of either sex or of any age, he would not be listed among this class. In **Rosman and Resnick**'s[9] series of 122 cases, the authors could find only six cases that could be listed in this class.

QUICK FACT 3.4

Class X necrophiles are *impotent with respect to living subjects.* They either do not get erection or lose it soon after they attempt penetration. With dead subjects, they can achieve both erection and penetration.

Brill[37] mentions the case of a blind necrophile, **H,** whose sister thought she could cure her brother (whom she loved very much) of necrophilia if she provided herself to him for intercourse. However, despite every help she provided him, **H** could not have sexual intercourse with her. Whatever little erection he did get after much effort, used to dwindle as soon as he attempted penetration. He was also unable to have sexual intercourse with prostitutes. One could say, H was *impotent quoad hoc vitus* (impotent with respect to the living). His sister was finally convinced that H needed *only a dead body for sexual intercourse.* (Please see Sidebar 3.2, "The Case of a Blind Necrophilic Fantasizer.")

Some Important Caveats

It is important to realize that a given necrophile may not necessarily be restricted to just one class throughout his entire lifetime. Quite often, with time, symptoms will intensify and the necrophile may start displaying behavior belonging to a different class, generally a higher one. In some cases, a necrophile displays behaviors belonging to different classes during the same time interval. Such necrophiles may be classified according to their predominant behavior. **Lancaster**[83] describes a case of a 23-year-old male necrophile (whom he refers to as **G.M.B.**), who on two occasions had had sexual intercourse with dead bodies (both times by breaking into the mortuary at a local general hospital). He was thus a class VIII necrophile. However, he was finally convicted not because of those acts of necrophilia, but because he stabbed a 21-year-old nurse and allegedly had sexual intercourse with her corpse. (Necrophilia was never actually proven. The only pointers to this were (1) the victim's body, when found, was in a position for sexual intercourse with the legs widely open and the buttocks supported on a pile of clothing and (2) semen was found in the vagina. However, the victim had had intercourse with her husband on the previous evening. DNA profiling was not available at the time.) If sex with the corpse did occur, he would be a class IX necrophile, but since his predominant behavior belonged to class VIII, he may be taken to belong to that class.

Merits of the New Classification

At this point, it might be useful to compare and contrast the modern classification with the earlier classifications (Table 3.8). The current classification system attempts to do away with subjective terms such as *pseudonecrophilia,* which has been the cause of great confusion earlier. It introduces a more scientific *mathematically graded system,* whereby necrophilic tendencies are rated from the most innocuous to the most heinous.

This classification appears to have an intuitive appeal, ranging all necrophiles from minimal to maximum severity. The lowest rung in the proposed classification, class I, belongs to role players—people who merely act out their fantasy. This kind of behavior is seen not only with necrophiles, but with many other paraphiliacs. For instance, many zoophiles are merely role players; that is, they want to have sexual intercourse with their partners only when they act out or position themselves as animals. These persons are fantasizers; that is, they merely fantasize about a particular paraphilia, without actually carrying out their activity. People with exhibitionist and voyeurist tendencies merely fantasize about their paraphilia, without actually carrying it out in reality.[84] From a legal standpoint, these people have no criminal liability.

The highest rungs—class IX and X—belong to those people who are almost exclusive necrophiles. Class IX necrophiles need to kill people in order to acquire a corpse for sexual intercourse. Class X people are exclusive necrophiles, in the sense that they are so dependent upon a dead body for expression of their sexuality that even if a willing living partner were available to them, they would be unable to form a romantic relationship with him or her. Table 3.9 summarizes the major characteristics of each class of necrophilia.

This classification could be useful for other purposes, too, most notably for uniform statistical compilation of data from around the world, epidemiological surveys, calculation of incidence and prevalence of this phenomena, and treatment.

Table 3.8 Modern Classification of Necrophilia Compared and Contrasted with Earlier Classifications

Modern Classification	Krafft-Ebing's Classification[1] (1886)	Wulffen's Classification[3] (1910)	Jones's Classification[4] (1931)	Hirschfeld's Classification[8] (1956)	Rosman & Resnick's Classification[9] (1989)
I. Role players	Left unclassified	Left unclassified	Left unclassified	Left unclassified	Left unclassified
II. Romantic necrophiles	Left unclassified	Left unclassified	Left unclassified largely; his **inhibited necrophilia** displays some elements of this class	Left unclassified	Left unclassified
III. Necrophilic fantasizers	Left unclassified	Left unclassified	Left unclassified	Left unclassified	Left unclassified
IV. Tactile necrophiles	Left unclassified	Left unclassified	Left unclassified	Left unclassified	Left unclassified
V. Fetishistic necrophiles	Left unclassified	Left unclassified	Left unclassified	Left unclassified	Left unclassified
VI. Necromutilomaniacs	Left unclassified	Necrophagy	Overt necrophilia	Left unclassified	Necrophilic fantasy (genuine necrophilia)
VII. Opportunistic necrophiles	Class I-KE	Left unclassified	Inhibited necrophilia	Class I-Hf	Pseudonecrophilia
VIII. Regular necrophiles		Necrostuprum	Overt necrophilia		Regular necrophilia (genuine necrophilia)
IX. Homicidal necrophiles	Class II-KE	Lust murder or necrosadism	Left unclassified	Class II-Hf	Necrophilic homicide (genuine necrophilia)
X. Exclusive necrophiles	Left unclassified	Left unclassified	Left unclassified	Left unclassified	Left unclassified

Table 3.9 Major Characteristics of Each of the 10 Classes of Necrophiles

Class	Tentative Name	Major Characteristics	Chief Protagonists
I	Role players	Do not want to have sex with a dead person. Enjoy sex with a living person pretending to be dead.	Austrian sex offender **Josef Fritzl** (1935–)
II	Romantic necrophiles	Bereaved people who would mummify a part of the body of their recently departed loved one and keep it with them in order to get psychosexual stimulation. Would not show a similar interest in any other dead body, i.e., the body of a person with whom they were not romantically involved in life.	**Sir John Pryce** (c. 1698–1761); Italian princess **Christina Trivulzio Belgiojoso** (1808–1871)
III	Necrophilic fantasizers	Fantasize intercourse with the dead. May visit cemeteries and funeral parlors and may masturbate in the presence of the dead. Some would like to have sexual intercourse in the presence of a coffin, or even a corpse.	**Pietro Pacciani** (1925–1998)
IV	Tactile necrophiles	Interest in dead bodies increases to the level of touching them. Like to stroke erotic parts of a dead body, such as breasts. May manipulate sexual organs of the dead in order to get an orgasm.	**Ed Gein** (displayed characteristics of some other classes of necrophilia, too)
V	Fetishistic necrophiles	Cut up parts of a dead body—e.g., a breast—mummify it, and keep it in their possession to use it as a fetish for their necrophilic activities. Differ from class II necrophiles in the sense that they (class V) do it with the bodies of strangers with whom they held no romantic relationship in life. Thus they do not do it merely to fill a psychosexual vacuum left by the death of their loved ones.	**Park,** a South Korean man who stole an urn containing ashes of actress **Choi Jin-sil**
VI	Necromutilomaniacs	Interest in dead bodies is *more* than merely touching them. Necrophilic pleasure comes from mutilating an already dead body.	Unnamed 63-year-old male (**R**) described by Rajs and colleagues[26]

Table 3.9 Major Characteristics of Each of the 10 Classes of Necrophiles (Continued)

Class	Tentative Name	Major Characteristics	Chief Protagonists
VII	Opportunistic necrophiles	Actual sexual activity with the dead starts from this class. Normally these necrophiles would be content to have sexual intercourse with the living, but if an opportunity arose, would not refrain from having sexual intercourse with the dead. Necrophilic mortuary attendants belong to this class.	**Kenneth Douglas** (1953–)
VIII	Regular necrophiles	The so-called classic necrophiles. They do not enjoy sexual intercourse with the living and prefer dead bodies for intercourse. Thus, they need to rob fresh bodies from graveyards. They can, however, have sex with both living and dead persons. In this sense they differ from class X necrophiles, who can have sex *only* with dead persons.	**Nicholas** and **Alexander Grunke** and their friend **Dustin Radke; Sergeant François Bertrand** (showed Class VI traits, also)
IX	Homicidal necrophiles	This penultimate category is the most dangerous of all, in the sense that they would kill a person in order to have intercourse with him or her. They are, however, capable of having sexual intercourse with the living, but the need for sexual intercourse with the dead is so great that they must kill human beings in order to have sexual intercourse with their dead bodies.	**Jeffrey Dahmer, Mark Dixie, Gary Leon Ridgway, Ted Bundy, Albert Fish, Ed Gein, Serhiy Tkach, Edmund Emil Kemper, Sergei Isaac Carlson** (incestuous homicidal necrophilia)
X	Exclusive necrophiles	Sexual intercourse is possible *only* with the dead, with the complete exclusion of living partners. They may or may not kill in order to get corpses.	Possibly **H** (Please see sidebar—**The case of a Blind Necrophilic Fautasizer**)

Combinations with Other Paraphilias

Necrophilia may occasionally be found in combination with other paraphilias or sexually odd behaviors. These behaviors can be "mapped" onto one or more of the 10 classes of necrophilia. Thus these are not *additional* classes, but merely variations within the already described ones.

Anal Necrophilia

Anal necrophilia, which consists of anal intercourse with the cadaver, has been described[24] (p. 118). Anal necrophilia may not necessarily involve penile-anal intercourse with the cadaver. It includes penetration of the anal canal by any body part (tongue, fingers), or perhaps by some inanimate object. It may be with the **cadaver of the opposite sex,** or with the **cadaver of the same sex.** The latter is a type of **homosexual necrophilia.** (Please see Sidebar 3.9.) Anal necrophilia with the cadaver of the opposite sex has been discussed earlier in this chapter (Rosman and Resnick's case[9] under class VII necrophilia, where a 37-year-old male had anal intercourse with the dead body of a 49-year-old woman; Torre and Varetto's case[57] under class VIII necrophilia, where anal necrophilia was performed on a 15-year-old girl; and Schlesinger's case[72] under class IX necrophilia, where a 16-year-old boy murdered his mother and had anal intercourse with her).

SIDEBAR 3.9 Types of Homosexual Necrophilia

Homosexual necrophilia has also been called **necrophily of inversion** by earlier writers.[83] (The term **sexual inversion** was used by sexologists, primarily in the late nineteenth and early twentieth centuries, to refer to homosexuality.) **Homosexual necrophiles** may be of **three** types. First—as described by Brill[44]—are those who perform homosexual acts with live people (chiefly as catamite), but do not engage in any anal intercourse with the dead. These may be called **homosexual necrophiles, Type I**. The second—**homosexual necrophiles, Type II**—are those, who are predominantly heterosexual with live partners, but who commit anal intercourse with the cadaver.[9,57,72] The third type, **homosexual necrophiles, Type III** (there do not seem to be any reported cases), is homosexual with respect to both the living and the dead (Table 3.10).

Each type of homosexual necrophile would fall under one or the other classes discussed above. Thus, the necrophile D, described by Brill,[44] is primarily a class IV necrophile. Among the homosexual necrophiles, he belongs to Type I.

Table 3.10 Three Types of Homosexual Necrophilia

Homosexual Necrophile Type	Homosexual Acts with Live People	Anal Intercourse with a Male Cadaver
Type I	Yes	No
Type II	No	Yes
Type III	Yes	Yes

Bartholomew and colleagues[86] describe two cases of homosexual necrophilia. In only one of these cases did the perpetrator admit his guilt. The case falls under class IX necrophilia (homicidal necrophilia). In this case (*R v. Forbes*), the accused Forbes was placed on trial for murder before the Supreme Court of Victoria, Australia (sitting at Wangaratta on May 1, 1974) before Justice Kaye. The accused was a 22-year-old white married male who had been a homosexual since he was 13 years old. His homosexual practices continued after his married life. Even during intercourse with his wife, he would fantasize about having a homosexual relationship with a male. Gradually his homosexual urges became more aggressive. He wanted a man wholly in his power (e.g., a drugged or an unconscious man, or best of all a dead man). This fantasy grew stronger and stronger, until once—when his wife was in the hospital for an infertility operation—he invited a suitable male friend (a muscular man with a large penis) to go up with him in the mountains. Once alone, he shot his friend through the head, stripped the body, "played" with the naked body, and then had anal intercourse with it. Finally he threw the body down a mine shaft and returned home, where he continued his normal life as if nothing had happened. When finally caught and asked whether he would have committed the offense had a policeman been present, he replied that he might have shot both of them. He said,

> I might have shot both of them, so that I could carry out what I had started to do. I was really excited inside me, and beyond myself, and did not ... I do not think anything would have stopped me. I was mad with power. I had him in my power and nothing could stop me.

The case illustrates how strong anal necrophilic tendencies may be. At his trial, the accused took the insanity defense, but it was not admitted. He was sentenced to death. The sentence was later commuted to a term of imprisonment for 50 years, with a minimum term of 40 years before becoming eligible for parole.

The second case[86] describes a necrophile by the name of **Isaacs,** a 47-year-old single white male who came from a strictly religious home of little warmth. His case (*R v. Isaacs*) was tried for murder before the Supreme Court of Victoria (sitting in Melbourne on March 17, 1975) before **Justice Gowans**. He was a heavy drunkard and a known homosexual. He had been convicted thrice for homosexuality and once for indecent assault. He tried to commit suicide at least five times by drug overdose, hanging, drowning, and driving cars into fixed objects such as telegraph poles.

His necrophilic offense involved the abduction of a 9-year-old boy, with whom he had anal intercourse three or four times over a period of about 8 hours while they drove about in his car. Finally the boy escaped from the car. Isaacs threw a stone at him, which hit him on the back of the head, causing him to fall down. Isaacs approached the fallen boy and hit him over the head with a rock, ensuring that he was dead. He then partially buried the body and went home. He returned after 15 hours and had anal intercourse with the dead body. The boy's anal canal was found dilated. Two fingers could be admitted freely, and in the lining inside there were two small abrasions. It was opined by the pathologist that while the abrasions were as a result of homosexual acts during life, the widely dilated anal canal indicated postmortem anal interference. Like the earlier case, this case too falls under class IX necrophilia (homicidal necrophilia).

The jury found Isaacs guilty and sentenced him to death. However, before the death sentence could be considered by the Executive Council and possibly commuted, he committed suicide in his cell by hanging.

Jacobus[85] describes a case of homosexual necrophilia that he refers to as **necrophily of inversion** and **sodomy.** The incident occurred when Jacobus was posted in **French Guiana** and was entrusted—among other things—with conducting postmortems. The attendant in the dissecting room was an old man who had been in the prison for 30 years. He had formerly been a medical student, and was condemned to penal servitude for life for the murder of his mistress so he could commit sexual intercourse with her dead body (**class IX necrophilia**). As part of his medical studies, this prisoner saw corpses of women laid out on slabs. This produced in him instantaneous erection (Jacobus uses the term **internal priapism**). Since he wanted to have intercourse with a dead woman, he suffocated his mistress under a pillow and copulated with her dead body several times during the night. Before the *Cour d'Assises* (a French criminal court), however, he maintained that both of them had got drunk, and during his drunkenness, he copulated with her thinking that she was motionless because she was drunk. The court gave him benefit of doubt, and condemned him only to 10 years. However, when he made several attempts at escape from prison, the court finally condemned him to life imprisonment.

While in prison, he became the attendant at the dissecting room where Jacobus worked. On several occasions, while dissecting genitalia of women, Jacobus noted that they were not in as perfect state of integrity as they should have been. One day he found the vulva and vagina of a child, aged 7 or 8, almost as much dilated as those of a full-grown woman, and the rectum also bore traces of similar maneuvers. The absence of characteristic lesions (Jacobus fails to mention them specifically) convinced him that these maneuvers had not been performed during life. Therefore, the suspicion fell on the mortuary attendant, especially keeping in mind his earlier love of the dead.

Jacobus's suspicions were confirmed one day when he received the body of a young convict who was a passive homosexual (catamite) during life. He had been murdered through jealousy by one of his lovers whom he had deserted. The death occurred at 6 AM. The body was brought to the dissecting room immediately thereafter. Jacobus obtained permission to make a special study of the genital organs, and then informed the mortuary attendant that he would come at 3 PM to dissect the body. Instead he turned up unexpectedly at 1 PM and started with the dissection. The anal sphincter was considerably dilated (as would be normal if the subject was indeed a catamite). However, in the rectum, Jacobus found a quantity of **fresh sperm,** which had evidently been **introduced a short time before** (no mention is made of how he came to this conclusion). The attendant, who was present, was immediately embarrassed. Ultimately Jacobus got the attendant to confess that he had indeed indulged in homosexual necrophilia with the dead man. He also admitted that he was in the habit of having sexual intercourse with the cadavers of women and girls, too. Usually he took care to carefully wash the internal parts, so as to remove traces of sperm, but Jacobus's unexpected arrival 2 hours earlier prevented him from doing so.

Incestuous Necrophilia

Incestuous necrophilia consists of necrophilic behavior with a close blood relative. **Masters and Lea**[24] (p. 118) describe a Louisiana case of necrophagia, in which a woman opened the caskets in her family vault and devoured the genitals of her husband, her brother, and a son. Schlesinger has described a case[82] where a 16-year-old boy murdered his mother and had anal intercourse with her. **Camille Allaman**'s[58] case (mentioned previously) is also that of incestuous necrophilia. **Masters and Lea**[24] (p. 117) report the case of a man who was not a necrophile, but when he saw the dead body of his sister he could not resist temptation, and had sexual intercourse with it. He would be classified as a class VII incestuous necrophile.

Other Paraphilias in Association with Necrophilia

Tsheryaskin[46] has described the case of a 19-year-old woman who displayed **sadomasochistic** tendencies, as well as **zoosadism,** along with necrophilia (case described above under class V necrophilia). Some cases are recorded where necrophilia is associated with **taphephilia** (sexual stimulation from being buried alive).

QUICK FACT 3.5

Necrophiles who also wish to be buried alive are called **taphephiles.** Incidentally, in both of the following cases, the necrophiles wanted to be buried with the dead bodies of their girlfriends.

- Necrophile **H** described by Brill.[37]
- Necrophile **D.W.** described by Karpman.[54]

John Christie (1898–1953) displayed fetishism (for female pubic hair and underwear) along with necrophilia. **Ed Gein** (1906–1984) suffered from multiple paraphilias; most notable were **fetishism, transvestism,** and **necrophilia.** Brill[37] mentions the case of a necrophilic fantasizer who was also a **masochist, sexual vampire, coprophile,** and **urophile.** He also had a **breast fetish** and suffered from **taphephilia, osmolagnia** (arousal caused by bodily odors, such as sweat), and **salirophilia** (arousal from ingesting sweat). (For details, please see Sidebar 3.2, "The Case of a Blind Necrophilic Fantasizer.")

References

1. Krafft-Ebing RF. *Psychopathia Sexualis*, 1st ed. FA Davis, Philadelphia, 1886 [reprinted by Bloat Books, 1999].
2. Jaffé PD. Necrophilia: love at last sight, in *Psychology and Criminal Justice: International Review of Theory and Practice (Publications of the European Association of Psychology and Law)*. Eds., J Boros, I Münnich, M Szegedi. Walter de Gruyter, Berlin, 1998, pp. 242–247.
3. Wulffen E. *Enzyklopädie der Modernen Kriminalistik*. Erich Langenscheidt, Berlin, 1910.
4. Jones E. *On the Nightmare*. International Psychoanalytic Library, No. 20. Hogarth, London, 1931.
5. Bonaparte M. Deuil, necrophilie, et sadisme propos d'Edgar Poe. *Rev. Française de Psychoanalyst*. 1931;**4**:716–734.
6. Bonaparte M. *The Life and Works of Edgar Allan Poe—A Psychoanalytic Interpretation*. Imago Publishing, London, 1949.
7. Mayor H. Deuil, nécrophilie, et sadisme: par Marie Bonaparte. (Les Editions Denoël et Steele, Paris, 1932. pp. 19. Prix frs. 3.). *Int. J. Psycho-Anal.* 1933;**14**:421.
8. Hirschfeld M. *Sexual Anomalies*. Emerson, New York, 1956, p. 425.
9. Rosman JP, Resnick PJ. Sexual attraction to corpses: a psychiatric review of necrophilia. *Bull Ame Acad Psychiatry Law*. 1989;**17(2)**:153–163.
10. Rosman J. (j.rosman@comcast.net) (16 December, 2009). *Re: From Anil Aggrawal — Help needed with your paper on necrophilia*. Email to: Aggrawal, A. (anil@anilaggrawal.com).
11. Shaffer L., Penn J. A comprehensive paraphilia classification system, in *Sex Crimes and Paraphilia*, 1st ed. Ed. EW Hicky. Pearson Prentice Hall, New Jersey, 2006, chapter 8, p. 87.
12. Segal H. A necrophilic fantasy. *International Journal of Psychoanalysis*. 1953;**34**:98–101.
13. Rauch HJ. Über Nekrophilie. Ein beitrag zur kenntunis der variationen des geschlechtstriebes. *Archiv für Psychiatrie un der Nervenkrankeiten*. 1947;**179**:54–93.
14. Lazarus AA. A case of pseudonecrophilia treated by behavior therapy. *J Clin Psychol*. 1968 Jan;**24(1)**:113–115.

15. Prins H. Vampirism—a clinical condition. *Br J Psychiatry*. 1985 Jun;**146**:666–668.
16. American Psychiatric Association. *Diagnostic and Statistical Manual of Mental Disorders*, 4th ed. Text rev. American Psychiatric Association, Washington DC, 2000.
17. World Health Organization. *The ICD-10 Classification of Mental and Behavioral Disorders: Clinical Descriptions and Diagnostic Guidelines.* World Health Organization, Geneva, 1992.
18. Aggrawal A. A new classification of necrophilia. *J Forensic Leg Med.* 2009;**16(6)**:316–320.
19. Bloch I. *The Sexual Life of Our Time in Relation to Modern Civilization.* Rebman, New York, 1908.
20. Kronfeld A. *Handwörterbuch der Sexualwissenschaft* [*Hand Dictionary of Sexology*]. Ed., M Marcuse. Marcus and Weber, Bonn, 1926, p. 523.
21. Mulchrone P, Miller E. Cellar beast told callgirls pretend you are dead; horror of family in dungeon. *The Mirror.* May 7, 2008, Wednesday, p. 5.
22. Holmes ST, Holmes RM. *Sex Crimes—Patterns and Behavior*, 2nd ed. Sage Publications, London, 2002, p. 148.
23. Allen C. A. *Textbook of Psychosexual Disorders*, 2nd ed. Oxford University Press, London, 1969.
24. Masters REL, Lea E. *Perverse Crimes in History: Evolving Concepts of Sadism, Lust-murder, and Necrophilia—From Ancient to Modern Times.* The Julian Press, New York, 1963.
25. Heasman A, Jones E. Necrophilia, in Sex *Crimes and Paraphilia, Ed., Hickey EW.* Pearson Prentice Hall, New Jersey, 2006, chap. 30.
26. Rajs J, Lundström M, Broberg M, Lidberg L, Lindquist O. Criminal mutilation of the human body in Sweden—a thirty-year medico-legal and forensic psychiatric study. *J Forensic Sci.* 1998 May;**43(3)**:563–580.
27. Schurig M. *Spermatologia Historico-medica.* Johannis Beckii, Frankfort, 1720, p. 357.
28. Ellis HH. *Studies in the Psychology of Sex, Volume V: Erotic Symbolism, The Mechanism of Detumescence, The Psychic State in Pregnancy.* FA Davis, Philadelphia, 1923.
29. Browne WAF. Necrophilism. *J Ment Sci.* 1875;**20**:551–560.
30. Whitehouse HR. *A Revolutionary Princess—Christina Belgiojoso-Trivulzio, Her Life And Times 1808–1871.* T. Fisher Unwin, London, 1906, pp. 235–236.
31. Masters REL, *Lea E. Perverse Crimes in History: Evolving Concepts of Sadism, Lust-murder, and Necrophilia—From Ancient to Modern Times.* The Julian Press, New York, 1963, pp. 140–141.
32. Taylor GR. *Sex in History*, 1st ed. Harper & Row, New York, 1973.
33. Anon. Woman kept dead husband by bed for a year. *Reuters.* Aug 2, 2007. Available at http://www.reuters.com/article/oddlyEnoughNews/idUSN0135228220070802
34. Anon. Wife kept dead husband's body on couch for months. KTLA News. June 5, 2009. Available at http://www.39online.com/news/ktla-decaying-body,0,360825.story. Accessed October 4, 2009.
35. Anon. Woman keeps husband's body in house for three days. Chennaionline. Sep 2, 2009. Available at http://news.chennaionline.com/newsitem.aspx?NEWSID=8dc7ab39-e8f1-49a2-9e5d-9bb0ebfe8508&CATEGORYNAME=NATL. Accessed October 4, 2009.

36. Anon., Man slept with dead wife for five years. *The Irish Times*, November 27, 2009, Friday, Section: World; Other World Stories, p. 18.
37. Brill AA. Necrophilia—Part II. *J. Criminal Psychopathol.* 1941;**3(1)**:51–73.
38. Drzazga J. Necrophilia, in *Sex Crimes and Their Legal Aspects*. Charles C Thomas, Springfield, IL, 1960, pp. 199–204.
39. Bauer M, Tatschner T, Patzelt D. Digital imaging of the dissection and sexual abuse of a corpse—an exceptional case of necrophilia. *Leg Med (Tokyo)*. 2007 May;**9(3)**:143–146.
40. Newton M. *The Encyclopedia of Unsolved Crimes*, 1st ed. Facts on File, New York, 2004, p. 201.
41. Thoinot L. *Medicolegal Aspects of Moral Offenses*. FA Davis, Philadelphia, 1923.
42. Stekel W. *Sadism and Masochism*. WW Norton & Co, New York, 1953, p. 278.
43. Rapoport J. A case of necrophilia. *J Criminal Psychopathol.* 1942;**4**:277–289.
44. Brill AA. Necrophilia—Part I. *J. Criminal Psychopathol.* 1941;**2(4)**:433–443.
45. Klaf FS, Brown W. Necrophilia, brief review and case report. *Psychiatric Q.* 1958;**32(4)**:645–652.
46. Tsheryaskin WG. Zur Frage der Nekrophilie [The Question of Necrophilia]. *Zeitschrift für sexual wissenschaft-wiss.* 1929;**16**:386–392.
47. Ehrlich E, Rothschild MA, Pluisch F, Schneider V. An extreme case of necrophilia. *Leg Med (Tokyo)*. 2000 Dec;**2(4)**:224–226.
48. Thompson LS. Tanned human skin. *Bull Med Libr Assoc.* 1946 April; **34(2)**:93–102.
49. Ham JY. Mystery of stolen remains of late top actress goes unsolved. *Yonhap English News*. 18 August 2009.
50. Si-soo P. Suspect caught over actress urn theft. *The Korea Times*, 26 August 2009.
51. Wulffen E. *Enzyklopadie de Modernen Kriminalistik*. Langenscheidt, Berlin, 1910.
52. De River JP. *The Sexual Criminal: A Psychoanalytic Study*. Charles C Thomas, Springfield, IL, 1951.
53. Meloy JR. Pseudonecrophilia following spousal homicide. *J Forensic Sci.* 1996 Jul;**41(4)**:706–708.
54. Karpman B. *The Sexual Offender and His Offenses*. Julian Press, New York, 1957.
55. Setia P, Tabin M. An unusual case of a man having necrophilia with his own wife, in *Proceedings of the XXIX Annual Conference of Indian Academy of Forensic Medicine*, 2008, Mumbai. pp. 17.
56. de Boismont B. *Gazette Medicale*, July 21, 1859.
57. Torre C, Varetto L. An exceptional case of necrophilia. *Am J Forensic Med Pathol.* 1987 Jun;**8(2)**:169–171.
58. Allaman C. *Des Aliénés criminels*. H. Jouve, Paris, 1891.
59. Quigley C. *The Corpse—A History*. McFarland, Jefferson, NC, 1996, p. 298.
60. Moreau P. *Des aberrations du sens génésique*. Asselin & Houzeau, Paris. 1884.
61. Moreau L. Viol, in *Les aberrations du sens génésique*. Asselin et Houzeau, Paris, 1887, pp. 258–275.
62. Krafft-Ebing RF. *Psychopathia Sexualis with Especial Reference to the Antipathic Sexual Instinct—A Medico-Forensic Study*, 12th ed. Trans. FJ Rebman. Rebman Company, New York, 1903.

63. Chan HC, Heide KM. Sexual homicide: a synthesis of the literature. *Trauma Violence Abuse.* 2009 Jan;**10(1)**:31–54.
64. Bartholomew A, Milte K, Galbally A. Sexual murder: psychopathology and psychiatric jurisprudential considerations. *Aust N Z J Criminol.* 1975;**8**:152–163.
65. Burgess AW, Hartman CR, Ressler RK, Douglas JE, McCormack A. Sexual homicide: A motivational model. *J Interpersonal Violence.* 1986;**1**:251–72.
66. Burgess AW, Hartman CR, Ressler RK, Douglas JE, McCormack A. Sexual homicide: a motivational model, in *Profilers—Leading Investigators Take You Inside the Criminal Mind.* Eds., JH Campbell, D DeNevi. Prometheus Books, New York, 2004, chap 3.
67. Geberth VJ. Anatomy of a lust murder. *Law Order Mag.* 1998; **46(5)**:98–102.
68. Geberth VJ. *Sex-Related Homicide and Death Investigation—Practical and Clinical Perspectives,* 1st ed. CRC Press, Boca Raton, FL, 2003, chap 7, p. 309.
69. Geberth VJ. *Sex-Related Homicide and Death Investigation—Practical and Clinical Perspectives,* 1st ed. CRC Press, Boca Raton, FL, 2003, chap 9, p. 431.
70. Holmes RM, Holmes ST. *Murder in America,* 2nd ed. Sage, Thousand Oaks, CA, 2001.
71. Meloy JR, Gacono GB, Kenney L. A Rorschach investigation of sexual homicide. *J Pers Assess.* 1994 Feb;**62(1)**:58–67.
72. Ressler RK, Burgess AW, Douglas JE. *Sexual Homicide: Patterns and Motives.* Free Press, New York, 1988.
73. Douglas J, Burgess AW, Burgess AG, Ressler RK. *Crime Classification Manual: A Standard System for Investigating and Classifying Violent Crimes,* 2nd ed. Jossey-Bass, San Francisco, CA, 2006.
74. Holmes RM, DeBurger J. *Serial Murder.* Sage, Newbury Park, CA, 1988.
75. Geberth VJ. *Sex-Related Homicide and Death Investigation—Practical and Clinical Perspectives,* 1st ed. CRC Press, Boca Raton, FL, 2003, p. 26.
76. Palermo GB. Narcissism, sadism, and loneliness—The case of serial killer Jeffrey Dahmer, in *Serial Murder and the Psychology of Violent Crimes.* Ed., RN Kocsis. Humana Press, Totowa, NJ, 2008, chap. 6.
77. Meloy JR. The nature and dynamics of sexual homicide: an integrative review. *Aggression and Violent Behavior.* 2000;**5(1)**:1–22.
78. Schlesinger LB. *Sexual Murder-Catathymic and Compulsive Homicides,* 1st ed. CRC Press, Boca Raton, FL, 2004.
79. Canter D, Alison L, Wentink N, Alison E. Organized/disorganized typology of serial murder: myth or model? *Psychology, Public Policy & Law.* 2004; **10**:293–320.
80. Douglas J, Burgess AW, Burgess AG, Ressler RK. *Crime Classification Manual: A Standard System for Investigating and Classifying Violent Crimes,* 2nd ed. Jossey-Bass, San Francisco, CA, 2006, p. 238.
81. Kolpack D. Teenager pleads not guilty in sister's death in Fargo. *The Bismarck Tribune.* November 21, 2007. Available at http://www.bismarcktribune.com/news/state-and-regional/article_f833bc98-3ed5-5e84-bcec-2b57188abb05.html. Accessed October 4, 2009.
82. Schlesinger LB. Adolescent sexual matricide following repetitive mother-son incest. *J Forensic Sci.* 1999 Jul;**44(4)**:746–749.

83. Lancaster NP. Necrophilia, murder and high intelligence: a case report. *Br J Psychiatry*. 1978 Jun;**132**:605–608.
84. Aggrawal A. *Forensic and Medico-legal Aspects of Sexual Crimes and Unusual Sexual Practices*. CRC Press, Boca Raton, FL, 2009.
85. Dr. Jacobus, French Army Surgeon. *The Abuses Abberations, and Crimes of the Genital Sense*. Charles Carrington, Paris, 1900.
86. Bartholomew AA, Milte KL, Galbally F. Homosexual necrophilia. *Med Sci Law*. 1978 Jan;**18(1)**:29–35.

Epidemiology of Necrophilia

4

Necrophilia is generally presumed to be rare.[1] However, it has been argued that it may be more prevalent than statistics imply. Given that the act would be carried out in secret with a victim unable to complain, cases only come to light when the subject gets caught.[2] Even among those, not all cases would be reported in medical journals or textbooks. The fact that **Rosman** and **Resnick**[3] could compile 122 cases of necrophilia (88 from world literature and 34 unpublished case reports from colleagues) despite these drawbacks implies that necrophilia may be far more common than has been believed until now.

Rapoport[4] finds it difficult to understand why there is a dearth of literature on necrophilia. To him, it seemed unlikely that the number of cases was as small as the absence of literature suggested. **Brill**[5,6] has suggested that perhaps there are more cases than are known and that possibly people dislike to report them because of the "abhorrent nature of this perversion." In fact, the rarity of reporting this disorder is due to a number of reasons.

QUICK FACT 4.1

Why there is a dearth of reporting on cases of necrophilia:

- Seemingly no harm is caused to anyone.
- Victims cannot complain.
- Only class IX necrophilia would get reported, because it involves killing.

A major reason is that most acts of necrophilia do not seem to cause harm to anyone. Even paraphilias such as frotteurism, which are committed on live victims, are not usually reported to the police, because apparently little harm to the victim is caused.[7] When a crime is committed on a dead victim, the possibility of it getting reported is virtually nil.

Housden[8] mentions a study by East and Hubert[9] whereby in a group of prisoners investigated for psychiatric treatment, just one case of necrophilia was found. Table 4.1 lists the distribution of sexual deviations reported in this study.

Table 4.1 Incidence of Paraphilias as Found by East and Hubert[9] in a Group of Prisoners Investigated for Psychiatric Treatment

Sexual Deviation	Frequency
Homosexuality (no longer considered a paraphilia)	79
Exhibitionism	35
Sadism	17
Masochism	8
Arson (sexual)	1
Necrophilia	1
Transvestism	2
Fetishism	5
Bestiality	4
Pornography (no longer considered a paraphilia)	2
Pygmalionism	1
Total	155

Offender Characteristics

Perhaps the best source to study the offender's characteristics is the classic Rosman and Resnick's[3] series, where they describe the following characteristics in a sample of 122 necrophiles.

KEY POINT 4.1

Regarding the **Rosman and Resnick** series,[3] an important point to remember is that they collected cases mostly from the literature, and thus had at their disposal only the data that was reported. Thus their sample size in relation to each parameter (e.g., age, sex, intelligence level) is not constant. If, for instance, a case from the world literature had not reported the intelligence level of the necrophile, the authors would have had no way to determine that, and that case would have had to be excluded. Thus it will be seen that sample size (*N*) will keep changing as different parameters are studied.

Hucker[10] also describes offender characteristics in some detail.

Age

According to Hucker,[10] the youngest offender described in literature was 16 years old, and the oldest 58 years old. (The ages typically denote the age at which the offenders committed the necrophilic acts, or in the case

Table 4.2 Some Notable Female Necrophiles

There have been very few reports of female necrophiles. Many of them belong to class II (romantic necrophiles). Some notable female necrophiles include the following:
Christina Trivulzio Belgiojoso
Joanna of Castile
Karen Greenlee
Lakshmi Ammal
Mercedes Velarde
TP, a 19-year-old necrophile reported by **Tsheryaskin**[12]
M, a 28-year-old necrophile reported by **Masters** and **Lea**[14] (pp. 229–230)

of fantasizers, when their fantasies were revealed.) According to him, most cases, however, fall between 20 and 50 years of age. In Rosman and Resnick's[3] series of 122 cases, they could explicitly determine ages of offenders in 68 cases ($N = 68$). The range was 16 to 65 years. The mean age was 34 years.

Sex

Like most other sexual deviations, necrophilia appears to be an almost exclusive domain of males, although a few authors have described necrophilia in females, too.[3,11,12] Sex of offenders could be gleaned from 115 cases out of 122 in Rosman and Resnick's[3] series. Of these **95%** (N = 109) **were males** and **5%** ($N = 6$) **were females.** Of the 14 necrophiles who committed homicide to obtain corpses for intercourse (homicidal necrophiles or class VIII necrophiles according to proposed classification), none was a female. Of the six female necrophiles described, three were regular necrophiles (class VII necrophiles according to proposed classification), one was a fantasizer (class V necrophile according to proposed classification), and two were of undetermined class.

Quigley maintains that of all necrophiles, **10% are females**[14] (Table 4.2).

QUICK FACT 4.2

Between 5 and 10% of all necrophiles are females.

Intelligence

Case reports do not always mention the **intellectual capacity** of the offenders, but from the reports that do mention intellectual capacity, the offenders' intellectual capacities seem to range from the mentally retarded[15,16] to exceptionally high intelligence.[17]

Camille Allaman[15] describes the case of a **class VIIIb necrophile** who was severely mentally defective. (Please see Chapter 3, "Classification," for characteristics of this class.) On October 15, 1890, at Binteniac in the arrondissement of Saint-Malo, the corpse of a woman **X** was found in the loft of a small homestead. She died suddenly of an attack of apoplexy when she went up to her garret, looking for her son. Her son soon discovered her dead body, performed sexual intercourse with it, and then mutilated it in a most unusual manner. He passed his arm into her vagina, lacerated its upper end, penetrated into the abdominal cavity, reached the intestines, grabbed them, and pulled out two meters of brutally torn intestines. He reached as far as the liver, of which he brought out some shreds. Then he lay down beside his mother and slept. He was discovered lying by her side in a deep and calm slumber. A part of her intestines was thrown over his shoulders. When he was woken up, he appeared quite stupefied. It was clear that his mental faculties were in complete disorder. It turned out that madness was a heritage in the family. A year before his necrophilic act, a doctor had certified his mental state to be very dangerous. **Dr. Porre** examined the corpse and determined that there had been a sexual violation of the corpse, and subsequently the mutilation. For reasons that are not quite clear, the culprit's confinement in an asylum was postponed.

The case of **Giuseppe Alessandro** as described by **Masters and Lea**[14] (p. 222) is also of a psychotic individual who transported the dead body of his fiancée to his home and made amorous overtures to her. (For a full description of this case, please see Chapter 3, "Classification," under the heading "Class II Necrophiles.")

Bernardi and Ponti[18] describe a very strange case in Italy, where a 15-year-old boy had sexual intercourse with a stillborn female baby by inserting his penis between her thighs. The crime occurred in the mortuary of the hospital. To conceal his crime, he threw the body in a well afterward. The boy was in the hospital for the treatment of tuberculosis of the knee. On examination, he was found to have the mental age of an 8-year-old, and no moral sense. He was not prosecuted. The authors conclude that necrophilia is generally associated with a low intelligence level, and this is the reason for the relative absence of prosecutions. The exceptionality of the case is the age of the victim (stillborn at 7 months' gestation).

Table 4.3 lists measured levels of intelligence of necrophiles, wherever reported in the literature. According to **Hucker,**[10] the offenders mostly appear to be of average intelligence. In Rosman and Resnick's[3] series, the IQ could be gathered or gleaned only from 13 case reports ($N = 13$). All 13 had an IQ above 80, and 69% of these had an IQ above 100.

Table 4.3 Levels of Intelligence of Necrophiles, as Reported in Literature

Necrophile	Reported by	Intelligence
John Christie (1898–1953)	Kennedy L[19]	IQ of 128. At the age of 11, Christie won a scholarship to Halifax Secondary School.
Jeffrey Dahmer (1960–1994)	Discovery Communications, LLC[20]	Dahmer was considered bright, possessing an IQ of about 145, but his grade-point average suffered because of the wide spread of his grades, which ranged from A to D.
	Davis JA[21]	WAIS-R (Wechsler Adult Intelligence Scale Revised), Full-Scale IQ score of 121.
26-year-old, married African-American male, 6'8" tall, and weighing 290 pounds. Committed necrophilia on his wife after killing her.	Meloy JR[22]	WAIS-R intelligence testing indicated a full-scale IQ of 81 (PIQ 80, VIQ 85).
Isaacs (1928–)	Bartholomew and colleagues[23]	IQ 100 (verbal 97; performance 106).
K.M., a 16-year-old high school sophomore. Had incestuous relationship with his mother (at her insistence mainly) for about 7–8 years. Committed vaginal and anal necrophilia on his mother after killing her.	Schlesinger LB[24]	Full-scale WAIS-R IQ of 113 (bright-normal).
W.R. (1890–?), a 50-year-old tactile necrophile who liked kissing lips and touching the breasts of female corpses in funeral parlors.	Rapoport[4]	IQ of 104 on the Bellevue Adult test.
40-year-old black male (1918–?)	Klaf and Brown[25]	IQ of 115.

Lancaster[17] describes the case of a 23-year-old male necrophile (whom he calls G.M.B.), who had had two known acts of sexual intercourse with corpses, and a third possible act of intercourse with the corpse of a 21-year-old bride of 2 months, whom he killed by stabbing (at least 13 times). He was a music student and had taken five "O" levels without tuition. He was very precise with words and had passed the Mensa entrance test with an IQ of 153.

KEY POINT 4.2

It is wrong to think that necrophiles are morons or idiots. Some **necrophiles** may be **extremely intelligent** people. One of the most notorious necrophiles, **Serhiy Tkach** (1951–), also known as the **Pologovsky Maniac,** was a former Ukrainian police criminal investigator. He was so intelligent, and covered his tracks so intelligently, that he could not be apprehended for more than two decades.

Bauer and colleagues[26] describe the case of a 40-year-old necrophile who was a civil engineer. Although the paper does not mention his intelligence levels, from the mentioned profession he appears a fairly intelligent individual.

From these reports it appears that the distribution of intelligence levels among necrophiles is virtually similar to that found in the general population; that is, intelligence among necrophiles varies from very low to very high.

Sexual Orientation

In Rosman and Resnick's[3] series of 122 cases, the sexual orientation of necrophiles could be determined in 71 cases ($N = 71$), and it was quite comparable to what prevails in the general population: 79% ($N = 56$) were heterosexual, 13% ($N = 9$) were bisexual, and 9% ($N = 6$) were homosexual.

Association with Alcohol and Drugs

Alcohol

Alcohol reduces people's ability to engage in complex, higher order cognitive processes and encourages them to focus on their immediate feelings of sexual desire and entitlement rather than on more distal cues such as their own sense of morality.[27] Alcohol consumption thus is known to contribute to sexual assaults. It has even been hypothesized that the quantity of alcohol consumed would have a *curvilinear relationship* to the severity of sexual assault.[28] Although there are a number of studies linking alcohol consumption with sexual assaults in general,[29–41] studies linking alcohol consumption with necrophilia in particular are rare.

Rosman and Resnick's[3] classic series of 122 cases studied alcohol consumption among necrophiles. In their 122 cases, they could determine the presence or absence of alcoholism in only 28 cases ($N = 28$). This was because many published studies did not mention alcoholism at all. Table 4.4 summarizes the consumption of alcohol by the necrophiles *before* committing their acts.

Table 4.4 Consumption of Alcohol by Necrophiles before Committing Their Acts

Rosman and Resnick's[3] Classification	Equivalent Classification (Chapter 3)	Total Number	Nonnecrophilic Intercourse Reported (N)	Percentage Involved in Nonnecrophilic Intercourse
	Genuine (True) Necrophiles			
Necrophilic homicide	Class IX	10	6	60
Regular necrophilia	Class VIII	8	2	25
Necrophilic fantasy	Class III, VI	—	—	—
	Pseudonecrophiles			
	Class VII	10	8	80

The necrophile may be an inveterate alcoholic, and his consumption of alcohol may be very large before the necrophilic acts. In Lancaster's case[17] the necrophile (whom Lancaster refers to as G.M.B.) had been drinking very large amounts of alcohol for over 8 years. At age 15 he used to drink eight pints of beer in an evening, and later he often drank up to 15 double Bacardi and Cokes in one session. He lost his driver's license for drinking and driving on two occasions; for 1 year in 1970 and for 3 years in 1972. Interestingly, alcohol, even in very large amounts, did not cause any slurring of speech or any obvious uncoordination of movement. His three known acts of necrophilia occurred in 1974—on October 18, November 2, and November 27—and on **all three occasions** he had consumed large amounts of alcohol before the necrophilic acts. On October 18, he first went on his own to a public house and had several alcoholic drinks. Then he had five double whiskies in the same public house with a friend. Then at a friend's house he had two bottles of whiskey of either a quarter- or half-bottle size. Later that night he broke into the mortuary at a local general hospital and had sexual intercourse with a corpse. On November 2 the amount of alcohol consumed was unknown, but the author asserts it was not small. Before his last act of necrophilia, on November 27, he had three pints of beer and one double whiskey at the college bar. He then went to the house of a friend, where he had three-quarters of a bottle of whiskey. Then he stole six **clonidine** tablets (0.025 mg each) from his landlady, and consumed them.

In his defense, it was even suggested that the **chemical agents** (alcohol on October 18 and November 2, and alcohol and clonidine on November 27) had brought about a temporary change in his personality with (1) development of a confusional state with impairment of consciousness and (2) a change of personality of a Jekyll-and-Hyde type, whereby patterns of behavior completely foreign to the defendant's normal character manifested themselves.

The jury did not accept his defense and on June 10, 1975, he was convicted and sentenced to imprisonment for life.

QUICK FACT 4.3

Instances of necrophilia under the influence of alcohol:

- **G.M.B.**, a necrophile described by Lancaster.[17] He committed three acts of necrophilia in 1974. All were performed after he had consumed large amounts of alcohol.
- **Eli Ulayuk**, a necrophile from Igloolik. In August 1988, after having consumed "home brew," he had a sudden urge to have sex with a 23-year-old female. So he stabbed and strangled her, and then possibly had sexual intercourse with her dead body. The police recovered the victim's body with her underwear removed and torn. (See Chapter 5, "Case Studies," for details.)

Other Drugs

Just like alcohol, although the interrelationship of drug consumption and sexual assaults in general has been studied,[42] studies linking the use of drugs and necrophilia are lacking. Although this relationship has been explored in the literature,[43] implications of such an association are less clear in real-life situations.

In Lancaster's[17] case study, the necrophile consumed six **clonidine** tablets before his necrophilic acts. Although he never took drugs such as amphetamine, LSD, or narcotics, he had occasionally taken his mother's or landlady's **diazepam** or **chlorpromazine** tablets to slow himself down.

Sex of the Corpses

Interestingly, not all necrophiles choose a corpse of the opposite sex for sexual intercourse. In Rosman and Resnick's[3] series, the sex of the corpse in relation to the sex of the offender could be gleaned from 91 case reports ($N = 91$). Of these, 85% ($N = 77$) used corpses of the opposite sex. But, significantly, 10% ($N = 9$) used same-sex corpses. (The authors do not mention if all of these nine cases belonged to males choosing male corpses for sex, but it appears so. One would imagine that if there were any case of a female necrophile choosing a female corpse for necrophilia, the act would be so bizarre that the authors would have mentioned it.) Five percent ($N = 5$) used corpses of both sexes. The highest percentage of same-sex corpses was among the necrophilic killers ($N = 14$), and 50% of these ($N = 7$) used same-sex corpses.

Marital Status

Marital status could be determined in 78 cases of Rosman and Resnick's[3] series ($N = 78$). Of these, 60% ($N = 47$) were single, 26% ($N = 20$) were married, and 14% ($N = 11$) were either divorced or widowed.

History of Sadistic Acts

In Rosman and Resnick's[3] series, histories of acts prior to their necrophilic act were available in 42 cases ($N = 42$), out of which 29 were true necrophiles, 11 pseudonecrophiles, and two were of undeterminable group. Out of all 42 cases, a total of 64% ($N = 27$) had a history of prior sadistic acts. All 11 of the pseudonecrophilic killers had a history of sadistic acts. Among the true necrophiles, the rate was 52% ($N = 15$). The highest rate of sadistic acts among the true necrophiles was in the necrophilic homicide group, where as many as 78% showed a history of prior sadistic acts. (The total offenders in the necrophilic homicide group was nine, of which seven showed a history of prior sadistic acts.)

Nonnecrophilic Intercourse

A significant question is whether necrophiles engage in nonnecrophilic intercourse (i.e., intercourse with regular living partners). According to the classification mentioned in Chapter 3, except class X (exclusive necrophiles), all other classes are theoretically able to have intercourse with the living. Up to class VII (opportunistic necrophiles), the necrophiles routinely engage in sex with the living. Class VIII (regular necrophiles) and class IX (homicidal necrophiles) can theoretically have sexual intercourse with a living partner, but whether it does actually occur is not clear.

Among Rosman and Resnick's[3] series, this fact was determinable in 56 cases ($N = 56$). Of these, 36 were genuine (also referred to as "true" by the authors) necrophiles (class VI, VIII, and IX) and 20 were pseudonecrophiles (class VII). Of the 36 true necrophiles, 31 had a history of nonnecrophilic intercourse. Of the 20 pseudonecrophiles, 19 had a history of nonnecrophilic intercourse.

Table 4.5 describes the distribution of nonnecrophilic intercourse as described by them. From the last column of the table, it is clear that an overwhelming percentage of necrophiles actually do engage in nonnecrophilic intercourse.

Is it possible that the remaining necrophiles (the ones who did not have a history of nonnecrophilic intercourse) were exclusive necrophiles (possibly belonging to class X)? It cannot be determined clearly from the paper. The authors simply refer to a history of "prior nonnecrophilic intercourse"; that is, a history of nonnecrophilic intercourse prior to their necrophilic acts or fantasies. The *key characteristic* of class X necrophiles is that it is *impossible*

Table 4.5 Frequency of Nonnecrophilic Intercourse among Various Classes of Necrophiles

Rosman and Resnick's Classification		Equivalent Classification (Chapter 3)	Total Number (*N*)	Nonnecrophilic Intercourse Reported in	Percentage Involved in Nonnecrophilic Intercourse
Genuine (True) Necrophiles	Necrophilic Homicide	Class IX	13	12	92
	Regular Necrophilia	Class VIII	12	9	75
	Necrophilic Fantasy	Class VI	11	10	91
Pseudonecrophiles		Class VII	20	19	95

for them to have sex with the living. Whether they displayed this characteristic is not clear from the paper.

Psychopathology

Many older texts mention that necrophiles are psychotic individuals.[44–46] However, this was not substantiated by Rosman and Resnick's[3] study. In their classic series, state of **psychosis** could be determined in 64 cases ($N = 64$). Of these only 11 (17%) were psychotic. Thus it is *incorrect to assume that most necrophiles are psychotic individuals.*

Assessment about **personality disorders** could be made in 32 cases ($N=32$). Of these, 18 individuals (56%) had a diagnosis of personality disorder.

The authors tried to determine the presence or absence of **unusual belief systems,** such as **parareligious beliefs** or **devil worship.** This determination could be made in 33 cases ($N = 33$). Unusual beliefs were found in 18 individuals (55%).

Occupation

No occupation seems immune to necrophilia. Michéa[47] reports the case of a **monk** performing necrophilia:

> In 1787 at Citeau near Dijon, one of my grandfathers, who was the physician for that celebrated abbey, left the convent one day to go to a cabin in the midst of the woods, to see the wife of a woodcutter, whom he had found dying the night before. The husband was occupied with his rough work far from the cabin, and had to leave his wife, who had no children or relatives or neighbors about her. On opening the door of the place, my grandfather was struck by a monstrous sight: a mendicant monk was performing the act of coitus on the body of the woman, who was then merely a cadaver.

A case is described by the French psychiatrist **Henri Legrand du Saulle** (1830–1886), where a **priest** was convicted of having satiated his passion upon the still warm corpse of a woman, near whom he had been placed to recite the prayers.[48]

Reports of monks and priests being involved in necrophilic acts seem to prove that having strong religious beliefs provides no immunity against this paraphilic behavior. **Masters and Lea**[14] (p. 125) report that the notorious necrophile **Victor Ardisson** was of a religious temperament. (For details, please see Chapter 1, "Necrophilia—Overview and Historical Aspects.") He always kept in his possession a prayer book and a clay angel, along with an ornament that he had stolen from a grave.

French physician and psychiatrist **Brierre de Boismont**[49] relates the case of a young man of **excellent education, good family,** and **good income** who used to bribe death chamber attendants to let him enter rooms where the corpses of young girls were laid out, so that he could have sexual intercourse with them. He was eventually caught when he attempted intercourse with a recently dead 16-year-old girl, the daughter of a very distinguished family. During the night the family heard a noise in the death chamber similar to the noise of an overturned chair. The mother of the deceased young girl entered the room and saw a man in his shirt who had just jumped from the deathbed. At first he was taken for a robber, but soon they perceived what he really was. It was learned that he belonged to a very good family and had an excellent education. He was sentenced to hard labor for life.

In the **Rosman and Resnick**[3] series, the occupations of necrophiles were listed as in Table 4.6.

Table 4.6 Occupations of Necrophiles as Reported in Rosman and Resnick Series

Occupation	Number
Hospital orderlies	8
Cemetery employees	8
Morgue attendant	8
Funeral parlor assistant	5
Soldier	3
Cleric	2
Pathologist	1
Anatomy student	1
Ambulance driver	1
Volunteer fireman	1
Total	38

References

1. Smith S, Dimock, J. Necrophilia and anti-social acts, in *Sexual Dynamics of Antisocial Behavior*. Eds., LB Schlesinger, E Revitch. Charles C Thomas, Springfield, IL, 1983, chap. 13.
2. Prins H. *Dangerous Behavior, The Law and Mental Disorder*. Tavistok, London, 1986.
3. Rosman JP, Resnick PJ. Sexual attraction to corpses: a psychiatric review of necrophilia. *Bull. Am Acad. Psychiatry Law*. 1989;**17(2)**:153–163.
4. Rapoport J. A case of necrophilia. *J Criminal Psychopathol*. 1942; **4**:277–289.
5. Brill AA. Necrophilia—Part I. J *Criminal Psychopathol*. 1941;**2(4)**:433–443.
6. Brill AA. Necrophilia—Part II. *J Criminal Psychopathol*. 1941;**3**:51–73.
7. Aggrawal A. *Forensic and Medico-legal Aspects of Sexual Crimes and Unusual Sexual Practices*. CRC Press, Boca Raton, FL, 2008.
8. Housden J. The relative frequency of the sexual paraphilias as demonstrated by 159 graffito. *Br J Criminol*. Jan 1963;**3**:290–293.
9. East N, Hubert J. *Report on the Psychological Treatment of Crime*. H.M.S.O., London, 1939.
10. Hucker S. Necrophilia and other unusual philias, in *Principles and Practice of Forensic Psychiatry*, 1st ed. Eds., R Bluglass, P Bowden. Churchill Livingstone, Edinburgh, 1990, chap. VIII.9.
11. Foerster K, Foerster G, Roth E. Nekrophilie bei einem 17 jährigen Mädchen [Necrophilia in a 17-year-old girl]. *Schweizer Archiv für Neurologie, Neurochirurgie und Psychiatrie*. 1976;**119(1)**:97–107.
12. Tsheryaskin WG. Zur Frage der Nekrophilie [The question of necrophilia]. *Zeitschrift für sexual wissenschaft-wiss*. 1929;**16**:386–392.
13. Quigley C. *The Corpse: A History*, 1st ed. McFarland & Company, Jefferson, NC, 2005, p. 300.
14. Masters REL, Lea E. *Perverse Crimes in History: Evolving Concepts of Sadism, Lust-murder, and Necrophilia—From Ancient to Modern Times*. The Julian Press, Inc., New York, 1963.
15. Allaman C. *Des Aliénés criminels*. H. Jouve, Paris, 1891.
16. Spoerri T. Nekrophilie: strukturanalyse enies falles. *Psychiatrica Neurologica*, 1959 (suppl 55). Karger, Basel.
17. Lancaster NP. Necrophilia, murder and high intelligence: a case report. *Br J Psychiatry*. 1978 Jun;**132**:605–608.
18. Bernardi L, Ponti G. Un caso eccezionale di necrofilia [An exceptional case of necrophilia] [Article in Italian]. *Minerva medicolegale*. 1957;**77(2)**:64–68
19. Kennedy L. *Ten Rillington Place*. Victor Gollancz, London, 1961, p. 225.
20. *Jeffrey Dahmer: The Butcher of Milwaukee's Human Slaughterhouse*. http://investigation.discovery.com/investigation/true-crime-stories/jeffrey-dahmer/jeffrey-dahmer-10.html. Accessed Feb 7, 2010
21. Davis JA. Profile of a sexual predator: a psychological autopsy of an American serial killer. *Forensic Examiner*. 1998 Jan-Feb;**7**:28–33.
22. Meloy JR. Pseudonecrophilia following spousal homicide. *J Forensic Sci*. 1996 Jul;**41(4)**:706–708.
23. Bartholomew AA, Milte KL, Galbally F. Homosexual necrophilia. *Med Sci Law*. 1978 Jan;**18(1)**:29–35.

24. Schlesinger LB. Adolescent sexual matricide following repetitive mother-son incest. *J Forensic Sci.* 1999 Jul;**44(4)**:746–749.
25. Klaf FS, Brown W. Necrophilia, brief review and case report. *Psychiatric Q.* 1958;**32(4)**:645–652.
26. Bauer M, Tatschner T, Patzelt D. Digital imaging of the dissection and sexual abuse of a corpse—an exceptional case of necrophilia. *Leg Med (Tokyo).* 2007 May;**9(3)**:143–146.
27. Abbey A, Zawacki T, Buck PO, Clinton AM, McAuslan P. Alcohol and sexual assault. *Alcohol Res Health.* 2001;**25(1)**:43–51.
28. Abbey A, Clinton-Sherrod AM, McAuslan P, Zawacki T, Buck PO. The relationship between the quantity of alcohol consumed and the severity of sexual assaults committed by college men. *J Interpers Violence.* 2003 Jul;**18(7)**:813–833.
29. Davis KC, Schraufnagel TJ, George WH, Norris J. The use of alcohol and condoms during sexual assault. *Am J Mens Health.* 2008 Sep;**2(3)**:281–290.
30. Howard DE, Griffin MA, Boekeloo BO. Prevalence and psychosocial correlates of alcohol-related sexual assault among university students. *Adolescence.* 2008 Winter;**43(172)**:733–750.
31. Ledray LE. Alcohol and sexual assault: what can/should we do in the emergency department? *J Forensic Nurs.* 2008;**4(2)**:91–93.
32. Horvath MA, Brown J. The role of drugs and alcohol in rape. *Med Sci Law.* 2006 Jul;**46(3)**:219–228.
33. Markos AR. Alcohol and sexual behaviour. *Int J STD AIDS.* 2005 Feb;**16(2)**:123–127.
34. Testa M. The impact of men's alcohol consumption on perpetration of sexual aggression. *Clin Psychol Rev.* 2002 Nov;**22(8)**:1239–1263.
35. Miranda R, Jr, Meyerson LA, Long PJ, Marx BP, Simpson SM. Sexual assault and alcohol use: exploring the self-medication hypothesis. *Violence Vict.* 2002 Apr;**17(2)**:205–217.
36. Abbey A. Alcohol-related sexual assault: a common problem among college students. *J Stud Alcohol Suppl.* 2002 Mar;**(14)**:118–128.
37. Abbey A, Zawacki T, Buck PO, Testa M, Parks K, Norris J, Martin SE, Livingston JA, McAuslan P, Clinton AM, Kennedy CL, George WH, Davis KC, Martell J. How does alcohol contribute to sexual assault? Explanations from laboratory and survey data. *Alcohol Clin Exp Res.* 2002 Apr;**26(4)**:575–581.
38. George WH, Stoner SA. Understanding acute alcohol effects on sexual behavior. *Annu Rev Sex Res.* 2000;**11**:92–124.
39. Moncrieff J, Drummond DC, Candy B, Checinski K, Farmer R. Sexual abuse in people with alcohol problems. A study of the prevalence of sexual abuse and its relationship to drinking behaviour. *Br J Psychiatry.* 1996 Sep;**169(3)**:355–360.
40. Allnutt SH, Bradford JM, Greenberg DM, Curry S. Co-morbidity of alcoholism and the paraphilias. *J Forensic Sci.* 1996 Mar;**41(2)**:234–239.
41. Ranieri-Collins S. Alcohol-related sexual assault. *Trends Health Care Law Ethics.* 1995 Summer;**10(3)**:37–40.
42. Baltieri DA, de Andrade AG. Drug consumption among sexual offenders against females. *Int J Offender Ther Comp Criminol.* 2008 Feb;**52(1)**:62–80.

43. Visagie A. Secrecy, drugs and necrophilia: taboos in contemporary Afrikaans gay literature. Paper presented at the 4th Conference of the International Association for the Study of Sexuality, Culture and Society (IASSCS), June 22–25, 2003, held at the University of the Witwatersrand, Johannesburg, South Africa.
44. Minovici M. *Tratat complect de medicina legala cu Legislatia si jurisprudenta Romaneasca Si Steina* [*A Complete Forensic Treatise with Romanian Legislation and Case Law*] [in Romanian]. Atelierele grafice SOCEC & Co., Societate Anomina, Bucuresti, 1928, pp. 761–783.
45. Castro LD. Un caso de necrofilia. *Revista de la Sanidad de Policia.* 1943;**3**:10–31.
46. Tomarug E, Rotescu I, Sirbu V. Un cas peu commun concernant les rapports sexuels avec des cadavres exhumés [An unusual case concerning sex with exhumed corpses]. *Acta Med Legalis Soc.* 1966;**19(1)**:109–114.
47. Michéa, *Union Médicale.* 17 July, 1849.
48. Legrand du Saulle H. *La Folie devant les Tribunaux*, Paris, 1864.
49. de Boismont B. *Gazette medicale*, July 21, 1859.

5 Case Studies

If I kissed her I'd have to kill her first.

—Ed Kemper to his sister, when she once joked with him about wanting to kiss his teacher

Introduction

Many necrophiles have attracted lay attention in the past. Most notable among them are Carl Tanzler, Douglas Clark, Ed Gein, Edmund Kemper, Gary Ridgway, Graham Coutts, Jeffrey Dahmer, Jerry Brudos, John Christie, John Wayne Gacy, Karen Greenlee, and Ted Bundy. A study of their early lives and how they grew up into being necrophiles sheds some valuable insights on this phenomenon.

Jerry Brudos

Jerome Henry "Jerry" Brudos (1939–2006) was an American necrophile who suffered from a number of additional paraphilias—most notably **fetishism** and **transvestism.** He is more often known for his foot and shoe fetishism and for this reason is often known as "The Shoe Fetish Slayer." He is also sometimes referred to as "The Lust Killer."

Brudos developed a particular fetish for women's shoes, especially black, spike-heeled shoes, from the age of 5, after having played with spike-heeled shoes at a local junkyard. This unique fixation with shoes persisted for life. Toward the end of his life, while incarcerated, Brudos had piles of women's shoe catalogs in his cell. He even wrote to major shoe companies asking for catalogs, and claimed they were his substitute for pornography.

At age 17, he abducted and beat a young woman, threatening to stab her if she did not follow his sexual demands. These included disrobing her and taking pictures of her in the nude. For this crime, he was institutionalized in a psychiatric ward at Oregon State Hospital for 9 months. There it was found his sexual fantasies revolved around his hatred and revenge against his mother and women in general. He told therapists there that one recurrent fantasy he used to have involved putting women into freezers so that he could arrange their stiffened bodies into pornographic poses.

In 1961, he married **Ralphene,** a 17-year-old girl with whom he would father two children. He asked his new bride to do housework naked except for a pair of high heels while he took pictures of her. He occasionally dressed in her panties and bra.

Between 1968 and 1969, Brudos bludgeoned and strangled four young women. He committed his first murder on January 26, 1968. On that day, while he was standing in his back yard, **Linda Slawson,** 19, who was going door to door selling encyclopedias, ran into him. He invited her into his garage-workshop, and once she was in, he bludgeoned her with a two-by-four, then strangled her to death. He then sent his family out for hamburgers, so he could play around with her corpse for a while. He removed her clothes and dressed her up in items from his own underwear collection. Then he severed her left foot, slipped a stolen spike-heeled shoe on it, and stored it away in his freezer. Finally, he tied an engine block to the corpse and threw it in the nearby Willamette River. Her body was never found.

He murdered again 11 months later—on November 26, 1968. The car of **Jan Whitney,** 23, had broken down and he offered to give her a ride. Instead of dropping her where she wanted, he took her home and hung her in his garage with a postal strap, effectively strangling her to death. He then anally raped her corpse and spent hours dressing it up and admiring it. He decided to keep her body and hung her from a hook in the garage ceiling (much like Ed Gein). A few days later he went away for Thanksgiving with his family. Upon returning, he discovered that a car had smashed into his garage, damaging a corner. A police officer came and inspected the damage, but did not look inside very well. Brudos lost his nerve after this incident and decided to get rid of the body. He sliced off one of the dead body's breasts as a trophy, took pictures of the corpse, and then threw the body in the Willamette River that night. Later he made Whitney's amputated breast into a paperweight by treating it with epoxy.

On March 27, 1969, Brudos abducted his third victim, **Karen Sprinkler,** 19, from a department store parking lot. He took her home and victimized her for quite some time. He raped her, forced her to pose for him, and eventually hung her, effectively strangling her. He then sexually assaulted the corpse a number of times. Then he sliced off both her breasts, took a bra from his own collection, filled its cups with scrunched up brown paper, and put it on her mutilated chest. Then he dumped her body in the Long Tom River. When the police divers found her body on May 12, 1969, they found it had been weighed down by an automobile cylinder head and had been in the water for approximately 2 months. Her body was fully clothed but when the clothes were removed, her amputated breasts and the "falsies" given by Brudos were discovered.

Brudos claimed his fourth—and final—victim on April 23, 1969. While posing as a police officer, he approached **Linda Salee,** 23, telling her she was being arrested for shoplifting. He had a fake police badge and she accompanied him. He took Salee back to his garage, where he strangled and raped her simultaneously. She died while he was raping her. He again kept the dead body and continued to violate the corpse. He wanted to cut off her breasts, too, but did not because her nipples were pink and he thought "nipples should be brown." So he tried to do the next best thing—make plaster molds out of them. He could not get a good cast, however. He then suspended her body from the ceiling, rigged up wires to a pair of hypodermic needles, stuck them in her chest, and **jolted her dead body with electricity** to see if he could make her "dance." On May 10, 1969, her bloated corpse was found floating in the Long Tom River. It had been weighed down by an automobile gearbox. The investigators found needle marks on her body where he had tried to administer electric current to the dead body. The coroner found that she had been strangled with a surgical thread and had been in the water for at least 2 weeks.

Brudos was apprehended on May 25, 1969, when he was hanging around the local college. In June 1969, he was charged with three counts of first degree murder for the murders of Jan Whitney, Linda Salee, and Karen Sprinker. (He was not charged with the murder of Linda Slawson, as her body was never found.) Since there is no death penalty in Oregon, he could not be given a capital sentence, but was sentenced to three consecutive life sentences. He spent his next 37 years in Oregon State Penitentiary, where ultimately he died from liver cancer on March 29, 2006, at the age of 67.

Conclusions and Impressions

Jerry Brudos suffered from multiple paraphilias. He may be seen primarily as a fetishist, with additional paraphilias (transvestism and necrophilia). His hatred toward his mother and women in general compelled him to turn into a lust killer and a necrophile. Brudos would typically have sex with his victims during their life, but would not torture or mutilate them during life. After death, almost all of his victims were sexually assaulted and mutilated (Table 5.1). Brudos was thus a **class IXe** necrophile.

Table 5.1 Summary of Jerry Brudos's Necrophilic Activities with His Victims

Victim/Age	Date When Killed	Activity during Life of Victim	Activity after Death of Victim
Linda Slawson, 19	January 26, 1968	No activity	Played around with corpse, removing clothes and dressing her up with his own collection of clothes
Jan Whitney, 23	November 26, 1968	No activity	Anally raped her corpse; hung corpse from ceiling
Karen Sprinker, 19	Mar 27, 1969	Raped her; forced her to pose for him	Sexually assaulted corpse; sliced off both breasts; put a bra (stuffed with paper) from his own collection on her mutilated chest
Linda Salee, 23	April 23, 1969	Raped her, killing her in the process	Sexually assaulted the corpse a number of times; tried to make plaster casts of her breasts; gave electric shocks to the dead body

Ted Bundy

Of all necrophiles, **Ted Bundy** and **Jeffrey Dahmer** are perhaps the most notorious. *Time* magazine listed the crimes of Ted Bundy[1] and Jeffrey Dahmer[2] among the top 25 crimes of the last century.

Theodore Robert "Ted" Bundy (1946–1989) was born at a home for unwed mothers in Burlington, Vermont, to Eleanor Louise Cowell. No one is really sure who his biological father was. Bundy's mother spoke of being seduced by a war veteran named Jack Worthington. Bundy displayed weird behavior right from his childhood. His Aunt Julia, Louise's younger sister, recalled incidents of lying down for a nap in her home and waking up to find knives surrounding her and a smiling 3-year-old Bundy at her side.

Between 1973 and 1978—his main period of homicidal activity—he is believed to have killed between 30 and 40 victims, all young girls. His homicidal activity spanned six states: Washington, Oregon, Utah, Idaho, Colorado, and Florida. His typical victim was a young, white, slender, single woman who was wearing slacks and had long brown or blond hair, parted in the middle. Smart, educated, intelligent, attractive, and suave, he would often deceive his victims by wearing a sling around his arm or a plaster cast around his leg and asking them for help with his books or to unload something from his Volkswagen. As the unsuspecting victim drifted along with him, he would bludgeon or strangle her at a lonely spot and then sexually assault the corpse. He was a true necrophile. He used to go back to the places where he left bodies in order to rape the rotting corpses. In fact, one could argue that he had killed women for the sole purpose of having an object to exploit sexually.[3]

Bundy was arrested on August 16, 1975, in Granger, Utah, but escaped on June 7, 1977. He was caught the second time on June 13, 1977, but managed to escape yet again on December 30, 1977. On January 8, 1978, while still on the run, he managed to reach Tallahassee, Florida, where he rented a room at a boarding house under the alias of "Chris Hagen."

Conclusions and Impressions

Bundy appears to be a **class IXf** necrophile. Torture and sexual activity with the victims started during life. After the killing, sexual activity continued and the bodies were mutilated, too. Many of his victims were abducted and were never found, so one can never be sure how Bundy treated them. But the fact that he kept handcuffs in his car—when police in Utah searched his car on August 16, 1975, a coil of rope and handcuffs were recovered from his car among other items—and he tried to handcuff some of his victims who survived (e.g., Carol DaRonch in Utah, on November 8, 1974) indicates that his torture of victims started during life. Some of his victims were abducted and kept alive for several days, during which rape and torture would continue. On October 18, 1974, **Melissa Anne Smith,** the 17-year-old daughter of Midvale police chief Louis Smith, vanished inexplicably from Midvale, Utah, after leaving a pizza parlor. Her nude body was found 9 days later near Summit Park, many miles east of Salt Lake City in the Wasatch Mountains. She had been strangled, raped, and sodomized. Postmortem examination indicated that she had been kept alive for at least 5 days after she disappeared. The postmortem examination also revealed that she had been beaten savagely, possibly with a crowbar, about the head. But despite such massive injuries, very little blood was found near the body, indicating that she was killed elsewhere.

The skulls of many of his victims were found at Taylor Mountain, Washington, after more than a year (mutilation after death). Some of the skulls were found with the front teeth broken out. Bundy would visit his victims' bodies over and over again at the Taylor Mountain site. He would lie with them for hours, all night at times, applying makeup to their corpses and violating their remains until putrefaction forced him to abandon the remains. Before his death, Bundy admitted to returning to the corpse of Georgann Hawkins for purposes of necrophilia.

Why did Bundy become a necrophile? When he was a student at the University of Washington, he began a relationship with **Stephanie Brooks,** a fellow university student whom he met in 1967. She was a beautiful and highly sophisticated woman from a wealthy Californian family.[4] Ted initially could not believe someone from her "class" would have an interest in an ordinary person like him, but they did have common interests. They both loved to ski and it was during their many ski trips together that he fell in love with her. She was possibly the first woman with whom he became involved with sexually.[4] However, she dumped him later, and Bundy seemed to have been deeply hurt. All his victims looked like her, and it is possible that he was trying to get even with her vicariously by murdering and sexually assaulting women who had her appearance.

Thor Nis Christiansen

Thor Nis Christiansen (1957–1981) was born in Denmark on December 28, 1957. His parents emigrated to Inglewood, California, when he was 5, and then on to Solvang. His father, Nis, ran a restaurant in Solvang.

Christiansen was initially a good student and had a high IQ. However, in his junior year of high school, he began smoking marijuana, drinking, and neglecting his schoolwork. He moved out of his parents' house, dropped out of high school, and began working as a gas station attendant. At this time, he also put on a lot of weight, at one point weighing 275 pounds.

During his teens, Christiansen began to be obsessed with fantasies of killing women and having sex with their corpses (typical class IX necrophilic behavior). He had a particular fetish for girls who wore their hair long and straight and had a certain kind of build and taste in clothes. He stole a .22 caliber pistol from a friend and began frequenting the University of California campus looking for girls wanting to hitchhike.

On November 20, 1976, he committed his first murder, when he picked up 21-year-old **Jacqueline Anne Rook** from the Isla Vista area near the University of California campus. On December 6, 1976, he picked up **Mary Ann Sarris,** 19, who was hitchhiking in the same area, and killed her. On January 18, 1977, he picked up **Patricia Marie Laney** and murdered her. All girls had been shot in the head by a .22 caliber pistol. Their bodies had been sexually violated after death.

Laney's corpse was discovered on January 19, in nearby Refugio Canyon, near Goleta. The police recognized the pattern when Jacqueline Rook was found dead, in the same area, on January 20.

Christiansen first came to the attention of police in February 1977, as one of several hundred persons questioned in the case. Cited as a minor in possession of alcohol, he was not considered a suspect at the time, although authorities confiscated a .22-caliber pistol from his car. Christiansen was not on the suspect list, even on May 22, 1977, when the skeletal remains of **Mary Sarris** were discovered in Drum Canyon, north of Santa Barbara. Homicide investigators wrote him off as just one more teenager picked up with liquor on his breath.

After these three murders, Christiansen moved to Oregon, lost weight, and moved back to Santa Barbara County and completed his high school diploma at a junior college. He moved into an apartment in Goleta with **Kerry Soliz,** a woman in her 20s whom he met while she was hitchhiking. While he was living with her he committed his fourth and last murder, when he killed **Laura Sue Benjamin,** 22, an African-American, on May 26, 1979. She was reportedly a prostitute. Her body was found in a culvert near Angeles Forest Highway and Big Tujunga Road in the San Gabriel Mountains, north of Los Angeles.

Before her killing, Christiansen had tried to kill another victim. On April 18, 1979, he shot **Lydia Preston,** 21, in the left ear in his vehicle, but she escaped, albeit severely injured. She was taken to Cedars-Sinai Medical Center, where the bullet was removed. She was released a few days later.

Preston met him again on July 11, 1979, in the Bottom Line Bar in Hollywood, and immediately reported him to the police. Christiansen was arrested. Because of Christiansen's address in Goleta, California, and the similarity of Preston's experience to the Rook, Sarris, and Laney cases, Christiansen became a suspect in the Isla Vista murders. After his apprehension, Santa Barbara County law enforcement realized they had investigated him as a suspect (among 100 others) in 1977, and had noted his possession of a .22 caliber pistol when he was arrested for drunk driving. On July 27, Christiansen was formally charged with three counts of first-degree murder in Santa Barbara. At the time of his trial, California did not have the death penalty, so he was sentenced to life and sent to Folsom State Prison. He was stabbed to death in prison on March 30, 1981. The perpetrator was not identified. Psychiatrists had predicted that he was likely to be killed in prison, as he was young, blond, and his last victim was African-American.

Conclusions and Impressions

Christiansen was a typical class IXb necrophile, who would kill his victims in order to have sex. He was able to have sexual relations with live women, evidenced by the fact that he was having a live-in relationship with a girlfriend. However, sex with corpses fascinated him and he killed for that purpose.

John Christie

John Reginald Halliday Christie (1898–1953) was born in Halifax, West Yorkshire. He murdered at least six women, possibly eight—including his wife Ethel and a 14-month-old baby girl, Geraldine—by gassing them with carbon monoxide or strangling them, or by combining both methods in his flat at 10 Rillington Place, Notting Hill, London.

His murders started in August 1943 with the murder of Ruth Fuerst, and lasted until March 3, 1953, with the murder of Hectorina MacLennan. His biography and murders are well known.[5,6,7,8,9] (For more details on Christie, please see Chapter 2, "Etiology", Chapter 6, "Medico-legal Investigation", and Chapter 8, "Expert Testimony in Necrophilia Cases".) Table 5.2 summarizes his killings, with some relevant details.

Table 5.2 Killings Attributed to John Christie

Victim (Name/Age)	Date of Murder	Body/Remains Discovered on/Autopsy Conducted by	Relevant Details
Ruth Margaret Christine Fuerst, 21	August 1943	March 28, 1953; remains of victims no. 1 and 2 examined by Francis Camps	Fuerst was an Austrian-born munitions worker and part-time prostitute. Had come from Vienna as a refugee in 1939.[10] Strangled during sex at 10 Rillington Place, London. Christie buried her body in his residence's garden at the backyard after initially hiding it beneath the floorboards of his front living room. Her skull, found broken in 110 pieces, was assembled under Camps' direction. It later stood in the laboratory of Professor R.J. Harrison of Cambridge, who supervised the work.[10]
Muriel Amelia Eady, 32	October 1944	March 28, 1953	Eady was Christie's coworker at a radio factory, where Christie had started working from 1944 as a clerk. He invited Eady back to his flat with the promise that he had concocted a "special mixture" that could cure her bronchitis. Eady was to inhale a mixture from his special jar. (Please see Chapter 2, "Etiology."). Once Eady was unconscious, he made sure she was dead by strangling her and then sexually assaulted the body. Buried the body alongside Fuerst's body in the back garden. When her skeleton was recovered, police found that Christie had used a femur (either from Fuerst or Eady) to prop up a trellis in the garden.
Mrs. Beryl Evans, 19	November 8, 1949	December 2, 1949; autopsy on victims 3 and 4 conducted by Dr. Donald Teare; he found evidence of strangulation by ligature in both;[11] both bodies were	In 1949, Beryl with her husband, a low-intelligence van driver, Timothy Evans (IQ of 70), moved into the top floor flat of the same building where Christie lived (10 Rillington Place; Christie lived in the ground-floor flat). They had a baby Geraldine in October 1948. She became pregnant again around July 1949. In November, when the pregnancy was around 16 weeks,[10] she wanted an abortion, but her husband did not. So she approached Christie, offering sex in return for an abortion. (Abortion was illegal in Britain at that time.)[10]

Table 5.2 Killings Attributed to John Christie (Continued)

Victim (Name/Age)	Date of Murder	Body/Remains Discovered on/Autopsy Conducted by	Relevant Details
		exhumed on May 18, 1953; second postmortem conducted jointly by Francis Camps, Donald Teare, and Keith Simpson	Realizing that an unsuspecting victim had herself walked into his net, he said he could abort the baby and offered her his notorious death jar, from which she could inhale carbon monoxide. She probably refused to inhale gas from the jar, whereupon Christie strangled her. Christie tried intercourse with the dead body, but could not raise an erection.[10] At her postmortem Donald Teare did not find any evidence of abortion,[10] nor did he find any signs of carbon monoxide poisoning.[12]
Geraldine Evans, 14 months	November 8, 1949	December 2, 1949; autopsy as above.	Geraldine was the young daughter of Timothy and Beryl Evans. For reasons that are not entirely clear, Timothy Evans claimed responsibility for the murder of both Beryl and Geraldine. After he was charged with their deaths, he withdrew his confession and accused Christie of being the murderer. On January 11, 1950, Evans was put on trial for the murder of his daughter, the prosecution having decided not to pursue a second charge of murdering his wife for a technical reason. Ironically, Christie, who later admitted to both murders, was a principal witness for the Crown against Evans. The jury found Evans guilty, and he was hanged at Pentonville on March 9, 1950.[10] When Christie admitted to both Beryl and Geraldine's murders, the question arose if Evans had been wrongly executed. An initial inquiry conducted by a senior QC, John Scott Henderson, revealed that Evans had indeed killed both, and Christie was lying. A subsequent inquiry by Mr. Justice Brabin found that while Evans had killed Beryl, Christie had killed Geraldine. Since Evans had been tried and hanged for the murder of Geraldine (a murder which he did not commit according to inquiry), he was

(*continued*)

Table 5.2 Killings Attributed to John Christie (Continued)

Victim (Name/Age)	Date of Murder	Body/Remains Discovered on/Autopsy Conducted by	Relevant Details
			granted a posthumous free pardon. His remains were exhumed from Pentonville Prison and reburied outside.[12] The continuing confusion has been about the extremely extraordinary coincidence that *two different stranglers (Christie and Evans) were living at the same address at the same time*, which makes many people still conjecture that both murders had indeed been committed by Christie.
Ethel Christie, 54	December 14, 1952	March 24, 1953; autopsy on victims 5, 6, 7, and 8 done by Francis Camps on March 25[10]; he did not find any sign of CO poisoning in Ethel's body, but there were signs of CO poisoning in victim nos. 6, 7, and 8; the last three victims also showed signs of strangulation and sexual intercourse before, during, or after death.[10]	Ethel was John Christie's wife. Christie strangled her in bed. Possibly committed necrophilia with her, as there seemed no other reason to kill her. It is also known that he kept her body in his bed for 2 days,[10] before finally hiding it under the floor boards of the front room, covering the body with buckets of soil brought in from the garden.[10] Christie said in court that he strangled his wife at 8 AM because she seemed to be choking. He could not see her in such discomfort, so he "put her to sleep with a stocking."[10] In the same breath, he gave a contradictory statement that the medicine bottle beside her bedside had contained 25 tablets of phenobarbitone the previous night, and next morning he found only two,[10] implying that Ethel had consumed 23 tablets in a kind of **drug automatism.** Camps in his postmortem, however, failed to detect any tablet in the stomach.[10] When the Attorney General **Sir Lionel Heald** asked, "If Dr. Camps is right, you must be wrong. Are you sure that is the truth of what happened?" Christie replied, "Yes, I am sure."[10]

Table 5.2 Killings Attributed to John Christie (Continued)

Victim (Name/Age)	Date of Murder	Body/Remains Discovered on/Autopsy Conducted by	Relevant Details
Rita Nelson, 25	January 2, 1953 (last seen alive)	March 24, 1953	Twenty-four weeks pregnant at the time of death. Christie possibly offered to abort her unborn baby and gassed her with his infamous death jar. Victims no. 6, 7, and 8 were prostitutes, and all had been treated for venereal disease in the same hospital in Southampton.[13] Engaged in necrophilic sexual intercourse with her dead body. Bodies of victims no. 6, 7, and 8 hidden in kitchen cupboard, where they were discovered on March 24, 1953.
Kathleen Maloney, 26	January 12, 1953 (last seen alive)	March 24, 1953	A prostitute he met in Ladbroke Grove. She asked him for a pound for "round the corner" intercourse and later increased her price to 30 shillings. When he did not agree, she followed him to his house, forced herself in, picked up a frying pan from kitchen, and attempted to kill him. Christie picked up a rope lying nearby and strangled her.[10] Christie's claim that Maloney started a fight seems unlikely.[14] Quite possibly Christie lured her to his house, killed her, and engaged in necrophilic sexual intercourse with her dead body. He kept her body in his bed for the whole night. The next morning, he washed, shaved, and made a cup of tea before putting the body in the kitchen cupboard.[10] Semen was detected in her vaginal canal.
Hectorina Maclennan, 26	March 3, 1953	March 24, 1953	Gassed. Engaged in necrophilic sexual intercourse with her dead body. Bodies of victim nos. 5, 6, 7, and 8 discovered by a new tenant, **Beresford Brown.**[10]

After his last murder, Christie left 10 Rillington Place on March 20, 1953, subletting the place to a Mr. and Mrs. Reilly, taking £7 13s in advance.[14] The owner, a Jamaican named Charles Brown, evicted the Reillys almost immediately, as it was illegal to sublet the flat, and rented the place to a new Jamaican tenant, who subsequently discovered the victims lying in the kitchen cupboard.

The hunt for Christie started immediately after March 24, when the bodies were discovered. On March 31 he was recognized by Police Constable Ledger on the embankment near Putney Bridge.[14] In light of his confessions, the bodies of Beryl and Geraldine Evans were exhumed on May 18. The pathologist who had been hired by Christie's defense team, Dr. Keith Simpson, did not find much in his favor.[12] Christie's trial started on June 22. The jury found him guilty and he was executed 23 days later, on July 15, 1953.

Conclusions and Impressions

Christie was a **class IXb** necrophile. He was impotent from his teens and did not have sexual intercourse even with his own wife. (For details please see Chapter 2, "Etiology.") Thus it is quite clear that he did not (in fact, he could not) have sex with his victims during life. Nor were any of the bodies mutilated. The only evidence is of postmortem sex with his victims. Semen was found in the vaginal canals of several of his victims and also in the seams of his shoes, indicating that he masturbated standing over the bodies of his victims and then, having gathered more confidence, engaged in sexual intercourse with the dead bodies.

His killings were undoubtedly a result of his necrophilic urges. He even killed his own wife for necrophilic activities. (According to his own admission, he could not have sex with her when she was alive.) Christie later confessed regarding his murders, "I remember experiencing a strange, peaceful thrill." He also admitted that the only way he could attain potency was with victims he rendered helpless. (There is no known way he rendered them helpless except by killing.)

He also displayed symptoms of **class V** (fetishistic) necrophilia. A *two-ounce tobacco tin containing four lots of pubic hair* was recovered in his house during police raids. It is inconceivable that women allowed him to clip their pubic hair. Most probably he clipped them from his victims after they died. The hair had not been stuffed carelessly in the tin, but in a highly artistic fashion. They had been teased out so that they formed *interlocking ringlets*, each ringlet occupying one corner of the tin. High Court Judge **Sir Daniel Brabin** described them as an "artistic display."[12]

Another curious thing was that *none of the dead bodies was wearing panties*. The best explanation for this is that the panties were removed after death for fetishistic activities.

Graham Coutts

Graham Coutts (1968–) was born in Leven, in the Fife area of Scotland. He went to Glenrothes School before his family moved south to Cheltenham. He never excelled academically. At the age of 15, he developed an interest in asphyxiophilia, and by the age of 21 he was practicing asphyxial sex, or as he called it, "breath control sex."

In 2003, he was living with his girlfriend, **Lisa Stephens,** in Hove, East Sussex. The couple was friendly with another couple, social worker **Malcolm Sentance,** 34, and his girlfriend, **Jane Longhurst,** 31, a music teacher by profession, living in Brighton, England. On **March 14, 2003,** Jane made a chance phone call to her friend Lisa. As Lisa was not at home, Coutts answered the phone. As talks went on, he convinced Jane to go swimming with him at a local bath.

As planned, Coutts picked her up from Shaftesbury Road in Brighton, but instead of taking her swimming, he drove her to his home and persuaded her to come in for a cup of tea.

It is not clear what happened after that. Coutts maintained that he wrapped a pair of nylon tights around Jane's neck as part of a **consensual sexual practice** (breath control play), which he had undertaken on numerous previous occasions with several different partners. During this erotic practice, Jane died accidentally, perhaps as a result of vasovagal shock.

The prosecution gave a completely different story. According to them, there was nothing to suggest that Coutts and Longhurst had ever been lovers. He invited Longhurst to his flat under false pretenses, and then killed her. After Longhurst died, Coutts first stored her body in his car and then in his shed. Eleven days after her death he enclosed the body in a cardboard box, rented a commercial storage facility, and stored the body there.

On April 19 he bought a can of petrol, took her body to an area of woodland some distance away, poured petrol over the body, and set fire to it. When the body was found, it was unclothed and burning. It had a ligature made from a pair of tights tied twice around the neck, with a knot on the right-hand side. Suspicion mounted on Coutts. When Detective Constable David Wright went to Mr. Coutts' flat on April 24 to question him about his movements on March 14 and April 19, he could not provide satisfactory answers. He said that on April 19, between 7 PM and 10 PM, he was delivering goods for the cleaning firm Kleeneze in Brighton. But he could not tell where he had been or whom he had visited, despite knowing names of roads in the city well. When asked for receipts for the Kleeneze rounds done on April 19, he could not provide any. He was arrested, interviewed, and released on bail, but was rearrested on April 28, when he was charged with murder.

Coutts was convicted of murder at **Lewes Crown Court** on February 3, 2004, and sentenced to a life term, to serve a minimum of 30 years. He appealed on the grounds that the jury was not offered a manslaughter alternative and that the jury was inadequately directed on the **Internet evidence.** It was dismissed by the Court of Appeal, but on appeal the House of Lords overturned the murder conviction, ruling that the jury should have been presented with a possible manslaughter verdict.[15] A new trial started on June 12, 2007. He was again found guilty on July 4, 2007, and was sentenced to a life term.

Conclusions and Impressions

It appears that Coutts was primarily an asphyxiophile who got sexual stimulation through asphyxia. He used to ask his lovers to strangle him so he could pass out. He also achieved sexual stimulation while trying similar asphyxiation on his partners. In the court, two of his former lovers—**Sandra Gates** and **Nicola Stainthorpe**—testified that Coutts used to put his hands around their throats and asked them to fulfill his desires for asphyxial sex. Stainthorpe said he wanted to continue squeezing until she blacked out. She also said, "He asked me to put my hands around his neck. He wanted me to press harder and harder with a view to hopefully making him pass out, black out." It turned out that on a few occasions he engaged in similar practices with his then-current partner, **Lisa Stephens,** too.

It is possible that while trying a similar experiment on **Longhurst** (quite possibly forcefully), he killed her accidentally. However, the fact that he kept the body in his possession for 5 weeks is a clear indication that he harbored necrophilic tendencies, too. Since he did not kill Longhurst specifically for necrophilic purposes, he is not a homicidal necrophile. Nor did he actively seek out a dead body for necrophilia. His behavior is more in line with **class VII necrophiles,** who are normally quite content having intercourse with the living but if an opportunity arose, they would have sex with the dead. That he had necrophilic tendencies is also proven by the fact that he paid hundreds of pounds in subscriptions to **necrophilia Web sites.**

At the time Coutts engaged in necrophilic acts with Longhurst's dead body, **necrophilia was not a criminal offense.** It became an offense when the *Sexual Offences Act 2003* came into force in May 2004. Thus, Coutts was never charged with necrophilia. In any case, he was charged with a more serious offense, so charging with necrophilia was never really required. However, the fact remains that if he had engaged in similar acts *with an already dead body,* it would have been difficult to convict him of any crime (except perhaps for possessing violent pornographic images in his computer).

Jeffrey Dahmer

Jeffrey Dahmer (1960–1994) is arguably the most celebrated of all necrophiles. His surname is now synonymous with "monster." More academic papers and theses have been written on him than on any other necrophile.[16–25] His crimes have been included by *Time* magazine as one of the top 25 crimes of the last century.[2] In all, Dahmer murdered 17 men and boys between the ages of 14 and 33 (ten Black, three White, two Hispanic, one Native American, and one Laotian[22]) between 1978 and 1991. Some believe that he was a racist, but quite possibly he chose predominantly black and other minority victims because he lived in a predominantly ethnic area.

Dahmer suffered from **exhibitionism,** too. He was arrested twice for indecent exposure, in 1982 and 1986; in his second offense, he masturbated before two boys. The majority of his necrophilic murders occurred between 1987 and 1991. His murders involved a number of deviant behaviors including rape, torture, dismemberment, necrophilia, and cannibalism.

Dahmer was born on May 21, 1960, in Milwaukee to **Lionel,** an analytical chemist, and **Joyce Dahmer.** His mother Joyce had a difficult pregnancy (it was her first pregnancy) with him. His father Lionel recalls that during pregnancy, her jaw would go sideways and lock, and her eyes would bulge—symptoms akin to epilepsy. A doctor would usually have to intervene, giving Joyce injections of barbiturates and morphine, which would finally relax her. Lionel believed that it was these injections that caused a behavioral abnormality in Jeffrey. Joyce, however, strongly denied that she had any such symptoms during her pregnancy.

At approximately age 4, he developed a hernia and underwent successful surgical repair.[20] In 1968 he was sexually molested by a neighbor boy in rural Bath Township. His parents had a troubled relationship, which ended in divorce in 1977. Both these incidents may have had a role to play in his subsequent psychopathology.[26]

Dahmer became increasingly withdrawn and uncommunicative between the ages of 10 and 15, showing little interest in any hobbies or social interactions. In fact, it has been proposed that Dahmer suffered from **Asperger syndrome,** and that this disorder was the cause of his homicidal necrophilic behavior.[20] While still in elementary school, Dahmer received an introductory chemistry set as a present. He developed an extraordinary interest in collecting dead insects, and later higher animals, using his chemistry set to store animal skeletons in bottles of formaldehyde. Biking around the neighborhood, he looked for animals that had been killed by cars, and soon had quite a collection of bones from cats, dogs, chipmunks, raccoons, and squirrels that he kept stored in jars. From time to time, he would pick a few of the bones, then let them fall with a brittle crackling sound that seemed to fascinate him. Over and over, he would pick up a fistful of bones, then let them drop back into the pile that remained on the bare ground. He seemed oddly thrilled by the sound they made.[27] Once he decapitated a dog, nailed its body to a tree, and impaled its head on a stick beside a wooden cross.

Dahmer also had a collection of stuffed rabbits, owls, and small birds. When his friends asked him about the stuffed animals, Dahmer would respond, "It's taxidermy. I used to do taxidermy . . . always wanted to do that to a human."

Dahmer also kept spiders, praying mantises, and other insects in jars that lined his clubhouse walls. He began drinking in his teens and was an alcoholic by the time of his high school graduation.

Murders

Dahmer's typical *modus operandi* was to go to gay bars and offer young homosexual and bisexual males money to pose for photos or to watch videos and drink beer at his place. He drugged victims into a deep sleep with spiked drinks before strangling or stabbing them to death. He then would have **oral** and **anal sex with the cadavers,** and then **dismember them with a hacksaw.** He would pose his dead victims in sexually explicit poses (**posing**) and take photographs. Their heads and genitalia were kept as souvenirs and trophies, biceps and other muscles were frozen for future consumption. Dahmer said human flesh tasted "like beef." The remainder was boiled with chemicals and acids before being washed down the drains. He tried to drill holes in the skulls of some living victims, and then pour acid into the skull. The idea was to make a **living zombie** who would obey his sexual commands without resistance.

Dahmer was smart (he had an estimated IQ of about 145), and was able to fool the police many times. In one incident, on the night of May 27, 1991, in Milwaukee, **Konerak Sinthasomphone,** a 14-year-old boy of Laotian descent, managed to escape and wandered into the streets with Dahmer in pursuit. When the cops started asking questions, Dahmer was able to convince the police that it was merely a lovers' quarrel. The police conclusion: "Intoxicated Asian, naked male. Was returned to his sober boyfriend." He was later strangled and dismembered and turned out to be Dahmer's 13th victim.

Dahmer again tried to fool the police on July 22, 1991, but was unsuccessful this time. On this day, he lured **Tracy Edwards,** an African-American male, into his home. Once in, Dahmer tried to handcuff him, but could put the cuffs on only one hand; he failed to cuff the wrists together. Then, wielding a large butcher knife, Dahmer forced Edwards into the bedroom, where Edwards saw pictures of mangled bodies on the wall and noticed the terrible smell coming from a large blue barrel. Edwards struggled and was able to free himself. Running through the streets, with the *handcuffs still hanging from one hand,* Edwards waved for help to a police car and led the officers back to Dahmer's apartment. As usual Dahmer tried to fool the officers by being friendly to them. However, when his bedroom was checked, Polaroid photographs of mangled bodies were discovered. In the refrigerator a human head and some other human remains were found. Further searching of the apartment revealed three more severed heads, multiple photographs of murdered victims and human remains, and severed hands and penises.

Trial and Sentencing

Dahmer was indicted on 17 murder charges, which were reduced to 15. His trial began on January 30, 1992. Dahmer pleaded not guilty by reason of insanity. The trial lasted 2 weeks. The court found Dahmer sane and he was sentenced to 957 years in prison. He served his time in Columbia Correctional Institution in Portage, Wisconsin, where he was killed by **Christopher J. Scarver,** an inmate, on November 28, 1994. Scarver is an African-American, but it was not revenge for Dahmer's killing of blacks. Scarver was a schizophrenic and thought he was carrying out orders from God.

Conclusions and Impressions

Dahmer was a **class IXf** necrophile. It is quite clear that he engaged in sex and mutilation of the dead bodies. A search of his house revealed many body parts and mutilated bodies. Dahmer tried to handcuff his last victim, indicating that he did engage in bondage and possibly torture during life. The photographs recovered from his house showed his sexual activities with both live and dead victims. Thus it is clear that Dahmer initiated torture and sexual activity during his victims' lives and continued sexual activity and mutilation after their deaths.

Mark Dixie

Mark Phillip Dixie (1970–) is a chef who has a long history of sex offending. Besides being a necrophile, he has shown **exhibitionistic** (like Dahmer) and **fetishistic** (like Christie) traits. At the age of 17, he indecently assaulted a female Jehovah's Witness in her 40s in London. Between 1993 and 1999 Dixie lived in Australia. During this time he worked in Western Australia, and it is believed that he might have been behind the **Claremont serial murders,** which involved the murder of three young Australian women during 1996 and 1997. The murders occurred in Claremont, a wealthy western suburb of Perth, Western Australia.

In June 1998, when in Australia, he stabbed and raped a 19-year-old Thai student studying economics (her name has been withheld by the court). Wearing a stocking mask over his head, Dixie broke into her house in Perth through a kitchen window and stabbed her eight times. He then raped her, convinced she was dying. A DNA sample from the woman's underwear was later matched to him. In 2001, in South London, he allegedly masturbated in front of a woman making a call from a public phone box.

Sally Anne Bowman's Murder

On September 24, 2005, a Saturday, 18-year-old model **Sally Anne Bowman** left her home in Croydon, South London, in the evening to have a night out with her friends. The next day, at about 6:30 AM, her partially naked body was found in a pool of blood in her driveway. She had been stabbed seven times and subjected to a gruesome sexual attack after she was dead. Neighbors had heard screams at about 4:20 AM, but dismissed them as either a simple domestic dispute or foxes' cries, which were common in that area at night.

Later it was discovered that she was dropped off outside her home in the early hours of September 25 by her boyfriend, 22-year-old Lewis Sproston. Initially he was suspected of murdering her, especially since the couple had had an argument for almost 2 hours, just before her death. He was indeed held for 4 days for questioning, but soon it became clear that he was not the murderer.

It was Dixie who killed her and then had sex with her dead body. He had been drinking and snorting cocaine all day as he celebrated his 35th birthday. In the early hours of September 25, he left his friends asleep and went looking for a victim. As Lewis left Sally in her driveway at 4:20 AM, Dixie leapt from the shadows and started hacking at her with a knife. Three of the blows went straight through her abdomen and came out through her back. After he had had sex with her dead body, Dixie took her underwear and her purse as trophies.

Dixie could not be caught immediately because the police had no clues about the killing. Quite by chance, he was brought to justice 9 months later. In June 2006, he got into a minor scuffle over a World Cup football match at Ye Olde Six Bells pub in Horley, Surrey, where he was working. His DNA was taken as a routine procedure. When put in a national police computer, it matched perfectly with that found on Bowman's body. Later his fingerprints were matched to a bloody fingerprint found on Sally's shoes and his bite marks were matched with those on her cheek, neck, and breast.

When apprehended, Dixie denied murdering Bowman but admitted he did have sex with her dead body, "taking advantage of the situation." It turned out that on an earlier occasion, he had masturbated over newspaper pictures of Sally Anne. Dixie filmed the act and the recording was discovered among his belongings in the barn of the Horley pub. This finding ultimately helped convict him.

On February 22, 2008, a jury of seven women and five men unanimously found him guilty of Bowman's murder. They took just three and a half hours to come to this decision. Dixie, a father of three children by two different women, was sentenced to life imprisonment at the Old Bailey, where the trial judge recommended that Dixie should not be released for a minimum of 34 years, by which time he will be 70 years old. This is among the longest minimum term ever imposed upon a single murderer.

Conclusions and Impressions

At various stages of his life, Dixie displayed necrophilic, exhibitionistic, and fetishistic tendencies. This is an instance of necrophilia coexisting with other paraphilias. It appears Dixie killed Bowman so that he could have sex with her dead body. This makes him a **class IX necrophile.** He is not a class X necrophile because he could have sex with the living (he fathered three children).

Kenneth Douglas

Kenneth Douglas (1953–) was a mortuary attendant at the Hamilton County, Ohio, morgue from 1976 to 1992. During this time he is believed to have had sex with several corpses. His sex act in 1982 with the dead body of **Karen Range,** 19, which was proved by his DNA found on the body, convicted him.

Karen Range of Roselawn, Ohio, had been murdered by **David Joseph Steffen** on August 19, 1982. Steffen came to her door under the pretense of selling cleaning products. He forced his way in and killed her by stabbing her. At autopsy, it was found that she had been severely beaten and had her throat slashed with a paring knife. Semen was found inside her body, and it was believed that it was Steffen who first raped and then killed her. Although Steffen admitted to killing Karen, he strongly denied having raped her. As DNA profiling had not been developed at that time, it was impossible to establish if he was speaking the truth. Blood tests, which were available at that time, were unable to eliminate him as a rape suspect. The jury believed that he did rape and kill her. In 1983, he was convicted of aggravated burglary, rape, and aggravated murder, and was sentenced to death.

Figure 5.1 From left to right, Kenneth Douglas, David Steffen, and Karen Range.

Almost a quarter of a century later, on March 17, 2007, Kenneth Douglas (Figure 5.1) was convicted of drug trafficking and as a routine procedure was ordered to provide a DNA sample. That DNA sample matched the 1982 semen sample gathered from Karen. Douglas was found guilty, and on September 8, 2008, he was convicted of gross abuse of a corpse. He was given a 3-year prison sentence, which included 18 months for corpse abuse and 18 months for a parole violation on an unrelated drug conviction (***State of Ohio v. Kenneth Douglas***, Hamilton County Court of Common Pleas Case No. B-0805963, Hamilton County, Ohio).

Investigators suspected that during his tenure as a mortuary attendant, Douglas may have had sex with other dead bodies, too. Subsequent investigation revealed that during the time Douglas worked as a morgue attendant, rape kit evidence was available to be tested in 29 cases. Douglas's DNA was found on two of them: on the bodies of **Charlene Edwards,** 23, and **Angel Hicks,** 24, both of Cincinnati. **Edwards** was strangulated by Mark Chambers in October 1991. On or about October 1, 1991, Douglas had sex with her dead body. **Hicks** died in December 1991 as a result of blunt injury to the head after being thrown from a third-story window. Douglas had sex with her body on or about December 8, 1991.

Conclusions and Impressions

Kenneth Douglas is a typical class VII (opportunistic) necrophile. His sex act with Karen's dead body in 1982 has been proved and he has been convicted in the case. Two additional necrophilic acts have been proved by DNA 9 years later. It is reasonable to infer that during his tenure at the Hamilton County morgue he must have had sex with several more bodies. Hamilton County officials believe that Douglas may have sexually violated more than 100 corpses during his 16-year employment at the morgue. Unfortunately this cannot be proved now, because DNA was not preserved in all cases.

Ed Gein

Edward Theodore Gein (1906–1984) was born on August 27, 1906, in La Crosse County, Wisconsin. He was the second child of George and Augusta Gein. Henry, his elder brother, was 7 years older. Gein's father held jobs as a tanner and carpenter when he was not working the farm. He was an alcoholic who would become enraged when inebriated.

Gein's mother Augusta was the main breadwinner and absolute matriarch of the Gein household. A fervent Lutheran, she was thoroughly disgusted with sex and tried to convince her children that all women were prostitutes and instruments of the devil. However, she was "not as strong" in her opposition to masturbation.[26]

Augusta operated a small grocery store and eventually purchased a 160-acre farm a few miles outside the small town of Plainfield, Wisconsin, which then became the Gein family's permanent home. Ed, quite devoted to his mother, left home only to go to school. Besides school, he spent most of his time doing chores on the farm.

Gradual Death of Gein's Family Members

During a short span of 6 years, from 1940 till 1945, Ed gradually lost all his three family members, which left him completely alone. The first to die was Ed's father George, who died of a heart attack in April 1940. Augusta gained greater control of her children after her husband's death. Ed's elder brother Henry died under suspicious circumstances during a brush fire on May 16, 1944. Some investigators suspected that Ed had killed his brother, but in the absence of any evidence, no charges were filed against him.

After his brother's death, Gein lived alone with his mother. Soon after, she suffered from a series of strokes that left her paralyzed. He would nurse her even as she verbally abused him. On December 29, 1945, she died, at which time Gein "lost his only friend and one true love. And he was absolutely alone in the world."[28]

Gein Lives Alone

Gein, devastated by his mother's death, remained on the farm, supporting himself with earnings from odd jobs. He sealed off rooms used by his mother, including the entire second floor, the downstairs parlor, and the living room, leaving them untouched. Only two places remained unsealed: a small room in which he lived, and a kitchen next to his room. He no longer worked the farm after the government began paying him as part of a soil conservation program. Doing local handyman jobs subsidized his income.

QUICK FACT 5.1

- **Ed Gein** never married and remained a bachelor throughout his life. This was perhaps because from childhood he had been ambiguous about his masculinity. He considered amputation of his penis on several occasions. **Christine Jorgenson,** a male-to-female transsexual, was much in the headlines in the 1950s. Influenced by her, Gein considered transsexual surgery, but could not do so as the process was costly.
- Eventually Gein discovered other ways to "become a woman." He haunted **three local cemeteries between 1947 and 1954** and **opened an estimated 40 graves.** The object was to steal dead bodies or sometimes simply some bits and pieces from the corpses. From these he carved out a number of fetish objects, which he would wear, imagining himself to be a woman. *Often he would dance underneath the moon wearing a woman's scalp and face, a skinned-out "vest" complete with breasts, and female genitalia strapped above his own.* By "putting on" another sex and personality, Gein seemed to find a measure of contentment.
- Gein later confessed that he enjoyed dressing himself like this and pretending he was his own mother. Interestingly his victims were roughly the age of his mother.
- Confirmation of Gein's grave robberies was obtained by opening three graves. In one, the corpse was mutilated as described by Gein; the second held no corpse at all; a casket in the third showed pry marks, but the body was intact.
- Gein appeared to be suffering from multiple paraphilias; most notable were **fetishism, transvestism,** and **necrophilia.**

Gein's Necrophilic Activities

On December 8, 1954, **Mary Hogan,** 51, disappeared from the tavern she managed in Pine Grove, Wisconsin. The police found a pool of blood on the floor, one spent cartridge from a .32-caliber pistol, and an overturned chair. Ed Gein became a suspect in this case, but no charges could be filed, as there was no concrete evidence against him. It was only 3 years later that the cartridge would be matched to a pistol found in his home.

Gein's necrophilic activities first came to notice on November 16, 1957, when Plainfield hardware store owner **Bernice Worden,** 58, disappeared. There was blood on the floor, and a thin trail of it led out back where the victim's truck had last been seen.

Alarmed, her son **Frank Worden** called police and recalled that Gein, whose farmhouse was 5 miles away, had been in the store the evening before his mother's disappearance and had inquired about the price of antifreeze. He also asked Bernice to go out on a date with him. To top it off, Gein had asked Frank a strange question—whether he would be gone all day. Frank had replied in the affirmative, saying he would be gone deer hunting.[29] A sales slip for a gallon of antifreeze made out to Ed Gein was the last receipt written by Worden on the morning she disappeared.

The investigators now had reason to suspect Gein. Upon searching Gein's property, investigators discovered Worden's decapitated body in a shed, hung upside down by ropes at her wrists, with a crossbar at her ankles. *The torso was "dressed out" like that of a deer.* It was cut from genitals to chest, and it had been disemboweled and washed; the breasts were intact. She had been shot with a .22-caliber rifle, and the mutilations performed after death. Her head was found under a mattress on one of the beds.[29] It had been turned into a macabre ornament, with twine attached to nails inserted in both ears.[26] Her heart was found in a saucepan on the stove.[26]

QUICK FACT 5.2 GEINERS

In the wake of Gein's arrest, macabre jokes called "Geiners" became a statewide craze. Some examples:

What did Gein say to the lawmen who arrested him?
Have a heart.
What did they find in Gein's cookie jar?
Ladyfingers.
Why won't anyone play cards with Ed Gein?
He might come up with a good hand.
Why did they let Ed Gein out of jail for New Year's Eve?
So he could dig up a date.

Limericks were made about him, too. The most famous is

There once was an old man named Ed
Who wouldn't take a woman to bed
When he wanted to fiddle
He cut out the middle
And hung the rest in his shed

Among other things found in his house were four human noses, bone fragments, nine death masks, a bowl made from a skull, ten female heads with the tops sawed off, human skin covering several chair seats, a belt made from human nipples,[26] pieces of salted genitalia in a box, skulls on his bedposts, and some organs in the refrigerator.[30]

QUICK FACT 5.3 FILM CHARACTERS BASED ON ED GEIN

Norman Bates in *Psycho* (1960), Leatherface in *The Texas Chain Saw Massacre* (1974), and Buffalo Bill in *The Silence of the Lambs* (1991) were all based on **Ed Gein.**

Sentencing

The police charged Gein with two murder counts: those of Mary Hogan and Bernice Worden. However, on January 16, 1958, the court ruled him mentally unfit for trial, confining him to Central State Hospital for the Criminally Insane at Waupun, Wisconsin (now the Dodge Correctional Institution). He was later transferred to Mendota State Hospital in Madison, Wisconsin.

In March 1958, Gein's shocking crimes prompted unknown arsonists to burn his home. When Gein learned of the incident, he simply shrugged and said, "Just as well." In 1968, Gein's doctors determined he was sane enough to stand trial. The trial began on **November 14, 1968,** and lasted just 1 week. He was found guilty of first-degree murder by **Judge Robert H. Gollmar,** but because he was found to be legally insane, he was sent to the Mendota Mental Health Institute in Madison, Wisconsin, where he died of respiratory and heart failure due to cancer on July 26, 1984.

Gein's gravesite in the Plainfield cemetery was frequently vandalized over the years (Figure 5.2). His gravestone was stolen in 2000. It was recovered in June 2001 near Seattle and is now in a museum in Waushara County, Wisconsin.[31]

Figure 5.2 Ed Gein's grave marker as it appeared in 1999. The number "666" has been carved in the stone, perhaps by some disgruntled vandal.

Conclusions and Impressions

It is doubtful if Gein ever had sex with the dead bodies he had collected. He certainly denied having sex with any of the bodies in his possession. And there is no reason to suspect his version. He did confess to more serious crimes—the murders of **Mary Hogan** and **Bernice Worden.** Gein had had doubts about his masculinity and had even considered sex change surgery at one time. Thus it is very likely that he never had sex with any of his victims. A study of Gein's crimes reveals that he shared characteristics of several different classes of necrophilia. He had in his possession the dead body of Bernice Worden (hanging upside down, quite an unlikely position for sexual intercourse), which he perhaps touched often for pleasure, displaying characteristics of a **class IV necrophile.** He wore fetishes, such as a belt made from human nipples, displaying characteristics of a **class V necrophile.** He raided cemeteries, removed corpses, and mutilated them, displaying characteristics of a **class VI necrophile.** Finally, he killed and mutilated his victims, **never having sex with them.** Thus he also displayed characteristics of a **class IXa necrophile.**

According to the scales suggested by Fromm,[32] Ed Gein seems to have maximal deviant traits on the *incestuous symbiosis-positive freedom* scale and on the *necrophilia-biophilia* scale. (Please see Chapter 2, "Etiology," for details of Fromm's theory of necrophilia.)

Karen Greenlee

Karen Greenlee (1956–) is one of the very few—and surely the most widely known—female necrophiles. She was employed at **Sacramento Memorial Lawn mortuary** as an apprentice embalmer. She came to public attention when in 1979 she stole the dead body of **John Mercure,** a 33-year-old man, apparently for necrophilic activities. She was to deliver his body to a cemetery for a funeral. Instead, she drove off in the hearse and kept the dead body for herself. She was discovered in the hearse with the dead man 2 days later in an adjacent county overdosed on codeine. As California at that time had no law related to necrophilia, she was charged only with stealing a hearse and interfering with a funeral. She received 11 days in jail, a $255 fine, 2 years' probation, and a recommendation for medical treatment. Mercure's mother, on her part, sued for severe emotional stress and received $117,000.[33]

It was not the first time Greenlee had felt such a sexual attraction to the dead. She had put a four-and-a-half page letter in Mercure's casket that detailed her earlier necrophilic episodes with between 20 and 40 male corpses. In the letter, she called herself a **morgue rat.** She wrote, "Why do I do it? Why? Why? Fear of love, relationships. No romance ever hurt like this . . . It's the pits. I'm a morgue rat. This is my rathole, perhaps my grave." On interrogation, she revealed that she did not understand why she felt so compelled to touch dead bodies; it was an addiction she could not seem to break.

Nicholas and Alexander Grunke, and Dustin Radke

In the late evening of September 2, 2006, twins **Nicholas** and **Alexander Grunke,** 20, and **Dustin Radke,** also 20 (Figure 5.3), went to **St. Charles Cemetery,** in Cassville, Wisconsin, intending to remove the body of **Laura Tennesen,** 20—who died in a motorbike accident on August 27—so that Nicholas Grunke could engage in sexual intercourse with the corpse. Nicholas Grunke had allegedly lusted after her when he spotted her picture in the obituary column of a local newspaper.

The three men used shovels to reach Tennesen's grave. The police were tipped off to suspicious activity in the cemetery. When an officer reached there, he found an abandoned vehicle parked near the cemetery. Minutes later he saw Alexander Grunke walking toward the vehicle, dressed in black and sweating profusely. When questioned, Grunke told the officer his brother and Radke were trying to dig up a grave. The grave was found partially dug up; the offenders had only managed to reach the top of the grave's concrete vault. Radke told police that Nicholas Grunke had asked him to help dig up Tennesen's body and take it to Grunke's house, so that Grunke could have sex with it. He also told him that on the way to the cemetery, they had stopped by a Dodgeville WalMart to buy condoms because Nick wanted to use them when he had sex with a corpse.

The defendants were charged with a number of offenses including damage to cemetery property (contrary to Wis. Stat. §943.012[1] and [2]), attempted criminal damage to property (contrary to Wis. Stat. §943.01 and 939.22), and attempted third-degree sexual assault (contrary to Wis. Stat. §§ 940.225[3]). Significantly, §940.225(3) by itself does not mention necrophilia; it mentions

Figure 5.3 From left, Nick Grunke, Alex Grunke, and Dustin Radke.

only third-degree sexual assault and states, "Whoever has sexual intercourse with a person without the consent of that person is guilty of a Class G felony. Whoever has sexual contact in the manner described in sub. (5)(b) 2. or 3. with a person without the consent of that person is guilty of a Class G felony." However, it was asserted by the prosecution that when this provision is read with §940.225(7), a charge of necrophilia could be established. §940.225(7) entitled "death of victim" states, "This section applies whether a victim is dead or alive at the time of the sexual contact or sexual intercourse."

Circuit Judge George Curry dismissed the sexual assault charges, noting that there was no law that addressed necrophilia. However, there was enough evidence to continue the case based on criminal damage to property and the alleged attempt to break into a burial vault. The State appealed against the decision. The Court of Appeals of Wisconsin opined that the decision of Circuit Judge Currey was correct and that section 940.225(7) indeed does not address necrophilia. However, on July 9, 2008, the Wisconsin Supreme Court in a 5–2 decision ruled that the statute does refer to necrophilia.[34,35]

Roderick Jones

Roderick Jones (1974–), a resident of Monessen, Pennsylvania, is a typical class VIII necrophile who used to break into funeral parlors to perform sexual intercourse with the dead. He had earlier abused a corpse in 1998, for which he was convicted in 1999. He also has a history of burglary, criminal trespass, and criminal mischief. On July 13, 2007, funeral director Johnny Draper was preparing a woman for burial at the Draper Funeral Home. He left for just about 10 minutes to talk to some friends across the street when Jones broke into the funeral parlor and attempted sexual intercourse with the female corpse.

When Draper noticed a light on in the basement, he went back inside, where he found Roderick Jones lying next to the coffin of the woman whom Draper had been preparing for burial. One of the deceased woman's legs was up in the air, her stockings had been removed, and the plastic covering her body had been torn open. Jones was lying down near the casket in an attempt to hide. Draper immediately informed the police and restrained Jones until police arrived. This happened despite the funeral home having a top-notch security system in place.

Conclusions and Impressions

Roderick Jones is a typical class VIII (regular) necrophile who seeks out corpses in funeral homes, cemeteries, mortuaries, and so on, to find corpses to have sexual intercourse with.

SIDEBAR 5.1 Necrophiles . . . Or Simply Serial Killers?

The behavior of many killers has been very much like those of necrophiles, although officially (i.e., in police records, court judgments), they have not been specifically mentioned as necrophiles. **Anthony Edward Sowell** (1959–) is a representative of this class. He pleaded guilty to attempted rape in 1989 and served 15 years in prison before his release in 2005. He was arrested again in October 2009 as a suspect in the murder of **11 women** whose bodies were found at his Cleveland, Ohio, duplex in the Mt. Pleasant neighborhood (including one skull). Two decomposing bodies were found in his living room, four in a shallow grave in the basement and in crawl spaces, four buried in his backyard, and a human skull in a bucket. An x-ray machine and miniature cameras were used by investigators to examine the spaces between the walls and floors of his home, and thermal imaging and radar were used to examine the ground near his house.

Neighbors used to complain about horrific stench emanating from his home, but no one investigated his house. The fact that he kept dead bodies in his home—including a skull, which he could easily have discarded—indicates that he might have been engaged in necrophilic activities. His behavior is very similar to that of known necrophiles John Wayne Gacy, Moninder Singh Pandher, and Surendra Koli, all of whom killed victims and kept their dead bodies in their homes. Sowell has been charged with at least five counts of aggravated murder.

Lam Kor-wan

Lam Kor-wan (1955–), sometimes referred to as **The Hong Kong Butcher,** is Hong Kong's most notorious necrophile. In 1982, at the age of 27, while working as a **taxi driver,** he is known to have abducted and killed at least four women. After killing, he would have sex with their dead bodies, often taking videos of his necrophilic acts. He would then mutilate their bodies and keep their sexual organs in Tupperware containers in his bedroom. For this idiosyncrasy, he was also known as **The Jars Murderer**. The rest of the bodies were disposed of via his taxi in the New Territories and on Hong Kong Island. As he would often attack his victims during inclement weather, he was also known as **The Rainy Night Butcher.**

Lam's Modus Operandi and His Victims

Lam's *modus operandi* was to pick up female passengers as a taxi driver, strangle them with electrical wire, take their dead bodies to his family home, have sex with the bodies, and then dismember them. In 1982, he killed at least four women in this way: dance hostess **Chan Fung-lan,** 21, on February 3; cashier **Chan Wan-kit,** 31, on May 29; waitress **Leung Sau-wan,** 29, on June 17; and student **Leung Wai-sum,** 17, on July 2.

Lam lived with his family and shared a tiny bedroom with his younger brother, but his family was unaware of his activities. This was because he worked the night shift, and when he returned home from work at 5 AM his family was asleep. When he got up the family members had already left for work. Each of his victims, all late-night passengers in his taxi, was strangled in his cab. The body was then hidden under a sofa in the living room until his family had left for work. Alone in the house, he lined his tiny bedroom with plastic sheeting and then carved up the body. He videotaped and photographed this whole act.

Lam's hobbies were photography and the collection of porn magazines that he kept locked in an old ammunition box at the bottom of the bunk bed he shared with his brother. Alone in the flat, he would get them out and spend hours poring over them, even rephotographing the pictures in the magazines.

Arrest

It was Lam's passion for photography that ultimately gave him away. In August 1983, a Kodak photo technician in Tsim Sha Tsui was processing a roll of film when he came across a series of close-up shots of a naked woman. Normally he would have dismissed the pictures as a couple's naughty snaps, but there was one photo he could not ignore. It was of a severed breast. He informed the shop manager, who in turn tipped off the police. As Lam returned to pick up the photos, he was caught by plainclothes officers. This was on **August 17, 1982.**

The policemen escorted Lam back to his flat in Tsim Sha Tsui, broke open the ammunition chest, and seized his porn magazines and photographs. The other boxes and trunks revealed an even more shocking collection: body parts of his victims, including breasts floating in Tupperware containers of formaldehyde.

The homicide detectives initially assumed they were dealing with a family of sex killers. They could not believe that one person could keep such a huge haul of body parts and pornography secret in such a small flat. They arrested Lam, his father, and his brother, and it was only when Lam broke down during interrogation and revealed the truth that his family was released. The bodies of all the victims were eventually located. Their identity was established by the Forensic Odontology Group, a group established in 1980, by using dental data and superimposition.[36]

Trial

At his trial in 1983, his mother, **Mrs. Lam Cheung Kim-ping,** appeared as a defense witness, and deposed that her husband (Lam's father) used to beat Lam when he was a child. She said that once when he was about 2 years old, he was slapped by his father so hard that his head banged against the wall, resulting in two black eyes and one side of his face turning red.[37] Many necrophiles are known to have suffered severe head injuries during the early part of their life, and this could have explained his necrophilic tendencies.

On his part, Lam admitted strangling the four women, dissecting them, and keeping parts of their remains. However, he told D.T. Barnes, a psychiatrist from Australia, that it was the power of God that had made him kill. He felt he could communicate with God when he was alone and that other people were "rubbish" and did not have this kind of communication.

Citing this, **Gilbert Rodway,** counsel for Lam, told **Mr. Justice Baber** and an all-male seven-member jury in the High Court that Lam "regarded himself as not himself" but a higher being when he committed the offenses. Furthermore, he acted as if his mind and body were two different parts. Accordingly Lam pleaded guilty to manslaughter on grounds of **diminished responsibility.**

Sentencing

In the case that the media labeled **The Horror Jars Case,**[37] the jury rejected Lam's plea. On April 8, 1983, he was found guilty of four counts of murder and sentenced to death by hanging. In August 1984, Lam's sentence was commuted to life imprisonment, as was the tradition before the abolition of the death penalty in 1993. He is currently serving his life sentence at Shek Pik Prison.

Conclusions and Impressions

Like many other necrophiles, Lam was abused and traumatized as a child. His father used to beat him as a child, and this caused severe head trauma, perhaps several times over. This could have been an etiological factor for his necrophilic tendencies. Lam is a **class IXc necrophile,** since he killed his victims and then had sex with and mutilated the dead bodies.

Anthony Merino

Anthony Merino (1983–) worked as a lab technician at Holy Name Hospital in Teaneck, New Jersey. He had another part-time job as a histology technician at Overlook Hospital in Summit, New Jersey. An industrious young man, Anthony was working those two jobs to help support his mother, who suffered from Alzheimer's, and his father, who suffered from colon cancer.

For 2 weeks, Anthony Merino worked well. Nobody complained about him, and nobody had a problem with the way he did his job. On October 28, 2007, he told a security guard that he needed to get into the morgue to check some human tissue samples, but that his morgue key was not working. The guard let him in and continued his rounds. On the way back, the guard sensed something odd, and when he went inside, he found Merino having sex with the corpse of a 92-year-old woman. The security guard called the police immediately. When the police arrived, they reportedly found Merino frantically washing his penis.

Merino was arrested on a charge of desecrating human remains, a second-degree crime in New Jersey. He was found guilty in September 2008

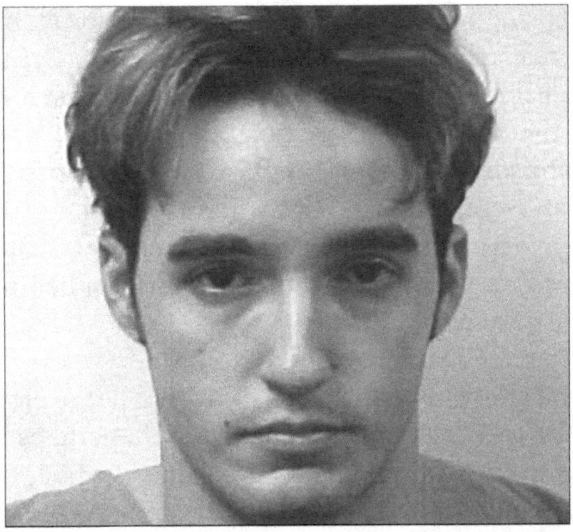

Figure 5.4 Anthony Merino.

and sentenced to 7 years in prison. However, under a complex plea deal, he will be able to seek a reduced sentence (Figure 5.4).

Tsutomu Miyazaki

Tsutomu Miyazaki (1962–2008), also known as The Otaku Murderer, The Little Girl Murderer, and Dracula, was a Japanese necrophile and serial killer who abducted and killed four young girls (between ages 4 and 7 years), mutilated them, ate parts of their flesh, drank their blood (vampirism), slept with their dead bodies, and sexually assaulted the corpse of at least one of his victims.[38] His victims were Mari Konno, 4; Masami Yoshizawa, 7; Erika Nanba, 4; and Ayako Nomoto, 5.

Winston Moseley

Winston Moseley (1935–) worked as a machine operator in Mt. Vernon in Westchester County, New York. He was a black man, twice married (first marriage ending in divorce), with two children. He owned a house in Richmond Hill, Queens, New York. He was apprehended on March 18, 1964, while trying to steal a television during a house burglary. He did not have any previous criminal record.

On interrogation he revealed that he had previously killed three women. He also indicated that he had had sex with at least two of them after their death, or at least when he thought they were dead. He killed **Barbara Kralik,** 15, on

July 20, 1963, in Springfield Gardens, Queens, and shot **Annie Mae Johnson** (also sometimes referred to as **Anna May Johnson**), 24, in South Ozone Park, Queens, on February 28, 1964, and **Catherine Susan Genovese** (**Kitty Genovese**), 29, in the Kew Gardens section of Queens, on March 13, 1964.

Annie Mae Johnson was killed about 2 AM on February 28, 1964. Moseley testified in the Genovese case that he saw Johnson in her car and followed it to near her small apartment house in South Ozone Park, Queens. When she got out, he followed on foot. She turned and saw him behind her. He asked for money and she gave it to him.

"Then I shot her. . . . I shot her in the stomach."

He said that he shot her again. Then "I turned her over and then I could see for sure that she was dead. Then I decided, well, perhaps I'd rape her now that she was dead so I took off all her clothes that she had, right there in the snow. . . . Then I decided it was too cold out in the snow so I rolled her up the steps on into the house into the middle of the living room floor. . . . So first of all I committed that cunnilingus, was it? But I was impotent . . . I laid on top of her. . . . I did have an orgasm." After that, he dragged her upstairs to her apartment.

"I set a fire in two places in the living room and I took the scarf that she had on and put that on the lower part of her body . . . on her genital organs and set fire to her."[39]

On March 12, 1964, he left work at 5:30 PM and came home. At about 2 AM on March 13, 1964, he left home in his 1960 white Corvair to find a woman whom he could kill and rape.[40] He drove around for an hour until he spotted Kitty Genovese, who was returning home from work (as a manager of a bar in Queens, New York), and followed her. At about 3:15 AM, she parked her car in a parking lot about 100 feet from her apartment's door and started walking toward her apartment. Moseley parked his Corvair somewhat haphazardly at a nearby bus stop and started walking toward her. As he approached Genovese, she halted, and tried to move away. Moseley ran after her, and quickly overtaking her, he stabbed her twice in the back. Genovese screamed, and her cries for help were heard by some neighbors. Robert Mozer, a neighbor who lived across the street from where the initial attack took place, called out to Moseley to "get out of here."[41]

Moseley was frightened. He jumped back into his car and drove away. He soon gathered courage, however, and returned. He found her lying in the hallway. When Genovese saw him, she started screaming again, upon which Moseley stabbed her a few more times. She became limp. He then lifted up her skirt and cut off her girdle. He cut her panties off, throwing away a sanitary pad.[40] He then stabbed her again in the stomach. He cut off her brassiere, and attempted to have sexual intercourse with her. But "I was unable to as I was impotent. I did have an orgasm, however."[40]

In his testimony, Moseley stated that the second time when he returned, he stabbed Genovese four or five times including one in the throat and "she didn't scream after that."[40] Apparently thinking she was dead, he tried to have sexual intercourse with her. Moseley's conduct after that is best described by his own sworn testimony.

Q. After you had disrobed her as you described you attempted to have sex relations with her?
A. Yes.
Q. Now, will you please describe it for me?
A. I laid on top of her and I attempted to have intercourse with her, but I was impotent and though I had an orgasm, I was not able to penetrate into her.
Q. Did you remove any articles of your clothing?
A. No.
Q. Did you have your penis exposed?
A. Yes.
Q. What do you mean by impotent?
A. I was unable to have an erection.
Q. Were you laying on top of her when you had the orgasm?
A. Yes.[43]

Genovese had been stabbed 17 times in all, and Moseley was confident she was dead. It turned out that she was not dead at that time; she died on her way to the hospital. Moseley is still in prison, his 13th parole bid having been rejected on March 13, 2008.

Conclusions and Impressions

Moseley committed necrophilia twice; the second time, as far as he was concerned, the victim was dead, although she was not. She was only breathing her last. He was a married man with two children and apparently had a satisfactory sexual relationship with his wife. However, he evidently got more thrill from having sexual intercourse with the dead. **Dr. Oscar Diamond,** director of the Manhattan State Hospital, a board certified specialist in psychiatry and neurology and a professor of psychiatry at New York Medical College and the New York School of Psychiatry, performed a pretrial psychiatric examination of Moseley. "He told me he got no thrill with live women he raped," he told the court later.[42] He preferred sex with the dead.[42]

From the two necrophilic acts that he was involved in, he appears to be a **class IXb** necrophile.

Why did he become a necrophile? Moseley has maintained that his wife-beating father was responsible for him turning into a killer necrophile. "My father was at the time stalking my mother and thinking about killing her." Dr. Oscar Diamond, who examined him and who appeared as a defense witness on Moseley's behalf, had the same opinion. He testified that Moseley was a schizophrenic exhibiting alternating symptoms of complete withdrawal and uncontrollable drives. According to him, Moseley's condition arose from several events in his family history. The contributing events included a traumatic abdominal operation on his mother followed by the breakup of his family while he was very young, his mother's infidelity to his father early on in his life, and a lengthy episode in which his father spent weeks following his mother around with a gun. Diamond testified that his deteriorating mental condition resulted in his hostility being directed toward women, focusing on female breasts and the abdomen, which represented the uterus.[41]

Moninder Singh Pandher and Surendra Koli

These two necrophiles who came to world attention in 2006 remind one strongly of John Wayne Gacy. Several children had disappeared mysteriously in the village of Nithari, a small hamlet on the outskirts of **Noida City,** in **Uttar Pradesh** (UP), near New Delhi, since 2005. The prime suspects were **Moninder Singh Pandher** (1957–), a rich and politically connected businessman, and his cook and aide, **Surendra Koli** (1970–).* However, presumably because of Pandher's strong political connections, the police dragged their feet and did not do anything.

The situation became unmanageable after **May 7, 2006,** when a 19-year-old girl, Payal, visited Pandher's residence at **D5, Sector 31, Noida,** and never returned. Because of public outcry and media blitz, the police had to arrest Pandher on **December 26, 2006,** and his aide Koli on the next day. When their house was searched, numerous pornographic CDs and pictures of naked children, mostly Indians, in the company of Pandher, were found.

Based on police interrogation of the men, on **December 29, 2006,** the skeletal remains of 15 children and fragments of clothes stuffed in gunny bags were recovered from a drain behind their bungalow.

A massive investigation followed, which was called **the Noida serial murder investigation** by the media. It included **brain mapping** and **narco analysis** of the offenders. In all there were 19 victims of necrophilia (Table 5.3). The table shows that four cases were filed against Koli and Pandher *before* the remains of victims were actually discovered (on December 29, 2006).

* Koli's first name is also variously spelled as **Surender** or **Subhash,** and his surname is also spelled as **Kohli,** which creates a potentially huge number of permutations and combinations of his name.

Table 5.3 Nineteen Known Victims of Notable Necrophiles Pandher and Koli*

Victim	Case Filed	Accused
Bina Halder*	April 5, 2005	Surendra Koli
Girl child Jyoti*	June 23, 2005	Koli and Moninder Singh Pandher
Male child Satyender, alias Max*	April 28, 2006	Koli
Alleged commercial sex worker Payal, 19*	October 10, 2006	Koli and Pandher
Domestic help Pinky Sarkar	December 30, 2006	Koli and Pandher
Domestic help Madhu Singh	December 30, 2006	Koli and Pandher
Male child Sheikh Raza	December 30, 2006	Charge sheet not submitted yet
Domestic help Nanda Bahadur	December 30, 2006	Koli
Anjali Sarkar	December 30, 2006	Koli and Pandher
Rachna Lal	December 30, 2006	Koli
Deepali	December 30, 2006	Koli
Nisha	December 30, 2006	Koli
Aarti	December 30, 2006	Koli
Male child Harsh	December 30, 2006	Koli
Pushpa Biswas	December 30, 2006	Koli
Unknown (remains beyond recognition)	December 30, 2006	No charge sheet filed in this case
Rimpa Halder (or Haldar), 14 (killed on Feb 8, 2005. Her body was found hacked.)	January 3, 2007	Koli and Halder (held guilty by court on Feb 12, 2009)
Girl child Sony	January 4, 2007	Charge sheet not submitted yet
Girl child Payal	December 30, 2007	Koli

*Asterisks denote cases that were filed before any remains of victims were discovered.

On March 2, 2007, Koli confessed, reportedly to unburden his conscience, at a Delhi court and admitted raping, killing, and having sex with dead bodies of children and women. He exonerated his employer Pandher, perhaps under pressure. Subsequently a case was registered against Koli under various sections of the Indian Penal Code, including rape, murder, kidnapping, and criminal conspiracy. Since necrophilia is not a crime in India, no case could be registered against him for having sex with the dead. (In India the only section that can possibly be invoked against necrophiles is section 297 of the Indian Penal Code [IPC], but to be able to invoke this section, the offender must have trespassed on burial places. Please see Chapter 7, "Legal and Ethical Aspects of Necrophilia.")

Following the statements of Koli, the Central Bureau of Investigation (CBI) had no choice but to give a clean chit to Pandher. However, it pressed lesser charges against Pandher for bribing police officials, indulging in prostitution, procuring call girls, and destruction of evidence.

Conclusions and Impressions

During interrogation Koli confessed to raping the children before killing them and then having sex with the bodies. There is no evidence that the children were tortured, too. Thus, Koli appears to be a class IXd necrophile. The sexual behavior of Pandher is less clear from his interrogations. Quite possibly he too belongs to class IXd necrophiles.

Gary Ridgway

Gary Leon Ridgway (1949–), known as the "Green River Killer," is an American necrophile and serial killer. Ridgway murdered 48 women in King County, Washington, from 1982 to 2001. (The exact number of his killings is not certain, as is the case with most serial killers. He did admit to having committed 71 murders, but the prosecution decided to press charges for only the 48 cases for which they had irrefutable evidence.[43]) Most of the murders took place during a 2 1/2-year period in the early 1980s. In 1983 alone, 27 women disappeared and 9 were found dead. His *modus operandi* was strangulation, mostly with his arm, but he would also use ligatures. After strangling the women, he would dump their bodies in one of four dump site areas in King County.

In 1983, Ridgway became a suspect for the Green River Killings. In 1984 the investigators administered a polygraph test on him, which he passed successfully. On April 7, 1987, the police took hair and saliva samples from him. It was this saliva that ultimately proved to be his undoing; the DNA profile from this sample matched that of semen found on four of his victims. (For details, please see Chapter 6, "Medico-legal Investigation.")

On November 5, 2003, Ridgway entered a guilty plea to 48 charges of aggravated first-degree murder as part of a plea bargain.

The skeletons of some of his victims were found with the leg bones raised and bent, or even broken, indicating he had been engaging in sex—possibly postmortem—with his victims.[44]

Serhiy Tkach

Serhiy Tkach (1951–), also known as the **Pologovsky Maniac** after one of the **Ukrainian** neighborhoods he lived and killed in, was a former Ukrainian police criminal investigator. He hailed originally from **Russia.** From 1984 until he was caught in 2005, he is claimed to have killed 100 women and performed sexual acts on their dead bodies. Tkach was able to commit his necrophilic acts undetected for more than two decades because, being a formal criminal investigator, he could hide his tracks skillfully. During the years that he remained at large, nine people were wrongly jailed for some of the murders of which he was found guilty. One of the wrongly accused men reportedly killed himself.

Tkach's murder tactic of choice was suffocation. At his year-long trial in Dnipropetrovsk, a city in southeastern Ukraine, Tkach, in a confessional statement, asserted that he was "a beast who deserved the death penalty." In December 2008, he was found guilty of murdering 36 women and was sentenced to life imprisonment.

Conclusions and Impressions

Tkach is a typical class IX (homicidal) necrophile. He needed to kill girls and women so he could perform sexual acts on their dead bodies. On intelligence level he would score rather high, as he was a former police criminal investigator.

Eli Ulayuk

Eli Ulayuk (1968–) is an Inuit from Igloolik, a small community in Nunavut, **Northern Canada.** In August 1988, when he was 20 years old, he killed a 23-year-old female in **Igloolik** by stabbing her repeatedly and finally strangling her. Upon arrest by the police, he gave an unusual account about his motivation, which he repeated in court and has acknowledged while in the Correctional Service of Canada (CSC). He stated that after consuming "**home brew,**" he had the sudden urge to have sex with the victim's dead body and killed her for that purpose.[45] The police recovered the victim's body with her underwear removed and torn but Ulayuk maintained that he changed his mind after killing the victim and did not actually have sexual relations with her body.

Ulayuk was given the maximum sentence provided by law—life imprisonment—in 1992 by the sentencing judge, the late **Justice Mark de Weerdt.** In 2000, Ulayuk was released on day parole in Yellowknife. His parole officer was **Louise Pargeter,** 34, whom he later killed. At one point she recommended that his parole be revoked. At her recommendation, Ulayuk was sent back to jail. He was released again on day parole in Yellowknife in April 2003 and was granted full parole in **June 2004.**

On **October 6, 2004**, Pargeter was at Ulayuk's apartment in Yellowknife for a prearranged meeting with him as his parole officer. At one point while Pargeter was seated on the couch, Ulayuk went behind the couch and while out of her line of vision picked up a hammer and hit her on the head from behind. She slumped over on the couch and then Ulayuk struck her four more times on the head with the hammer. He then wrapped some twine around her neck and strangled her. He then removed her clothing and had sexual intercourse with her.

After the necrophilic act, he took the keys to her vehicle from her jacket, left his apartment, and drove south on the highway out of Yellowknife. Several hours later, just after midnight on October 7, he was arrested by the Royal Canadian Mounted Police (RCMP) after he fled on foot from the highway. Following his arrest, Ulayuk, in due course, made a number of admissions to the RCMP including the details of the killing and the fact that he had for some time thought about killing Pargeter. He had also for some time fantasized about killing other women in Yellowknife and having sex with their dead bodies.

Conclusions and Impressions

Ulayuk is a typical **class IXb (homicidal) necrophile.** Twice (in 1988 and then again in 2004) he killed females in order to have sexual intercourse with them. On the first occasion, he was under the influence of alcohol ("home brew"). At the correctional facility in 1992, his criminogenic factors were identified as **substance abuse, education/employment,** and **emotional stability.** He participated in numerous programs but refused sex offender programming. He considered himself not to be a sex offender since he claimed he had not had sex with the victim's body. Thus he lived in a denial mode, but again performed a necrophilic act in 2004.

References

1. Chua-Eoan H. Crimes of the century—the top 25: Ted Bundy, 1978. *Time*. Available at http://www.time.com/time/2007/crimes/14.html. Accessed December 29, 2009.
2. Chua-Eoan H. Crimes of the century—the top 25: Jeffrey Dahmer, 1991. *Time* Available at http://www.time.com/time/2007/crimes/16.html. Accessed December 29, 2009.
3. Reichert D. *Chasing the Devil—My Twenty Year Quest to Capture the Green River Killer*, 1st ed. Little, Brown and Company, New York, 2004, p. 140.
4. Rule A. *The Stranger Beside Me—Ted Bundy, The Shocking Inside Story*. W.W. Norton, New York, 1980, pp. 17–18.
5. Kennedy L. *Ten Rillington Place*. Victor Gollancz, London, 1961.
6. Eddowes J. *Two Killers of Rillington Place*. Warner Books, London, 1995.
7. Brabin D. *Rillington Place*. Her Majesty's Stationery Office, London, 1999.
8. Marston E. *John Christie*. The National Archives, Surrey, 2007.
9. *The Trial of Evans & Christie: 10 Rillington Place* [audio book], 1st ed. Narrs., R Pickup, T Edmond, T Nichols, J Baddeley, R Welch, N Barber, E Mansfield. Mr Punch Ltd., 2009. Length: 3 hrs and 8 mins.

10. Jackson R. *Francis Camps—Famous Case Histories of the Celebrated Pathologist.* Panther Books, London, 1983, pp. 70–97.
11. Beeley JA, Harvey W. Pink teeth appearing as a post-mortem phenomenon. *J Forensic Sci Soc.* 1973 Oct;**13(4)**:297–305.
12. Simpson K. *Forty Years of Murder.* Grafton Books, London, 1988, pp. 234–252.
13. Jesse FT (Ed.). *Trials of Evans and Christie: Notable British Trial Series Vol. 82.* William Hodge, London, 1957.
14. Wilson C, Pitman P. *Encyclopedia of Murder.* Pan Books, London, 1984, pp. 165–171.
15. *R. v. Coutts* (2006) 1WLR 2154.
16. Owsley DW, Mann RW, Chapman RE, Moore E, Cox WA. Positive identification in a case of intentional extreme fragmentation. *J Forensic Sci.* 1993 Jul;**38(4)**:985–996.
17. Bennett KA. Victim selection in the Jeffrey Dahmer slayings: an example of repetition in the paraphilias? *J Forensic Sci.* 1993 Sept;**38(5)**:1227–1232.
18. Jentzen J, Palermo G, Johnson LT, Ho KC, Stormo KA, Teggatz J. Destructive hostility: the Jeffrey Dahmer case. A psychiatric and forensic study of a serial killer. *Am J Forensic Med Pathol.* 1994 Dec;**15(4)**:283–294.
19. Tithecott RF. Making monsters: Jeffrey Dahmer and the social construction of the serial killer [Thesis for the degree of Doctor of Philosophy]. University of Southern California, Los Angeles, 1995, 294 pages.
20. Silva JA, Ferrari MM, Leong GB. The case of Jeffrey Dahmer: sexual serial homicide from a neuropsychiatric developmental perspective. *J Forensic Sci.* 2002 Nov;**47(6)**:1347–1359.
21. Martens WH, Palermo GB. Loneliness and associated violent antisocial behavior: analysis of the case reports of Jeffrey Dahmer and Dennis Nilsen. *Int J Offender Ther Comp Criminol.* 2005 Jun;**49(3)**:298–307.
22. Nichols DS. Tell me a story: MMPI responses and personal biography in the case of a serial killer. *J Pers Assess.* 2006 Jun;**86(3)**:242–262.
23. Strubel A. Jeffrey Dahmer: his complicated, comorbid psychopathologies and treatment implications. *New School Psychol Bull.* 2007;**5(1)**:41–58.
24. White JH. Evidence of primary, secondary, and collateral paraphilias left at serial murder and sex offender crime scenes. *J Forensic Sci.* 2007 Sep;**52(5)**:1194–1201.
25. Pardue A, Arrigo BA. Power, anger, and sadistic rapists: toward a differentiated model of offender personality. *Int J Offender Ther Comp Criminol.* 2008 Aug;**52(4)**:378–400.
26. Newton M. *The Encyclopedia of Serial Killers*, 2nd ed. Facts on File, New York, 2006.
27. Dahmer L. *A Father's Story.* William Morrow and Company, New York, 1994.
28. Schechter H. *Deviant: The Shocking True Story of Ed Gein, The Original "Psycho."* Pocket Books, New York, 1998.
29. Philbin T, Philbin M. *The Killer Book of Serial Killers—Incredible Stories, Facts, and Trivia from the World of Serial Killers*, 1st ed. Sourcebooks, Naperville, IL, 2009.
30. Woods PA. *Ed Gein—Psycho!* St. Martin's Griffin, New York, 1995.
31. Bie M. *It Happened in Wisconsin*, 1st ed. Two Dot, Guilford, CT, p. 97.
32. Feist J, Feist GJ (Eds.). *Theories of Personality*, 6th ed. McGraw-Hill, New York, 2006, pp. 198–200.

33. Quigley C. *The Corpse: A History*, 1st ed. McFarland & Company, Jefferson, NC, 2005, p. 300.
34. *State v. Grunke*, 752 N.W.2d 769 (Wis. 2008).
35. Foley RJ. Court: Wisconsin law bans sex with dead bodies. *The Associated Press State & Local Wire*. July 9, 2008, Wednesday.
36. Lee S. Smile for new ID photos? Officials remain tight-lipped. *South China Morning Post*, July 6, 2003, p. 4.
37. Lowe S. Slice of life; from the *South China Morning Post* this week in: 1983. *South China Morning Post*, March 18, 2008, Tuesday, p. 2.
38. Takayama H. Will there be more? *Newsweek*. April 28, 1997, Atlantic Edition. p. 29.
39. Rosenthal AM. *Thirty-Eight Witnesses: The Kitty Genovese Case*. University of California Press, Berkeley, 1999.
40. Winston Moseley's confessional statement. Available at http://kewgardenshistory.com/kitty_genovese-3-Confession.pdf. Retrieved December 28, 2009.
41. *The People of the State of New York v. Winston Moseley*. Available at http://kewgardenshistory.com/kitty_genovese-3-Brief-2.pdf. Accessed December 29, 2009.
42. Tücke M. *Arbeitsbuch: Grundlagen der Psychologie für (zukünftige) Lehrer (Broschiert)*. Lit Verlag, Berlin, 2006, pp. 114–115.
43. Prothero M, Smith C. *Defending Gary—Unraveling the Mind of the Green River Killer*, 1st ed. Jossey-Bass, San Francisco, CA, 2006, pp. 472–473.
44. Prothero M, Smith C. *Defending Gary—Unraveling the Mind of the Green River Killer*, 1st ed. Jossey-Bass, San Francisco, CA, 2006. p. 315.
45. *R. v. Ulayuk*, 2006 NWTSC 10.

Medico-legal Investigation

6

If you want to understand the artist, look at his work.

John Douglas
Former head of the FBI's Behavioral Sciences Investigative Support Unit

Introduction

A sound medico-legal investigation of a case of necrophilia would involve (1) examination of the scene of crime, (2) examination of the dead body, and (3) examination of the suspect. The need for a multidisciplinary effort between crime scene specialists, forensic pathologists, serologists, biologists, DNA experts, forensic psychologists, psychiatrists, and behavior profilers cannot be overemphasized.

Examination of the Scene of Crime

A **crime scene** is a location where an illegal act takes place, and comprises the area from where most of the physical or trace evidence or any other kind of information leading to the solution of crime is retrievable. While in most cases there is just one crime scene (e.g., where an act of homicide occurred), in some cases there might be multiple crime scenes (e.g., one location where a homicide occurred and another location where the body was disposed of or dumped). Some experts refer to the first scene (i.e., where the homicide occurred) as the *primary crime scene* and the second (i.e., where the body was disposed of) as the *secondary crime scene.* According to others, the primary crime scene is *where the body was found, and where the police officers were called to respond.*[1] Later, if it is discovered that the homicide had occurred at another place, that scene would become *another primary crime scene.*[1] In this model, there is no *secondary crime scene.*

Crime scenes in necrophilia may be multiple (Figure 6.1). At least eight different crime scenes can be identified in Table 6.1. In any given single case of necrophilia, not all eight may be seen. In most cases, the investigator would be dealing with fewer crime scenes.

For instance, it is possible that a homicidal necrophile picks up a potential victim from a university campus (CS1a), transports her to his home in his vehicle

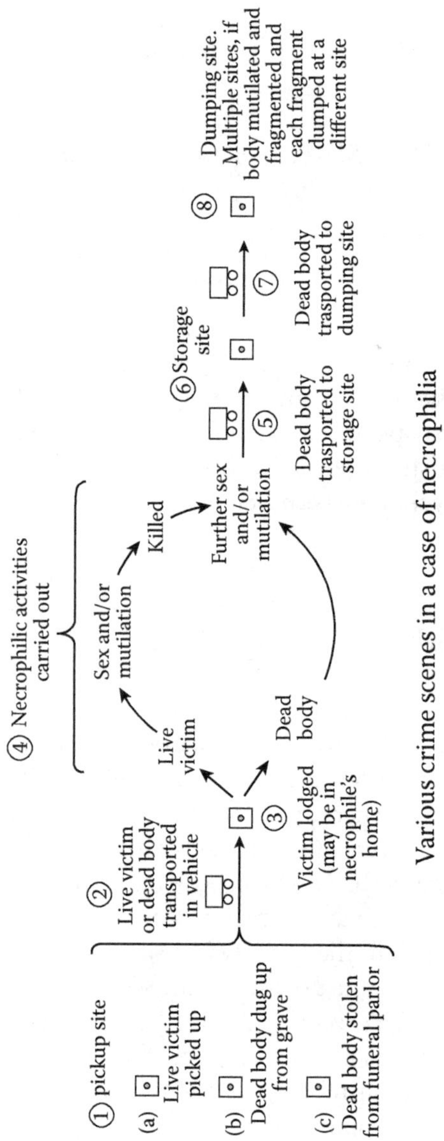

Figure 6.1 Crime scenes in necrophilia may be multiple.

Table 6.1 Various Possible Crime Scenes in a Case of Necrophilia

Crime Scene	Description
Crime scene-1a (CS1a)	Pickup site of live victim; may be a university, college, outside an office, or a hitchhiker
Crime scene-1b (CS1b)	Graveyard (or any other site where corpse is buried)
Crime scene-1c (CS1c)	Funeral parlor (or any other site where corpse is lying in the open)
Crime scene-2 (CS2)	Transport vehicle used by necrophile to carry live victim (or dead body) to the lodging site (mostly necrophile's home)
Crime scene-3 (CS3)	Victim's lodging place (necrophilic activities may take place here)
Crime scene-4 (CS4)	Place of necrophilic activities (this may be some place away from victim's lodging place)
Crime scene-5 (CS5)	Transport vehicle used by necrophile to carry dead body to storage site
Crime scene-6 (CS6)	Storage site of dead body
Crime scene-7 (CS7)	Transport vehicle used by necrophile to carry dead body from storage site to ultimate dumping site
Crime scene-8 (CS8)	Final dumping site; dumping sites may be multiple if body is mutilated and fragmented into several parts and each part thrown separately

(CS2), murders the victim and commits necrophilic acts with the dead body at his home (CS3), and then carries the body (CS7) to the final dumping site (CS8). Sometimes you might find, say, just five crime scenes (as in the case mentioned). An investigator may be tempted into renumbering them as CS1, CS2, CS3, CS4, and CS5. If we renumber them, a particular crime scene, for instance, "final dumping site" (CS8) would keep getting different numbers in different cases—in a case with five crime scenes, it would be CS5; in a case with six crime scenes it would be CS6 (if there were six crime scenes), and so on. I suggest that each crime scene should have a "fixed number," as shown in Table 6.1. This will give the advantage of better cross-communication between various experts involved in the case, when they are talking about a crime scene.

Necrophilic crimes generally begin at crime scene-1 (CS1). In the case of class IX (homicidal) necrophiles, it could be a university campus (CS1a); in the case of class VIII (regular) necrophiles, a dug-up grave (CS1b), and in the case of class VII (opportunistic) necrophiles, it could be a mortuary or funeral parlor. Necrophilic crimes end up at crime scene-8 (CS8), where the body was finally disposed of. If the body was mutilated and fragmented, and each fragment disposed of at a different place, there would be multiple crime scenes-8.

Victim Pickup Site

In **class IX necrophilia,** crime scene-1a is the site from where the necrophile picks up the potential victim. **Ted Bundy,** for instance, picked up victims by feigning physical disability. Such crime scenes should be canvassed for possible witnesses who may be able to give the physical description of the suspect, his car, and so on. Vehicles parked in the vicinity must be documented, their owners contacted, and their movements around the area recorded. The owner could be a potential suspect or perhaps a possible witness. Parking summonses issued in the neighborhood should be checked and the owners interviewed. Evidence from parking garages may include payment receipts and recordings from surveillance cameras, which must be examined closely. Toll plazas and electronic pass use (EZ Pass, Fast Lane, etc.) around the victim pickup site must be examined. Garbage and sewers along the possible route of escape must be searched for dead body or body parts. It may be useful to check the criminal record of the victim. **Thor Nis Christiansen, John Christie,** and **Robert Lee Yates, Jr.** used to pick up prostitutes for their necrophilic activities. **Dahmer** used to pick up homosexual boys and men; 71% of his victims (total 12) had criminal records, half of these for violent crime. Friends and relatives of the victim must be interviewed for possible information. **Graham Coutts** picked up Jane Longhurst—an acquaintance—for necrophilic activities. Longhurst was a friend of Coutts' girlfriend, Lisa Stephens.

Dug-Up Grave

A dug-up grave may be the crime scene-1b in class VIII necrophilia (regular necrophiles), where dead bodies are stolen from graveyards for necrophilic purposes (please see Chapter 3, "Classification" for details). If a dug-up grave is encountered, it may be vital to search the surroundings for clues. Torre and Varetto[2] describe a case of 15-year-old unmarried girl whose grave was violated two days after burial. Her hymen was intact, although the anus showed dilatation. When the surroundings were searched for additional clues, the lavatory of the cemetery showed a few pages of pornographic cartoons. One such page, curled up, showed some semitransparent, shiny dried stains. A laboratory examination revealed spermatozoa on this page. Pornographic material in a cemetery is a highly unusual finding. This discovery strongly pointed toward the fact that necrophiles were at work in that grave.

The crime scene may reveal other clues of importance. In Torre and Varetto's case, one point of contention was the number of offenders who violated the grave. The scene of crime revealed the presence of two shovels around the grave. Their presence indicated that it was the work of at least two people. Additionally, a large amount of earth had been displaced, which was consistent with more than one person digging the grave. Finally, the authors suggest that the tidy way in which the earth was removed indicated coordination which could have been achieved only by two or more persons working in collusion.

Suspect's Home

Necrophiles are known to keep bodies and body parts in and around their house. This gives rise to a very **offensive stench,** which is usually noticeable quite far from the suspect's house. In fact, in many cases, neighbors have complained of an offensive stench coming from a suspect's house, but police have often ignored it. The necrophile will often give plausible reasons for the smell. In the case of **Jeffrey Dahmer,** whenever neighbors complained about the bad smell, he always had a convincing explanation—his sewage system was leaking, his freezer, full of meat, was broken and the meat had spoiled, and so on. Notable necrophiles whose apartments and houses are known to have emanated an offensive stench are **Jeffrey Dahmer, John Wayne Gacy, Moninder Singh Pandher,** and **Surendra Koli.**

A search of the suspect's home, garage, basement, car, and so on can give vital clues, as necrophiles often like to keep the dead bodies of their victims in their possession for their sexual activities. Sometimes they collect trophies from their victims' bodies (their amputated breasts, for example) and keep them as fetishes. Between 1968 and 1969, **Jerry Brudos** killed and committed necrophilia on at least four women. When he was apprehended on May 25, 1969, he denied his involvement in any of the murders. However, when his garage was searched, the police found overwhelming evidence of his guilt, including photographs of his victims.

When **Ed Gein's** property was searched, investigators discovered his victim Bernice Worden's decapitated body in his shed, hung upside down by ropes at her wrists, with a crossbar at her ankles (Figures 6.2a and b).

Jeffrey Dahmer was able to fool the police officers a number of times, simply because they did not care to search his house thoroughly. (For complete case, please see Chapter 5, "Case Studies.") On July 22, 1991, when two

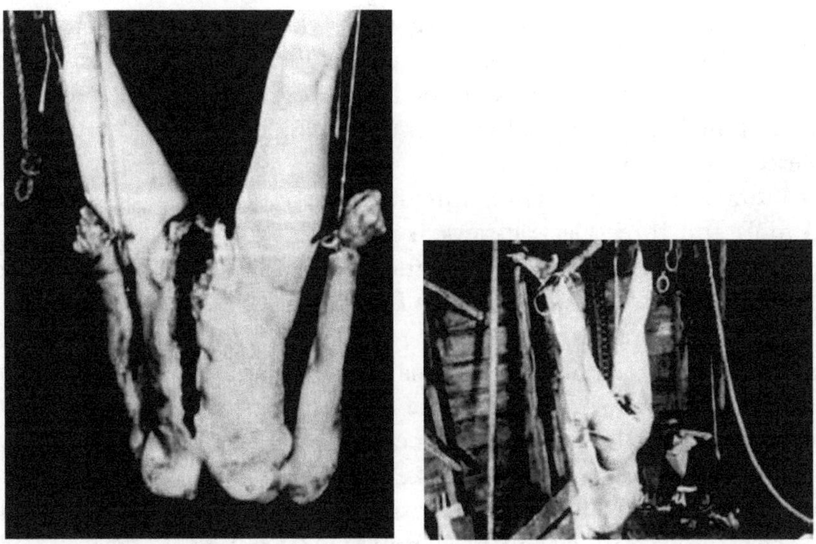

(a) (b)

Figure 6.2 Bernice Worden's body as found in Ed Gein's shed.

police officers, **Robert Rauth** and **Rolf Mueller,** decided to search his house, a number of incriminating pieces of evidence were found. The officers were led to Dahmer's apartment by a potential victim who had escaped. An offensive stench coming from the house made them suspicious.

In Dahmer's fly-infested bedroom, the police officers discovered a 12-inch butcher knife hidden under the bed. (It had previously been described to them by the victim.) They also noted a Polaroid camera lying on the bed, and several Polaroid photographs protruding from a drawer in a tall, eighteenth-century style chest of drawers. While some photographs showed nude men engaged in homosexual sex acts, numerous others showed corpses in various states of mutilation and dismemberment. When his refrigerator was opened, a **grotesquely severed human head** was found on the bottom shelf next to a box of Arm & Hammer baking soda.

A search warrant was issued after these discoveries so that a thorough search of his house could be made for more incriminating evidence. Over the next several hours, a hazardous materials team of police officers wearing oxygen masks and protective rubber suits began searching Jeffrey Dahmer's apartment. **Three additional human heads** and a **human heart** were recovered from a small lift-top freezer, along with a pair of lungs, a liver, a kidney, and bundles of frozen intestines. **Three headless torsos** were found in a 55-gallon plastic vat, submerged in chemicals, in Dahmer's bedroom. Some body parts, including bones, were found stored in cardboard boxes. A decomposed hand was found protruding from beneath the bed, male genital organs were found floating in a lobster pot in the kitchen, and five male skulls, boiled and scraped clean, were seized from a box and a filing cabinet. Two more skulls were found on a closet shelf, where several sets of hands and arms hung from the clothes rack. The two skulls in the closet were painted gray, apparently to give them a plastic-like appearance, like models used by artists and medical students. In all, remains of an estimated 11 victims were recovered from his apartment.

A number of other incriminating items were recovered. These included hand tools and three electric saws, a number of bottles of formaldehyde, hydrochloric acid, and chloroform, and horror films such as *The Exorcist*, *Friday the 13th*, and the *Nightmare on Elm Street* series.

A search of **John Christie**'s house revealed a tobacco tin containing four locks of pubic hair. Initially Christie maintained that they were from his wife (Ethel) and the three women that were found in his former coal cellar. On a subsequent occasion he claimed that one sample came from **Beryl Evans** (wife of Timothy Evans, a co-tenant). Dr. Lewis Charles Nickolls, director of the Metropolitan Police Laboratory, who examined this evidence, concluded that while one of the locks might have been from **Mrs. Christie,** the others were identical to those of the three dead young women found in the house. Two skeletons were recovered from Christie's backyard garden. (The bodies had been buried for 10 years, so they had been completely skeletonized.) Even if it is assumed that two locks came from those bodies, one set is still unaccounted for.

Sometimes the body of a victim may have to be exhumed in order to check the necrophile's allegations. In the case of **Christie,** his confession that one lock of his pubic hair collection had been taken from the body of **Beryl Evans** came in April 1953, while her body—after autopsy by **Donald Teare**—had been interred in December 1949. To confirm or refute his allegations, the body of Evans had to exhumed. The exhumation was done on May 18, 1953. The second postmortem was done jointly by Francis Camps, Donald Teare, and Keith Simpson—the latter representing Christie. The first thing Simpson noted was that no area of Beryl's pubes appeared to be denuded of hair. The hair found in the tobacco tin at Christie's house was quite substantial in volume, and if that much hair had come from her pubes, some pubic area would be denuded.[3] To be sure, Donald Teare had taken some **pubic hair** as samples in the earlier autopsy in December 1949, but even that denudation was not visible. Simpson asked Teare, who was standing right beside the body, how much he had taken and was satisfied when Teare told him that he had taken very few, and their absence would not be easily visible on the pubes.[3]

Simpson then took a representative sample of **Evans' pubic hair** and compared it with each of the four locks found in the tobacco tin. He could immediately rule out three locks. The fourth matched somewhat—it was identical in color, thickness, and general microscopic structure. The hair was mid-brown and of a very common type. Simpson estimated that the match was still inconclusive because 15–20% of the population would have those characteristics. Thus, he looked for some other peculiar characteristics. On detailed examination he found that in Christie's lot, the hair had been cut at both ends. One cut end was recent—obviously made by Christie when he took hair from his victim. The other cut had rounded off and was about 6 months old. The conclusion was that the victim had herself trimmed her hair 6 months ago. The hair in the sample from Evans's body was cut at one end (made by Simpson), but the other end was uncut, implying Evans had not been trimming her pubic hair. The conclusion was that the hair found in Christie's house was not Evans' and thus obviously Christie was telling a lie.[3] In this case, the official testimony that none of Christie's collection of hairs could have come from Evans was given by Dr. Nickolls. Simpson would have said the same had he been called.[3]

John Wayne Gacy, Moninder Singh Pandher, and **Surendra Koli** all kept dead bodies in and around their houses to carry on their necrophilic activities. In **Pandher** and **Koli**'s case, at least 19 child victims were missing from their village, and they were the prime suspects. Several of the children went missing after they reportedly went to Pandher and Koli's house for domestic chores. On February 8, 2005, a 14-year-old maid, **Rimpa Halder,** went to Pandher's house and never returned. Later, her body was found hacked up. The evidence in this case was the recovery of **Rimpa's clothes** from Pandher's house, where Koli worked as domestic help. The clothes were identified by the mother of the victim. The DNA samples from Rimpa's clothes were matched with the blood sample of her mother, father, and brother, positively identifying her. During the probe, Koli identified the buttons of Rimpa's dress.

Use of **cadaver dogs** may be helpful.[4] When Cleveland killer **Anthony Sowell** was caught, an **x-ray machine** and **miniature cameras** were used by investigators to examine the spaces between the walls and floors of his home, and **thermal imaging** and **radar** were used to examine the ground near his house. Using these devices, a total of 11 bodies (including one skull) were recovered from his home.

Excavations in and Around Suspect's House

Excavations in and around a necrophile's house may prove rewarding. In Christie's case, three bodies had been recovered from his kitchen cupboard, and initially it appeared that his mode of disposal of bodies was to tuck them away in the kitchen cupboard. However, a fourth body—that of his wife—was soon discovered under the floorboards of the front room. Four days later (March 28, 1953), two skeletons were recovered from the garden in his back yard. (For details, please see Chapter 5, "Case Studies.") Thus, finding one or more bodies in the necrophile's house must not lull the investigators into believing that everything has been discovered.

Efforts must be made to search for any ancillary material buried alongside the body, as this may be helpful in dating the material. In the Christie case, the skeletons that were discovered buried in the garden appeared quite old, but it could have been a difficult task to date them exactly. However, a newspaper dated July 19, 1943, was found buried alongside the bones, which appeared to date the discovery fairly accurately. (It turned out later that the female—Ruth Fuerst—had been killed in August 1943.)[5]

Closed Caption TV Footage

Necrophiles may like to store dead bodies at some safe place where they can visit them repeatedly for committing necrophilic acts. If the storage place happens to have CCTV cameras, a review of its footage can be quite helpful in investigations.

In 2009, a class V necrophile, 41-year-old man named **Park,** was arrested for stealing an urn containing the ashes of the late South Koran actress Choi Jin-sil, known as "Korea's sweetheart." He was caught after footage from a closed circuit camera revealed his vandalizing acts. (For details of this case, please see Chapter 5, "Case Studies.")

After murdering his victim, 31-year-old Jane Longhurst, on March 14, 2003, **Graham Coutts** kept her body for some time in his car, then in his shed, and finally in a commercial storage facility (Big Yellow Self Storage Company unit in Brighton). Security cameras revealed that during the time the body was stored there (for about 3 weeks), **Coutts** visited it at least nine times, ostensibly to commit necrophilic acts. On April 19, he finally took her body to Wiggonholt Common, West Sussex, and set fire to it. **CCTV footage** at the commercial storage facility showed him removing a large cardboard box the day before her burning body was found. This CCTV footage proved vital in ensuring his conviction. (For details of this case, please see Chapter 5, "Case Studies.")

Examination of the Dead Body

Examination must begin with an examination of clothing over the body (if present). If the body is naked, the examination begins with a general physical examination to determine all visible external injuries. In the case of **John Christie**'s victims, an examination of clothing revealed that none of the dead bodies was wearing underwear, indicating that they had been removed for fetishistic activities. (Christie's fetishism was confirmed later, when another fetish—a tobacco tin containing four ringlets of pubic hair—was recovered from his house.)

Christie was fond of killing his victims by **carbon monoxide poisoning.** (Please see Chapter 2, "Etiology," for details of a "death jar" he had invented for this purpose.) Thus, the first question that was put to **Francis Camps** (the pathologist who conducted the autopsy on all eight of Christie's victims) was whether he found signs of **gassing. Cherry red coloration** was present in his last three victims.[5]

In necrophile victims, a primary task for the pathologist is to confirm (or refute) the suspicion that the corpse was sexually abused. This is done by determining if the injuries found on the body were **antemortem** or **postmortem.** Necrophiles are known not only to engage in postmortem sex, but also to bite breasts and other parts of the body—Ted Bundy bit Lisa Levy's buttocks—and produce postmortem mutilations. A **histopathological** examination is vital to differentiate the antemortem from postmortem injuries. **Histochemical examination** may reveal the age of injuries. Tears in the hymen will be visible just as they are in any other case of rape. The important difference, however, is that there will be absence of any inflammation or bleeding (Figure 6.3) in postmortem cases.

If the body has been anally penetrated, it may show anal dilatation. Although anal dilatation is a common postmortem finding in many cases (due to muscular relaxation after death), its presence when rigor mortis is still present may indicate anal penetration. Additionally, when strong circumstantial evidence of necrophilia is present (e.g., a dug-up grave), anal

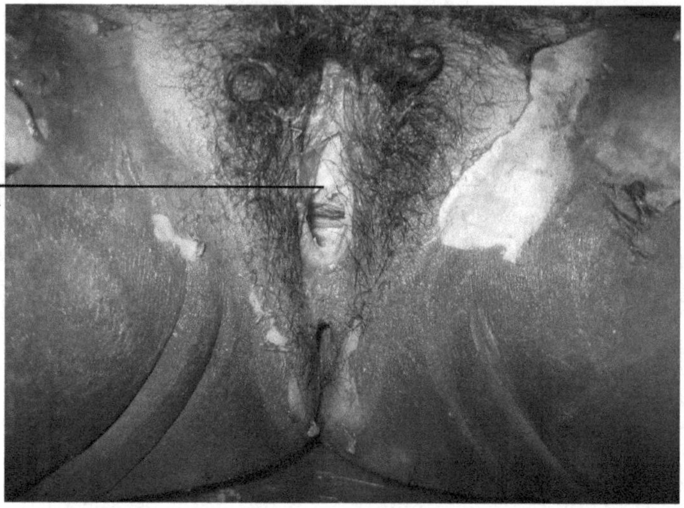

Figure 6.3 Postmortem tear in the hymen caused by suspected necrophilic activity. Note absence of any bleeding or inflammation around the tear. This tear was not present when the body was brought to the mortuary in the evening. It was noticed the next day at the time of postmortem examination.

dilatation may point strongly toward postmortem anal penetration. In Torre and Varetto's[2] case, the anus showed dilatation in the presence of rigor mortis in other parts of the body. The authors felt that all facts taken together indicated that the body had been anally penetrated. (For details of this case, please see Chapter 3, "Classification.")

DNA Profiling

DNA profiling can be very helpful in necrophilia investigation, for identification of both the victim and the suspect and in many other ways. It can help identify scattered body parts and link them as coming from the same victim. If the necrophile has left seminal or salivary stains on the body or at the scene of crime, DNA profiling can help establish his identity positively. In **Ted Bundy**'s case, seminal stains were indeed recovered from the crime scene, but as DNA profiling was not available at that time, his identity had to be established by other means (bite marks). At around the same time on the day Bundy killed two Chi Omega sorority coeds, **Margaret Bowman** and **Lisa Levy** (please see the heading "Bite Marks on the Dead Body" in this chapter for details), three other girls were attacked, but they survived. These were **Karen Chandler** and **Kathy Kleiner,** who lived in the same Chi Omega sorority house as Lisa and Margaret, and **Cheryl Thomas**, who lived eight blocks away. She was bludgeoned in her bed.

No semen was found on the body or clothes of Lisa, Margaret, Karen, or Kathy or around their bodies at the scene of crime, but a **semen stain approximately three inches in diameter** was found on **Cheryl Thomas**'s bottom sheet.[6] This happened in 1978, and DNA profiling was yet 6 years away. Otherwise Bundy could have been easily caught. However, blood type could still be obtained from the stain if the offender happened to be a secretor. (Bundy was a secretor, and had type O positive blood.)[6] Unfortunately Richard Stephens, the forensic serologist at the Florida Department of Law Enforcement's crime lab, could not determine the blood group, perhaps because of the effect of environment on the stain. Also, there was no detectable PGM enzyme activity.

Graham Coutts killed his victim, 31-year-old Jane Longhurst, on March 14, 2003, and kept the dead body in his possession for over a month before finally disposing of it on April 19. For the last three weeks, he kept the body in a cardboard box and stored it in a commercial storage facility, using a false name. When he was finally caught, and the storage facility searched, many pieces of incriminating evidence were found. Among them were Jane's clothes, including underwear and a swimming costume, a bloodstained rope, a bloodstained box, her mobile phone, and goggles. More significantly, a used condom was discovered at the same site. DNA on the outside of the condom matched that of **Jane Longhurst,** while the DNA of the semen inside matched **Coutts**'. DNA of bloodstains found on the shirt matched that of Jane.

In **Pandher** and **Koli**'s investigation, the victim **Rimpa** was identified by DNA profiling. Her clothes had been found in Pandher's house. The DNA recovered from the clothes was matched with that of her parents and brother.

Some necrophiles (e.g., Graham Coutts) have been known to dispose of their victims by burning. A DNA profile of the victim from burnt remains should be attempted, as it is now possible to prepare a DNA profile of the victim from even severely burnt bodies.[7,8,9]

Touch DNA

Humans shed tens of thousands of skin cells each day, and these cells are transferred to every surface the skin contacts. When any crime is committed where the perpetrator touches an object, he transfers many of these cells to the object. While technically this is known as **Low Template DNA (LTDNA)**, or **Low Copy Number DNA** (LCN DNA), it is sometimes also referred to as **Touch DNA** (DNA that is transferred by touch) or **Trace DNA**.[10] It has been shown that a DNA profile of the perpetrator could be made from touch DNA.[11,12] **Touch DNA** has been successfully sampled from countless items including gun grips, window sills, eating utensils, luggage handles, and the inside of cars such as steering wheels.[13]

Theoretically, if a necrophile has as much as touched a dead body (e.g., **class IV necrophilia**), he is likely to leave his DNA on the dead body, and his

DNA profile could be prepared from it. This possibility must be kept in mind. **Touch DNA** can be lifted from the body using sterile cotton swabs.

QUICK FACT 6.1

- DNA present in one haploid human cell (e.g., sperm head) = 3 pg (3×10^{-12} g).
- DNA present in one diploid human cell (e.g., buccal cell, skin cell, WBC) = 6 pg (6×10^{-12} g).
- 1 ng (1×10^{-9} g) of DNA would be contained in 167 diploid cells (e.g., WBC) or 333 haploid cells (e.g., sperm heads).
- Amount of DNA required for successful DNA profiling during initial days (1985–1995) = 50 ng to 1000 ng. This was done by RFLP method—no longer used in forensic casework.
- Development of PCR during early 1990s reduced the amount of DNA required to 0.5–2 ng. PCR amplification cycles typically required were 28.
- Development of Low Copy Number profiling (LCN profiling) during late 1990s reduced the amount of DNA required to less than 200 pg.
- 200 pg of DNA is contained in 33 WBCs or 67 sperm heads.
- In some instances LCN profiling is possible even from less than 100 pg of DNA.
- Typically, in LCN profiling, the number of PCR amplification cycles required is 34, instead of the conventional 28.
- Precautions with LCN profiling: Stochastic (or random) effects on DNA amplification. During PCR, the primer must bind to its cognate template before molecular Xeroxing can start. In LCN milieu, so few target templates are available that molecular collisions required between the primer and its cognate template may not occur at all. This may result in total loss of an allele (allele drop-out). Alternately an allele from contaminated DNA may be amplified (allele drop-in). This effect—commonly referred to as the stochastic effect—may result in false interpretation of results.

DNA typing is now possible with very minute quantities of DNA (LCN profiling). It has been carried out on **epithelial cells** that have been transferred from the hands of the suspect onto the neck of the victim during **strangulation,**[14,15] from **firearms** and **fired cartridge cases,**[16] and from **cigarette butts.**[17,18] This possibility must be kept in mind, as all these scenarios are quite common in **class IX necrophilia.**

Primary, Secondary, and Tertial Transfer of DNA

Depending on how people "shed" their skin cells, they have been broadly classified into two groups: **good DNA "shedders"** and **bad DNA "shedders."** When a good DNA shedder touches an object, even after a thorough hand washing, he would leave behind enough of his skin cells on the object touched for his full DNA profile to be made. A bad DNA shedder would not leave behind his full DNA profile immediately after hand washing. It may take up to 6 hours after hand washing for him to shed enough skin cells for his full DNA profile to be made.[19]

With the possibility of preparing profiles from touch DNA, the possibility of small quantities of DNA transfer from one object onto another must be kept in mind, as this possibility may be raised by the defense. The issue may be important when a **good DNA shedder** has, for example, shaken hands with a **bad DNA shedder**, and the latter in turn touched an incriminating object (for example, a knife during the course of a homicide). Shaking hands will transfer a large amount of the good shedder's skin cells onto the hands of a bad shedder. If the bad shedder then commits a homicide, it is possible that he *might not transfer any of his own cells to the knife* (as he is a bad shedder), but may *transfer a large amount of the good shedder's cells already collected on his hands*. This may falsely implicate the good shedder.

QUICK FACT 6.2

- **Primary transfer:** Hands of a person (**P_1**) touch the body of victim (**V**). His skin cells are transferred onto the body of the victim.
- **Secondary transfer:** Person **P_1** shakes hands with **P_2**. Skin cells of **P_1** are transferred onto the hands of **P_2** (primary transfer). **P_2** subsequently touches the body of a victim, perhaps during an act of homicide. Cells of **P_1** are found on the dead body (secondary transfer), although **P_1** had nothing to do with the murder.
- **Tertiary transfer**: **P_1** and **P_2**—husband and wife—share a towel. Skin cells of **P_1** are transferred onto the towel (primary transfer). **P_2** cleans her body with the towel. Cells of **P_1** are transferred from the towel onto the body of **P_2** (secondary transfer). A criminal **P_3** wearing gloves attacks **P_2** and kills her. During the scuffle, his (**P_3's**) gloved hands touch the body of **P_2**. Cells of **P_1**, which were present on the body of **P_2** (as a result of secondary transfer) are now transferred to the gloves worn by **P_3** (tertiary transfer). **P_3** leaves behind the gloves at the crime scene. Cells of **P_1** are recovered from the gloves, giving the impression that he (**P_1**) was the murderer, while he was not.

The issue of **tertiary transfer** was raised by the defense in *Commonwealth of Massachusetts v. Dirk K. Greineder*, in which a prominent physician was accused of killing his wife. Although the jury ultimately convicted Greineder—there was other incriminating evidence besides the DNA—the case presents a good example of how the possibility of tertiary transfer may be raised by defense. It presents a plausible alternative explanation for what might at first glance seem to be incriminating DNA evidence.

Sidebar 6.1 ***Commonwealth of Massachusetts v. Dirk K. Greineder*****—The Case of Tertiary Transfer**

Dr. Dirk Greineder, 60, was working as an allergist at Brigham & Women's Hospital (Boston, Massachusetts) in 1999. On the morning of October 31, 1999, he and his wife Mabel went for a walk with their dog in a wooded area. At 8:56 AM, police received a frantic call from Greineder from his cell phone. He said his wife had been attacked and was likely dead, and requested immediate assistance. When the police arrived on the scene, they found Greineder in a wooded area standing over the dead body of his wife, blood smudges on his yellow windbreaker, black jeans, and eyeglasses. Mabel Greineder had wounds on her head, neck, and chest. Drag marks led from the body to a path puddled with her blood. Mabel had been hit twice in the head with a hammer and stabbed ten times. Dr. Greineder claimed he separated briefly from Mabel during their walk and returned to find her mutilated body on the ground. Police searched the area and collected a bloody glove, a knife, a hammer, and several other items near the crime scene. The glove and knife revealed Dirk's DNA, indicating that he might have murdered her. There was strong motive for doing so. He led a secret sex life, including sex with prostitutes, Internet pornography, and solicitation of sex online. In the week before his wife's murder, Dr. Greineder had sex with Brooklyn prostitute Nora Lopez during a business trip to New Jersey, joined an Internet dating service called People2People, and chatted online with swinging couple Harry and Amy Page to set up a threesome. Computers taken from the home revealed reams of pornographic material accessed on a regular and continued basis. Mabel had discovered his sex life and it had become necessary to eliminate her.

During the trial, Dr. Greineder claimed that his DNA that was recovered from the knife and gloves was there as a result of tertiary transfer. He and his wife had shared a towel the morning of the murder. He claimed that his DNA was transferred from his face to the towel, and from the towel to his wife's face. His explanation was that his wife was later attacked by a glove-wearing stranger who struck her on the face, strangled her, and stabbed her, in the process transferring Dirk's DNA from his wife's face to the gloves and the knife.

To support the theory that his DNA could have been transferred innocently to the instruments of murder, Greineder commissioned a study. Forensic scientists Marc Taylor and Elizabeth Johnson, of Technical Associates (an independent laboratory in Ventura, California) simulated the sequence of events posited by the defense theory: A man wiped his face with a towel, then a woman wiped her face with the towel, then gloves and a knife like those used in the murder were rubbed against the woman's face. DNA tests on the gloves and knife revealed a mixture of DNA from the man and woman—exactly what was found in the Greineder case. Taylor was allowed to present his findings to the jury. The jury, however, convicted Greineder because of other overwhelming evidence against him.

Scattered Body Parts

If the necrophile has dismembered the body and scattered the parts, it may be necessary to ascertain that all recovered body parts belong to the same person. Sometimes the offender keeps certain body parts with him and disposes of the rest of the body, especially as it starts putrefying. In such cases also the identity of each body part needs to be established. This is best done by DNA profiling.

Bauer and colleagues[20] describe the case of a 40-year-old, married civil engineer with two children who once stole the dead body of a 14-year-old girl who had died in a railway accident. Since a number of eyewitnesses were available, the autopsy was not thought necessary. The body was kept in a casket, and the funeral was scheduled for three days later.

Meanwhile the offender—a necrophile who had previously stolen two dead bodies—came to know about the death of this young girl through reading her obituary in a newspaper. Using a general key, he entered the mortuary where the casket was lying. No security measures were in place. The offender stole the body, placed it in his car, and drove it to his property outside of town. During the next three days, he dissected the body and removed most of the internal organs (including heart, lungs, liver, spleen, kidneys, and uterus with ovaries). He preserved these organs in alcohol, placing them in several different vessels. These vessels were tucked away in his loft, where they were later discovered by the police. When the body began putrefying after three days, the offender disposed of the body in a shallow well on his property filled with water and mud.

Three months later, the offender was seen taking pictures of some intestines in a secluded industrial area. When questioned about the origin of the intestines, he replied that they were animal in origin. However, suspicion was aroused, and the offender was apprehended six weeks later. Vessels with organs preserved in alcohol were recovered from the loft in his house. On interrogation, he told where he had disposed of the body, which was duly recovered by divers. It was a partially skeletonized torso, with no limbs. Remaining soft tissues were in an advanced state of decomposition and showed early adipocere formation. The internal organs, including the brain, were missing. However, there were no signs of opening of the skull (except a linear fracture in the left temporal, parietal, and occipital bone, which was attributed to the railway accident). No brain was recovered from the offender's collection, so it was presumed that the brain had liquefied and flowed out of the foramen magnum.

A major problem was to establish whether the organs found in the offender's collection belonged to the same body, which was recovered from the shallow well, and also whether *both* matched the girl in question. This was achieved by performing DNA analysis of tissues from the torso and from all body parts. The DNA profile of both matched the DNA profile of the deceased girl as determined from blood stains in the casket. It was further verified by analyzing samples of the parents.

Vaginal, Oral, and Rectal Swabs

In many cases of necrophilia, the semen of the offender may be identified vaginally, anally, and orally, as well as on the body and on clothing items near the body. **Vaginal, oral,** and **rectal swabs** from the dead body must be taken according to standard protocols in live victims, and tested for **intact spermatozoa, P30,** and **restriction fragment length polymorphism (RFLP) typable DNA.** Detection of these markers does not necessarily mean acts of necrophilia; this may have been due to sexual activity during life. However, taken with other circumstantial evidence, this examination can corroborate necrophilia. Seminal stains should be searched for on the victim's body and clothing by UV light (254 nm).[21] If found, they should be swabbed and subjected to the same tests. Detection of semen on cloth may be difficult by fluorescence. If difficulty is faced, **phosphorescence** may be utilized instead of **fluorescence.**[21]

QUICK FACT 6.3

Fluorescence refers to emission of light that decays immediately upon removal of the exciting source (e.g., UV light). In contrast, **phosphorescence** is emission of light that *persists after the removal of the exciting source.* At normal room temperatures, *only* fluorescence is observable from most organic materials. However, when organic material is cooled, it usually exhibits phosphorescence as well. This principle is applied to detection of semen on cloth. At normal room temperature, both the fabric and seminal stains would fluoresce, making their detection difficult. When the cloth is cooled to 77 K (temperature of boiling nitrogen) phosphorescence is (once again) seen both in the fabric and seminal stains. However, while the semen phosphorescence persists for about 20 seconds after removal of the excitation lamp, that exhibited by the fabric is of much shorter duration. Thus, after a few seconds, only the semen phosphorescence is visible. Therefore phosphorescence (at 77 K) is a far more effective technique to visualize seminal stains than fluorescence.

Laboratory examination has been shown to reveal the presence of **intact spermatozoa, P30,** and **restriction fragment length polymorphism (RFLP) typable DNA** on a vaginal swab in a corpse as old as 34 days.[22] This was most certainly a case of sadistic murder (necromutilosexuality, as suggested in Chapter 3, "Classification") rather than of necrophilia, but it demonstrates the value of collecting trace evidence even from bodies recovered very late.

In the case of necrophile **John Christie** (1898–1953), four bodies were recovered from the cupboards of his house and two skeletons from his backyard garden on March 24, 1953. The bodies in the cupboards were more recently dead. Of these, **Hectorina MacLennan** had died most recently. She was killed on March 3, 1953 (about 3 weeks earlier). **Francis Camps,** the pathologist who conducted the autopsies on the bodies, found some whitish material exuding from the vulva of MacLennan and also inside her vagina. He took vaginal swabs from all four bodies and examined them under the microscope. Three of these showed presence of spermatozoa. The body that did not show spermatozoa was Christie's wife.[3]

SIDEBAR 6.2 DNA in Necrophile Investigations

Gary Ridgway killed an estimated 48 victims, committing acts of necrophilia on several of them. During much of the time of his activity, the science of DNA profiling was not known. It was only in 1984 that DNA profiling became possible. In four of his victims, semen had been found and preserved: 31-year-old **Marcia Fay Chapman** (murdered August 1, 1982); 17-year-old **Cynthia Jean Hinds** (murdered August 11, 1982); 16-year-old **Opal Charmaine Mills** (murdered August 12, 1982); and 21-year-old **Carol Ann Christensen** (murdered May 3, 1983). In September 2001, almost 20 years after those murders, DNA profiles were made from the semen samples preserved from those bodies using short tandem repeat (STR) analysis. The DNA profile could be matched exactly with that of Gary Ridgway, who worked at the Kenworth Truck Plant. Gary Ridgway ultimately was found to be the infamous Green River Killer, who killed a total of 48 women, including these four.

In another case, **Ted Bundy** was not responsible for the 1973 murder of Kathy Merry Devine, a killing for which he was long suspected. DNA testing linked that killing to an ex-con named William Cosden, who was subsequently tried and convicted of her murder.

If the pathologist fails to take vaginal swabs, not only would it be a grave mistake, but it may lead to unsavory allegations. In the same **Christie case** mentioned earlier, postmortem on two of the bodies (Mrs. Beryl Evans and her 14-month-old daughter Geraldine Evans, found in the washhouse at the back of Christie's flat) was performed in December 1949 by **Donald Teare,** a very respectable forensic pathologist of his time. He decided—for whatever reason—not to take vaginal swabs. It was later claimed by a person of no lesser eminence than the British journalist **Sir Ludovic Kennedy** (1919–2009) that "Had he done so, he would almost certainly have found traces of Christie's spermatozoa."[23] **Keith Simpson,** the British pathologist who was representing Christie, in turn, states, "I doubt if a more reckless overstatement can be found in all the millions of words written about the Evans-Christie case."[3] While allegations and counterallegations continue, the fact is that if vaginal swab had been taken in that case, such a controversy would never have arisen in the first place.

Breast Swabs

Examination of breasts may show postmortem lesions. **Breast swabs** for saliva are indicated as necrophiles are known to suck and/or bite breasts.[24] Since saliva contains nucleated squamous epithelia cells (NSEC),[25] DNA profile of the perpetrator can be prepared from it.[26,27,28]

KEY POINT 6.1

Examination of dead body in the investigation of necrophilia:

- Examine clothing for cuts, tears, seminal stains, other body fluids. Note if any part of clothing is missing, e.g., bra, panties, as they may have been removed for fetishistic activities. In **Christie**'s case, panties were found missing from all his victims.
- Detailed examination of the body, especially genitalia.
- Examine pubic hair closely. Determine if pubic hairs have been **clipped away.** They may have been removed for fetishistic purposes. (In **Christie**'s case, a tobacco tin was recovered containing four ringlets of pubic hair.) See if pubic hair is matted with semen. If yes, clip them away for DNA profiling.
- Look for other possible fetishes (e.g., missing scalp hair), which may have been removed from the body.
- Determine if the injuries on the dead body are antemortem or postmortem.
- Perform histochemical examination of all injuries.
- Perform histolopathological examination of all injuries.
- Perform vaginal, oral, and rectal swabs for DNA profiling.
- Perform breast swabs for salivary stains and possible DNA profiling from nucleated cells present. Determine secretor status. If secretor, determine blood group.
- If the body is skeletonized or is in advanced decomposition stage, use standard identification protocols, such as dental data and superimposition.

If the body is in advanced decomposition or skeletonized, standard identification protocols such as **dental data** and **superimposition** can be used for identification. The crimes of the notorious Hong Kong necrophile **Lam Kor-wan** occurred in the pre-DNA era (1982). The bodies of his victims were identified by the Forensic Odontology Group, a group established in 1980, by using dental data and superimposition.[29] (For details, please see Chapter 5, Case Studies.")

Price[30] mentions a very illustrative case (*Regina v. Ward*) where a **thorough postmortem examination** could lead to the arrest of the necrophile. The case is interesting because the killing and necrophilic acts had been done by different persons. While the killer could be caught by simple interrogation, the necrophile could be caught only when he was confronted with the scientific evidence.

The case involved the stabbing of a 68-year-old spinster, **Miss Ada Roberts,** who lived alone. She did not have a good relationship with one of her neighbors—a man called **Mr. Ward**—who was a known alcoholic and gambler. On August 5, 1960 (Friday), when Ada was returning from work at about 5:30 PM, Ward stabbed her on the left side of her chest. At the time of stabbing she was only about 20 yards from her house, but no one saw him stabbing her. Her neighbors saw her stagger toward their yard gate, open it, and collapse. A doctor who was called immediately missed the stab wound, diagnosed cerebral hemorrhage, and ordered an ambulance. She was brought to the hospital at 6:25 PM, where the casualty medical officer, having examined her within the ambulance, pronounced her dead and ordered her to be removed to the public mortuary. He also missed the chest wound. The public mortuary was closed, so the body was brought back to the hospital mortuary, where, with the assistance of a porter (whom the author refers to as "M"), it was placed, still fully dressed, upon a trolley and left in the mortuary chapel, where it remained for the rest of the night.

The next day, at about 8 AM, when the hospital mortuary attendant reported for work, he noticed bloodstains on the left side of her vest when trying to undress the body. He noticed two wounds: a deep wound on the left side of the chest and another, more superficial one, over the front of the left shoulder. H.M. Coroner was informed immediately, at about 9 AM on August 6, 1960 (Saturday). A detailed postmortem could start by 4 PM at the earliest. The chest wound had cut the fourth left costal cartilage, transfixed the heart, penetrated the diaphragm, and bruised the stomach. There was a hemopericardium and left-sided hemothorax. The wound had been caused by a single-edged knife. The other wound in front of the left armpit was more superficial.

Normally in such cases the pathologist does not pay much attention to the genitalia. In this case, however, the pathologist took care to examine the genitalia in detail. Herein lies the importance of the detailed examination of genitalia in every case. The examination revealed (1) a small apparently **incised nick of the left labia minora,** (2) **a one-inch tear with bleeding but no bruising on the back wall of the entrance to the vagina,** and (3) **a bruise at the right side of the entrance to the vagina** (Figure 6.4). This "bruise" later turned out to be an angioma on histological examination. A histological examination of all injuries is thus also necessary, so that none of the "injuries" gets wrongly interpreted.

Keeping in mind that the deceased was a virgin and that genitalia atrophy after menopause, an opinion was expressed by the pathologist that she was "violated at, or very shortly before, death and it was possible **that penetration had been made easier by the use of a knife.**"

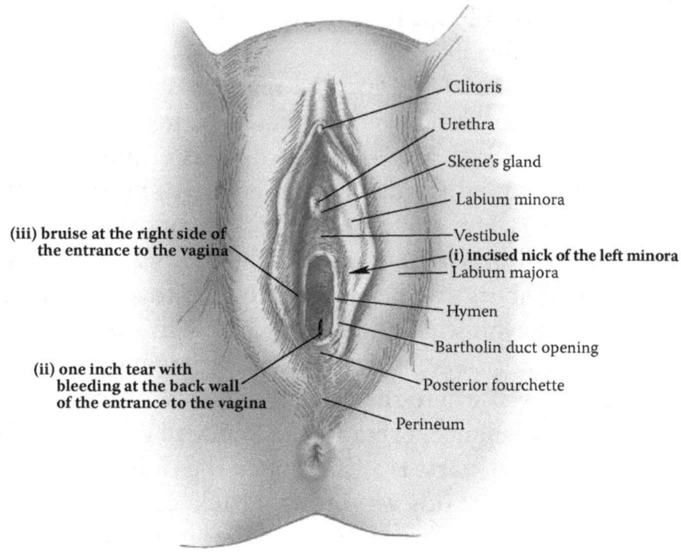

Figure 6.4 Three significant injuries on the genitalia found by Price[30] in an apparent case of necrophilia. Drawn by the author from description.

This discovery led to the taking of vaginal swabs. An immediate examination showed many spermatozoa, which confirmed sexual assault. At this time, there was no suspicion of necrophilia, and it was believed that sexual assault and stabbing were somehow related. Clothing was also examined at this point of time, and the examination showed incisions corresponding to the chest wounds.

At 6:45 PM on the same day (August 6, 1960) house-to-house inquiries were commenced. At 8:15 PM, Ward was interviewed and admitted that he had stabbed Roberts. However, he strongly denied any sexual assault on her either before or after death. His physical examination was conducted by an experienced police surgeon. It was found to be negative. Ward was charged with murder at 9:25 PM that Saturday evening.

Vaginal swabs were sent to laboratory for further forensic examination. By September 1, it was known that Roberts's blood group was A, and that the seminal fluid had been ejaculated by a secretor of the blood group B or AB. Quite fortuitously, Ward's blood group was O. Otherwise, in that pre-DNA era, it would have been virtually impossible for him to prove he had not sexually assaulted Roberts. He was also *not a secretor*.

Investigations up to this point indicated that the sexual assault on Roberts's body may have been done postmortem by some other individual. Male attendants and porters who had access to the body on that particular evening were interviewed. Each one (including M, who later turned out to be the culprit) denied having indulged in such an act. At this point in time, it was decided to re-interview 35 of the male staff, and to ask if they would allow their blood grouping. All agreed, including M, who was noticed to be nervous. At the conclusion of the interviews he was found to be waiting outside the room. Even before his blood grouping could be done, he confessed to the necrophilic act. He said that he had done it for the first time. He also said that the act was done immediately after the ambulance crew had left, that is, about 1 hour after death. He agreed that penetration was difficult, and that tearing had occurred during penetration, but denied having used a knife.

This case illustrates very well how a thorough postmortem examination backed with histological, serological, and laboratory examination could help catch the necrophile. The solution of the case is all the more praiseworthy since it occurred in the pre-DNA era. Ward was found to be suffering from attacks of confusion, loss of memory, and mania, and was thus found guilty of "manslaughter with diminished responsibility." He was sentenced to 10 years imprisonment. There was no appeal. Since at that time there was no law against necrophilia in Britain, M could not be sentenced. He was, however, removed from service. The case drew the attention of the government to make a law in this respect.

Past medical history of M revealed that he had been involved in a motorcycle accident in 1958, with consequent head injury and concussion. This may or may not have been a causative factor in his necrophilic tendencies.

Fingerprints on the Dead Body

Any crime involving human-to-human contact is likely to leave fingerprints of one person onto the other's skin and clothes. If a person is involved in necrophilic activities with a dead body, he is likely to leave his fingerprints on the cadaver. Fingerprints recovered from genital organs of the body, inside of thighs, buttocks, breasts, and so on, are highly likely to be those produced by necrophilic activities. Fingerprints of persons who handle a dead body, for example, mortuary attendants, are more likely to be on exposed areas of the cadavers and not on areas such as genital organs and breasts. If fingerprints of a suspect are recovered from such areas, it is highly likely that he was involved in necrophilic activities. Significantly, in the case of tactile (class IV) necrophiles, fingerprints on the dead body may be the *only* evidence.

One of the earliest attempts to recover fingerprints from cadavers was undertaken by Carl Gray of the University of Leeds.[31] He used the **iodine fume-silver plate** method to recover latent fingerprints on both living subjects (eight volunteers) and cadavers (four warm cadavers and five cadavers refrigerated at 4°C). Experimental fingerprints were placed using hands that had been impregnated with the operator's own skin oils by rubbing the oily skin of the forehead before each impression. Groups of fingerprints were imprinted in marked grids on the anterior surface of the forearms of living volunteers and on the anterior surface of the thighs in cadavers. While fingerprints from the skin of live subjects were recoverable only up to 15 minutes, those from the skin of cadavers were recoverable up to **18 hours** (warm cadavers) and **24 hours** (cold cadavers). Presumably fingerprints could not be lifted from live subjects because of sweating. In real-life situations, there could be increased sweating because of struggle. In addition, there is likely to be violent movement between the hands of the assailant and the body of the victim, causing the fingerprints to get smudged. These factors are absent in the dead, enabling the forensic scientist to lift the fingerprints from dead bodies for longer periods.

Interestingly it is precisely this combination that makes the technique **particularly useful for the investigation of necrophilia,** because all fingerprints that were placed on the victim's skin during life (e.g., during consensual intercourse with one's partner) would vanish within 15 minutes, but those that were placed after death (as during necrophilic activities) would be detectable up to 24 hours.

It is now possible to determine the DNA profile of the perpetrator from his fingerprints.[11] This possibility must be kept in mind.

Bite Marks on the Dead Body

It is well known that in sexual assault cases, offenders often inflict bite marks. Necrophiles are no exception and may leave bite marks on the dead body, especially around breasts or buttocks. The most notable necrophile caught and sentenced by virtue of bite marks was **Ted Bundy.**[32] On January 15, 1978, when Bundy was on the run—he had earlier escaped from a Colorado jail on December 30, 1977—he entered the Florida State University Chi Omega sorority house at Tallahassee at about 3 AM and killed two sleeping women, **Margaret Bowman**, 21, and **Lisa Levy**, 20, within a space of about 15 minutes. So swift were his killings that none of the almost three dozen girls who were present in the sorority at that time heard him.[6] Lisa Levy was also sexually attacked, possibly after she had been killed. **Dr. Thomas P. Wood,** the pathologist at Tallahassee Memorial Hospital who performed the postmortem examination on Levy, found one **deep bite mark on her right breast;** her right nipple was attached by only a thread of tissue. There was also a **class III double bite mark on her left buttock.**[6,33]

SIDEBAR 6.3 Classes of Bite Marks

Based on severity of bite, four classes of bite marks are generally recognized.[33]

- **Class I:** The mildest form of bite mark. The pattern is diffuse. Individual tooth marks cannot be identified. Often appears as a diffuse bruised ring and if DNA profiling cannot be done from associated mucosal cells, may be of little or no evidentiary value for matching to a suspect. However, if mucosal cells are recovered and DNA profiling is possible, these can provide positive evidence regarding identity of the suspect. Saliva from the marks can also sometimes be matched to the suspect. Arch forms can also be identified at times.
- **Class II:** Deeper than class I bite marks. Displays both class and some individual characteristics. Upper (maxillary) and lower (mandible) arches can be identified. Specific teeth may be identified. These bite marks are used more for exclusion than for inclusion of a suspect.
- **Class III:** Deeper than class II bite marks. Show excellent tooth morphology in at least one arch. Specific teeth shapes and their position in the dental arch can be identified. Can be used for both inclusion as well as exclusion. The third dimension or indentations may be present and can help estimate the time the bite was inflicted in relation to the time of death.
- **Class IV:** This is the severest form of bite mark. It takes the shape of an incised wound, and often the tissue is completely bitten off. Blood (from the victim) is present on the surface, and DNA (of the offender) may be contaminated. It is difficult, if not impossible, to match this bite to the suspect because no individual bite marks are discernible.

Sometimes **bite marks may be mixed.** For example, upper arch may inflict a class I bite, while lower arch may be a more severe class II bite. **Ted Bundy's bites were class III bites,** making it possible to positively identify him.

Bundy had bitten Levy's buttock twice with his teeth, leaving distinct rows of marks where those teeth had sunk in. The first bite showed a full and complete bite mark. Bundy then turned sideways and bit a second time. The top teeth stayed in about the same position, but the lower teeth—biting harder—left two rings. The second set of impressions gave investigators more points for comparison, increasing the probability of a match.

A Clairol hair spray bottle with a nozzle-top had been introduced in the victim's vaginal orifice, injuring both the vaginal vault as well as rectum. The bottle was later found in the room. It was stained with type O blood (Lisa's type),[6] fecal matter, and hair.

The bite mark was photographed at the scene with a ruler alongside it by **Sergeant Howard Winkler,** head of the Crime Scene Unit of the Tallahassee Police Department. This proved very valuable later, as the pieces of skin containing bite marks (from right breast and left buttock) that were excised by the pathologist at the time of postmortem examination were less helpful.[34] Although initially preserved in normal saline, they were later transferred to formalin without retaining rings, causing them to shrink.

Even from these "shrunken" pieces of tissue, forensic odontologist **Richard Souviron** could opine that the "biter would have had poorly aligned teeth." This information helped to establish the element of probable cause necessary for obtaining a search warrant. When this was accomplished, Souviron was able to take dental impressions, bite records, and photographs of Bundy's teeth. Souviron then compared Bundy's dental impressions with the photographs of the bite injury.[34] Because Bundy's teeth were particularly unique in many respects, a perfect match could be accomplished. Souviron could convince the jury by overlaying a transparent sheet bearing an enlarged picture of Bundy's teeth over an enlarged picture of bite marks on Lisa Levy's buttocks. They lined up exactly. This was more convincing because many of Bundy's teeth were crooked and thus created a unique bite mark.

Bite mark evidence also indicated that Levy was motionless when she was being bitten. Dr. **Lowell J. Levine,** the chief consultant in forensic dentistry to the New York City Medical Examiner, testified that he believed Lisa Levy had been "passive" when the bite marks were left on her body. "There is very little evidence of motion or swirling you'd normally get as tissue moves in various directions as the teeth move on the skin. These things were left slowly, and the person was not moving.[6]

The patterns produced by teeth in biting must be photographed. If it happens to be a class III bite mark, where indentations are clearly visible, the bite mark must be impressed for three-dimensional modeling by a trained technician or forensic dentist.[35] The analysis of the pattern's possible link to a particular necrophile biter is dependent on proper evidence collection at the beginning of the case. This kind of analysis must always be done by an experienced forensic dentist.

Toxicology

An important aspect of medico-legal investigation is determining if any depressants, deliriants, or other intoxicants were present in the body. Many necrophiles have offered alcohol to their victims, so that they can overpower their victims when they are tipsy. In the case of Christie's victims, it has been somewhat a mystery how Christie persuaded the three tough prostitutes (his last three victims) to sit quietly in a deck chair and be gassed. One possibility was that he offered alcohol to them, but only **Kathleen Maloney** was found to have been drinking.[5]

Christie also claimed that his wife Ethel Christie died of **drug automatism,** having taken 23 tablets of phenobarbitone during her sleep. **Francis Camps,** the pathologist who conducted the postmortem, failed to detect any tablets in the stomach.[5] Carbon monoxide poisoning was found in three of his victims (the last three).[5]

When **Beryl Evans**' body was exhumed, an important question was to determine whether she had been killed by carbon monoxide poisoning. (For details on Evans, Christie's third victim, please see Chapter 5, "Case Studies.") **Keith Simpson,** the pathologist who was engaged by the defense, was there to look for it. (Paradoxically, the defense was trying to prove that **Evans** was killed by **Christie,** thinking it would help them prove he was insane.) He did find some cherry red coloration on the front of Evans's thighs. He asked for the specimens from those areas for confirmation of carbon monoxide poisoning. He also took her teeth, which were pink in color. None showed carbon monoxide.[3]

Physical Evidence from the Corpses

Physical evidence from the corpse (e.g., hair, fibers) may be collected from the body or the scene of the crime and matched with those recovered from the suspect, according to standard protocols. Alternatively, victim may be positively connected to the necrophile if victim's hair is found on him or in his possession. When Ted Bundy was caught, hair was found in his car. These matched the hair of some of his victims: the pubic hair of **Melissa Smith,** 17 (disappeared October 18, 1974; nude body found 9 days later), and head hairs from **Caryn Campbell,** 23 (disappeared January 12, 1975; body found February 17, 1975) and **Carol DaRonch** (abducted on November 8, 1974, but managed to run away and survived).[6]

Modus Operandi

Most homicidal necrophiles (class IX) employ the same *modus operandi* (MO) to kill, and this can sometimes lead to their capture. **Thor Nis Christiansen**'s MO was to pick up a hitchhiking girl of a certain appearance (long, straight hair, and a particular build and taste in clothes) from the University of California campus, kill her by shooting her in the head with a small .22 caliber pistol, and then have sex with her body. He killed four girls in that manner. Before killing his final victim on May 26, 1979, he tried to kill another girl, 21-year-old Lydia Preston (on April 18, 1979), but she escaped, albeit severely injured. She identified him 3 months later in a bar (on July 11, 1979, by which time he had committed his fourth—and final—murder) and immediately notified the police. Christiansen was arrested. It was the similarity of his MO that helped the police link him with three earlier murders. (For details of the Christiansen case, please see Chapter 5, "Case Studies.")

Other Evidence

Palm prints are generally considered part of fingerprinting, and in some criminal cases have been found at crime scenes or on victims of crimes. In *State v. Inman,*[36] *United States v. Moore,*[37] and *Yelder v. State,*[38] palm prints were instrumental in obtaining convictions. To date, palm prints have not been used in any case involving necrophilia, but the possibility should be kept in mind. The crime scene and the body must be searched for palm prints.

Lip prints are also unique, much like fingerprints, although they have not been exploited in crime investigation to their full potential. The Appellate Court of Illinois ruled in *People v. Davis*, No. 2-97-0725, that a lip print is sufficient physical evidence to prove a person guilty of a serious crime.[39]

The possibility of a necrophile's lip prints being present on a dead body is certainly real, but there is also the possibility of lip prints being present on some materials used by necrophiles. Some necrophiles are known to use **duct tape** to bind their victims (when torture and sex start during life and continues after death, as in class IXd, IXe, and IXf necrophiles). In the Davis case, lip prints of the suspect were found on the **sticky side of a piece of duct tape.**

SIDEBAR 6.4 Importance of Lip Prints in Criminal Investigations

In 1993, during a crime scene examination of a homicide in Kane County, Illinois, a roll of duct tape was seized as evidence. Analysis of the tape discovered a **lip print on the sticky side. Leanne Gray,** an Illinois State Police lab forensic scientist specializing in latent print examination, obtained standards of the defendant's (Davis') lips using the sticky side of duct tape and lipstick on paper. Using a side-by-side comparison of the standards and the photograph of the latent print from the evidence, she along with **Steven McKasson** of the Southern Illinois forensic science lab in Carbondale, Illinois, concluded that the defendant made the lip print. In fact, **13 points of similarity** between the standard and the photograph were found. Gray testified that lip print comparison is not a new form of identification but **it is seldom used because lip prints are not readily available.** Although this print is the only case of which she is aware in Illinois in the past 10 years, the methodology of lip print comparison is a known and accepted form of scientific comparison. The methods used in her comparisons are accepted within the forensic science community, regardless of whether the comparison is a lip print or fingerprint. She opined, in accord with the Federal Bureau of Investigation (FBI) and Illinois State Police, that lip prints, like fingerprints, are unique and a positive means of identification.[39]

Examination of the Suspect

Examination of the suspect plays an important part. Unlike in rape, the dead body offers no resistance, and no injuries are expected on the body. However, local genital findings may be important; recent abrasions and bruises may point toward attempts at recent sexual intercourse. Washings from the penis may reveal squamous cells from the deceased's vagina from which DNA profiling can be done. At one time, **glycogenated squamous epithelial cells** were supposed to be specific to the vagina.[40] If recovered from the **urethral meatus, glans penis,** or **penile shaft,** and demonstrated by **Lugol's iodine staining technique,** they were supposed to be strongly indicative of penile vaginal penetration.[41] This is no longer true, as glycogenated squamous epithelial cells are now known to be present within the male genital system as well. Such cells have been recovered from the urethral meatus, glans penis, and even the shaft of penis from volunteers who have abstained from sex for more than 5 days.[42,43,44]

DNA examination is possible from these squamous cells, which can be irrefutable evidence in favor of the sexual act. It may, however, be difficult to opine whether the sexual act was performed before or after death. However, based on whether the local injuries found on the deceased's genitalia were antemortem or postmortem, this can reasonably be ascertained.

Suspect's Belongings

An examination of the suspect's belongings can give some useful leads. Eight bodies were recovered from the home of **John Christie,** with semen in the vaginal canals of many victims. At the time the bodies were discovered (1953), DNA profiling was not available. Otherwise Christie could have been positively linked with sexually assaulting the dead bodies. An examination of **Christie's belongings** helped reconstruct his necrophilic activities to some extent. Semen was found in the **seams of his shoes,** as well as **on his clothes,** indicating that Christie could have masturbated standing over his victims' dead bodies. Semen was also found in the vaginal canals of most victims, indicating that he had sexual intercourse with the dead bodies.[45] (Please see also Chapter 2, "Etiology," and Chapter 5, "Case Studies.")

Computer Forensics

If the suspected necrophile is found to have a computer or laptop in his possession (or on his premises), it may be worthwhile to search the **hard disk** for evidence related to necrophilia. The necrophile might have visited any of a vast number of Internet necrophile sites before committing his necrophilic acts. The hard disk may show other related evidence, the most incriminating of which may be pictures of the dead body itself. In the case described by Bauer and colleagues,[20] the (unnamed) offender's computer showed a number of incriminating images and other content that had been downloaded from the Internet and stored on a CD. The material included collections of autopsy images of unknown origin, a comic strip with cannibalistic content, images showing violent abuse of women, and more than **2000 pornographic pictures** showing adolescent and pre-adolescent girls. The offender had also collected Web sites describing the life and crimes of many previous offenders, among them the most notorious serial killers, for example, **Jeff Dahmer** and **Ted Bundy.** The hard disk of his computer and several CDs recovered from his premises showed more than **5000 password-protected digital images.** These had been taken during the dissection and abuse of the body of the 14-year-old girl whose dead body he had stolen. The images helped the police immensely to reconstruct his necrophilic acts in an exact sequence.

SIDEBAR 6.5 Reconstruction of Necrophiliac Acts Using Computer Forensics

Bauer and colleagues[20] describe a very interesting case of necrophilia in which 5000 password-protected digital images were recovered using **computer forensics.** The images were taken by a necrophile (who was also an engineer) with a camera with a self-timer for his own necrophilic pleasure. However, upon seizure, the very same images provided clinching proof of his necrophilic activities. They also provided a clear and ambiguous sequence of his necrophilic activities. The images had been taken in series of up to 200 each in small time intervals. The first series showed the body dressed and undressed in an upright position with cords fixed at the extremities or in a hanging position with a cord fixed around the neck in a trailer on the offender's property. (This and several subsequent behaviors are strongly reminiscent of **Ed Gein.**) In some pictures a paper tissue could be seen in the mouth of the body. In several others, the offender was seen **manipulating breasts** and **genitals** of the body and masturbating simultaneously. In some pictures, he was seen opening the body with an incision extending from the throat to the pubic arch (very much like Gein). There were images showing the sequential removal of the internal organs, breasts, and the entire head. Pictures also revealed that he tried to place the severed head in different artificial positions (including within the abdominal cavity and between the thighs).

In some pictures, the offender was seen extensively preparing the genital region. He also tried to engage in **vaginal intercourse with the body** but could not maintain a stable erection. Shots taken outdoors showed intestines strung over branches of trees and bushes.

About 800 images were devoted to careful arrangements of body parts such as intestines, uterus, or breasts on a plate with knife and fork as if he was ready to eat them. More than 1500 images were taken in the bathroom where he washed and cleaned the body parts. They showed him undressed in the bathtub abusing different organs in bizarre situations: uterus and ovaries were placed on his own genitals and intestines were strewn all over his body. He even tried to engage in oral intercourse with the victim's facial skin flap, penetrating its mouth with his genitals.

Based on this (and several other pieces of evidence), the offender was sentenced to 2 years and 3 months in prison. (The charge was "disturbing the peace of the dead," which in German law carries a maximum sentence of 3 years.) The court also accepted the recommendation of the psychiatric expert and ordered the committal of the defendant to a psychiatric hospital without setting a time limit.

When **Graham Coutts**' computer was examined, it was found to contain a series of violent images downloaded from a variety of Internet sites containing portrayals of sexual asphyxiation, rape, torture, and violent sex. (For a complete description of his case, please see Chapter 5, "Case Studies.") During his trial, the Crown Prosecution Service brought further evidence that Coutts's consumption of **violent Internet pornography** had been high on **March 13, 2003**, when he was visiting such sites as "necrobabes," "deathbyasphyxia," "hangingbitches," and "rapepleasure." His Internet activity had been markedly reduced from **March 14** onward.[46] Significantly, Coutts murdered **Jane Longhurst** on **March 14, 2003,** and after that he was in round-the-clock possession of her body. The implication is that he was quite possibly occupied with necrophilic acts, which caused a reduction in computer activity. This evidence was useful in securing his conviction.

Brain Mapping

Brain mapping is based on the principle that a complete record of all activities (including any crimes committed by the person) is stored in the brain.

This information can be detected by using **memory and encoding related multifaceted electroencephalographic response** (MERMER), even if the subject makes a conscious effort to conceal that knowledge.[47,48] This technique was used on Koli and Pandher with success.[49]

Narcoanalysis

It has been known for quite some time that certain drugs that tend to sedate—alcohol is the oldest example—may cause the person to speak the truth. For this reason these drugs are sometimes loosely referred to as "truth drugs" or a combination of them often called "truth serum." Some such drugs are scopolamine, 3-quinuclidinyl benzilate, temazepam, and various barbiturates including sodium thiopental (sodium pentothal) and sodium amytal (amobarbital).

Klaf and Brown[50] present the report of a 40-year-old black necrophile (KBP), who denied having any interest in the dead, but during **sodium amytal interviews** revealed a number of activities with the dead that he engaged in. (For full details of this case, please see Chapter 3, "Classification," under the heading "Class IV Necrophiles: Tactile Necrophiles.") Narcoanalysis was also conducted on Koli and Pandher with success.

Other Tests

Polygraphy, or "lie detector," may be attempted in necrophiles. This was used with success in the Koli and Pandher case. **Postmortem reports of necrophiles** depicting possible abnormalities have not been published extensively. **Moreau**[51] describes the case of a 23-year-old necrophile whose autopsy showed that the **meninges of the anterior lobes were thickened** and **adherent to the cortex.** (Please see Chapter 3, "Classification," under the heading "Class IX Necrophiles: Homicidal Necrophiles," for details.) It is not likely that this pathological lesion was the cause of his necrophilia; nevertheless, it is an interesting finding. Perhaps in the future more detailed autopsies on necrophiles would be able to throw more light on the anatomical and pathological causes of this behavior.

Psychological Assessment

A forensic psychiatric's assessment of a suspected offender is necessary (1) to establish a psychiatric diagnosis, (2) for scientific research, and (3) to assist courts in the question of legal insanity.[20] Both **projective** and **objective tests** have been used for the assessment of necrophilia.

QUICK FACT 6.4

A **projective test** is a personality test designed to let a person respond to **ambiguous stimuli,** such as an inkblot or a picture showing an ambiguous scene of people. The subject may be asked what the "item" represents. Since the item is vague and ambiguous, the subject is thought to "project" his own unconscious attitudes and motivations into the inkblot or picture. Hence the name "projective tests." In general, projective tests are open ended and relatively unstructured, allowing the subject ample freedom to respond. Major projective tests are the **Rorschach inkblot test, Thematic Apperception Test** (TAT), **Draw-A-Person test,** and **sentence completion test.** Interpretation of projective tests relies heavily on clinical judgment; the clinician must interpret in each individual case what the subject's responses signify. Projective tests have their origins in psychoanalytic psychology, which stresses that all humans have conscious and unconscious attitudes and motivations that are hidden from conscious awareness.

An **objective test** is that in which responses are analyzed according to a universal standard. These tests generally comprise structured questionnaires involving multiple choice or true/false questions. Unlike projective tests, these tests leave the subjects very little freedom and choice when responding. What is *objective* about these tests is that the psychologist administering the test does not need to rely on judgment to classify or interpret the subject's response; the intended response is clearly indicated and scored according to a pre-existing key. Because scoring is very straightforward and each answer receives a certain number of points based on a point scale, objective tests are more valid and reliable than are projective tests. A major criticism of objective tests is that subjects can lie and fake their answers. Some tests such as the **Minnesota Multiphasic Personality Inventory** (**MMPI-2**) have additional validity scales to counteract this drawback. The best known objective personality test is the MMPI-2. A combination of projective and objective tests may be the best way to test an individual's personality.

Rorschach Test

The Rorschach test is a projective test consisting of a set of ten bilaterally symmetrical inkblots. Five inkblots are of black ink, two are of black and red ink, and three are multicolored, on a white background. Subjects are asked to tell the examiner what the inkblots remind them of.

Since the inkblots are rather vague and cannot be interpreted in any particularly fixed way, it is thought that the subject projects his own personality, subconscious thoughts, hidden desires, and so on in his interpretation of the inkblots. Thus his overall personality can be assessed by this test.

The overall goal of the technique is to assess the structure of personality. The emphasis is on how individuals construct their experience (cognitive structuring) and the meanings assigned to their perceptual experiences. The interpretations on Rorschach data can provide information on the subject's motivations, response tendencies, cognitive operations, affectivity, and personal and interpersonal perceptions.

MMPI

The **Minnesota Multiphasic Personality Inventory (MMPI)** was developed in 1940 by **Starke R. Hathaway,** a psychologist, and **J. Charnley McKinley,** a psychiatrist, at the **University of Minnesota.** It consisted of **566** personality questions that could be answered "true" or "false." Items were worded so that persons with an elementary school education could take the test. The complete test could be administered in about 1–2 hours.

The test evaluates the subject on ten clinical scales and several subsidiary scales:

Scale 1 (formerly known as the **Hypochondriasis Scale [Hs]**) measures subject's perception of his or her health, or actual injuries or health issues.

Scale 2 (formerly known as the **Depression Scale [D]**) measures subject's discouragement level.

Scale 3 (formerly known as the **Hysteria Scale [Hy]**) measures the emotionality of the subject.

Scale 4 (formerly known as the **Psychopathic Deviate Scale [Pd]**) measures subject's need for control or his/her rebellion against control.

Scale 5 (formerly known as the **Femininity/Masculinity Scale [MF]**) measures a stereotype of the subject and how the subject compares.

Scale 6 (formerly known as the **Paranoia Scale [Pa]**) measures subject's ability to trust.

Scale 7 (formerly known as the **Psychasthenia Scale [Pt]**) measures whether the subject has entered into adulthood with or without unresolved issues.

Scale 8 (formerly known as the **Schizophrenia Scale [Sc]**) measures subject's ability to have original or unique thoughts and whether he or she can think outside the box.

Scale 9 (formerly known as the **Mania Scale [Ma]**) measures subject's psychic energy.

Scale 10 (formerly known as the **Social Introversion Scale [Si]**) measures whether the subject likes to be around other people.

SIDEBAR 6.6 Some Representative MMPI Items

1. I like mechanics magazines. (T/F)
13. I work under a great deal of tension. (T/F)
37. I have never been in trouble because of my sex behavior. (T/F)
69. I am very strongly attracted by members of my own sex. (T/F)
93. I think most people would lie to get ahead. (T/F)
101. I believe women should have as much sexual freedom as men. (T/F)
151. Someone has been trying to poison me. (T/F)
179. I am worried about sex matters. (T/F)
182. I am afraid of losing my mind. (T/F)
199. Children should be taught all the main facts of sex. (T/F)
231. I like to talk about sex. (T/F)
250. I don't blame anyone for trying to grab everything he can get in this world. (T/F)
297. I wish I were not bothered by thoughts about sex. (T/F)
315. I am sure I get a raw deal from life. (T/F)
302. I have never been in trouble because of my sex behavior. (T/F)
310. My sex life is satisfactory. (T/F)
320. Many of my dreams are about sex matters. (T/F)
430. I am attracted by members of the opposite sex. (T/F)
470. Sexual things disgust me. (T/F)
485. When a man is with a woman he is usually thinking about things related to her sex. (T/F)
519. There is something wrong with my sex organs. (T/F)
548. I never attend a sexy show if I can avoid it. (T/F)
558. A large number of people are guilty of bad sexual conduct. (T/F)
566. I like movie love scenes. (T/F)

Items used in the MMPI were developed using an *empirical keying approach*. This implies that the clinical scales were derived by selecting items that were endorsed by patients known to have been diagnosed with certain pathologies. The test provides clear, valid descriptions of people's problems, symptoms, and characteristics in broadly accepted clinical language. The profiles are easy to explain in court and appear to be relatively easy for people to understand. If a subject tends to lie deliberately, it can be detected by several validity scales built within the test. For example, Item 60 in the test is "I do not read every editorial in the newspaper every day." For most people the answer is "True," as one really does not read every editorial every day. If someone scored this "False," he is probably lying. Several such items are interspersed within the test to indicate whether the person was lying.

The **MMPI** was completely revised in **1989 (MMPI-2)**, and now consists of **567 items.**[52] In addition to ten clinical scales already mentioned, it has nine validity scales (or "lie" scales), assessing for lying, defensiveness, faking good and faking bad, and so on. These scales make it very difficult to fake the MMPI-2 results.[53]

The **MMPI** (and now **MMPI-2**) are the most frequently used personality tests in mental health, especially in forensic contexts. The tests have been used effectively in the evaluation of paraphiles[54,55] and sex offenders.[56–64] MMPI has been administered to necrophiles to assess their personalities.[65] The MMPI is *only one element* of psychological assessment, and is never used as the sole basis for a diagnosis.

The MMPI responses of Jeffrey Dahmer are illustrative. They did not reveal a violent killer. Instead the responses showed a mild-mannered, outwardly harmless, socially confident, and skillful person. His MMPI item responses endorse not minding meeting strangers, being inclined to initiate conversation and sustain it when he did so, making friends as quickly as others, and loving to go to dances.[65]

SIDEBAR 6.7 Some MMPI Responses by Jeffrey Dahmer[65]

9. I am about as able to work as I ever was—True
24. No one seems to understand me—True
67. I wish I could be as happy as others seem to be—True
128. The sight of blood neither frightens me nor makes me sick—True
131. I do not worry about catching diseases—False
133. I have never indulged in any unusual sex practices—False
180. I find it hard to make talk when I meet new people—False
239. I have been disappointed in love—True
270. When I leave home I do not worry about whether the door is locked and the windows closed—False
292. I am likely not to speak to people until they speak to me—False
305. Even when I am with people I feel lonely much of the time—True
309. I seem to make friends about as quickly as others do—True
327. My mother and father often made me obey even when I thought it was unreasonable—False
371. I love to go to dances—True
430. I am attracted by members of the opposite sex—False
458. The man who had the most to do with me when I was a child (such as my father, stepfather, etc.) was very strict with me—False
562. The one to whom I was most attached and whom I most admired was a woman. (Mother, sister, aunt, or other woman.)—False

Dahmer scored **considerably higher** on Scales 2, 4, 6, 7, and 8. He accepted his gay identity (item 430 of MMPI). To the question "The sight of blood neither frightens me nor makes me sick," Dahmer responded "true."[65] Significantly, he used to dismember corpses after he had killed his victims. Dahmer's MMPI further showed that he practiced safe sex and admitted to worrying about catching diseases. He always used condoms when engaging in sex with his guests or their corpses to prevent AIDS and other STDs. He also admitted to engaging in unusual sex practices.

Necrophiles who keep dead bodies in their homes may be security conscious—a trait revealed by MMPI (item 270 of MMPI). Dahmer installed two alarm systems and an artificial surveillance camera in his apartment and an extra lock on his front door, and admitted to worrying about whether he closed his windows and locked his door.[65]

Intelligence Testing

Intelligence testing of necrophiles may be done as part of their neuropsychological assessment. The best-known intelligence tests are the so-called Wechsler series of tests. The first in this series was the Wechsler-Bellevue

Intelligence Scale, which was introducted in 1939. In the 1950s, the standard test of intelligence was **Wechsler Adult Intelligence Scale (WAIS)**. In 1981, it was replaced by **WAIS-R,** in 1997 by **WAIS-III,** and in 2008 by **WAIS-IV.** Intelligence testing on a number of necrophiles has been done. The results are given in detail in Chapter 4, "Epidemiology of Necrophilia."

Phallometric Assessment

The most widely used physiological assessment of sexual behavior—albeit controversial—is **phallometry, penile plethysmography,** or **phalloplethysmography.**[66] The technique relies on the fact that sexual arousal causes penile erection. Thus any technique that could measure and quantify penile erection could in turn—in theory at least—quantify the levels of sexual arousal. The technique assumes that while a normal person would not be sexually aroused by aberrant sexual stimuli (say pictures of nude young children or dead bodies), a paraphile (e.g., a pedophile or necrophile) having an abnormal interest in such aberrant stimuli would. If a comparison were made of the levels of sexual arousal elicited by normal erotic stimuli (e.g., pictures of nude adult women) and aberrant erotic stimuli, a normal person would show a very high ratio in favor of normal erotic stimuli. A **necrophile,** however, would be much more intensely aroused by seeing **pictures of dead bodies** than by seeing similar pictures of nude adult women. Such arousals can be detected by **phallometry.**

Theoretically speaking, this technique could objectively diagnose any paraphile or sex offender. Thus a pedophile would be strongly aroused upon seeing pictures of nude young children, a homosexual upon seeing pictures of nude persons of the same sex, a fetishist upon seeing pictures of the object of his fetish (e.g., a shoe), a necrophile upon seeing pictures of a dead body, a zoophile upon seeing pictures of animals, and so on. This technique, however, has been most frequently used on pedophiles, homosexuals, and exhibitionists. Tichy,[67] for example, used this technique on pedophiles and exhibitionists and found it quite useful in differentiating this group from normal people.

There are two general methods for measuring changes in penis size: either measuring the change in penile volume or measuring the change in penile circumference. Both are equally satisfactory.

Not much has been published on whether necrophiles are really sexually excited by seeing pictures of the dead. Judging from the number of pictures and videos with overt necrophilic content on the Internet, however, it seems reasonable to believe that such pictures must be erotically stimulating to necrophiles. Trying phallometry on suspected necrophiles using pictures of the dead may be a good idea.

Rapoport[68] describes the case of a 50-year-old necrophile, W.R. (1890–?), who was sometimes stimulated by pictures. (For details of this case, please see Chapter 3, "Classification," under the heading "Class IV Necrophiles: Tactile Necrophiles.") Interestingly these were not pictures of the dead, but pictures of deceased people taken when they were alive. No phallometry was ever done on him, but from the description, it does appear that if it had been tried on him with the said pictures, the results would have been encouraging.

It appears that a vast variety of pictures with a necrophilic theme may be used for phallometry: pictures of dead persons, pictures of deceased people taken when they were alive, pictures of dead persons with nudity, pictures or videos of live persons having sex with the dead, pictures of persons mutilating a dead body, and so on.

Criminal Profiling

Criminal profiling is the process of inferring distinctive personality traits of an offender based on characteristics of the crime committed by him.

> **QUICK FACT 6.5**
>
> Criminal profiling is known by several names. Some of the more common ones are *behavioral profiling, crime scene analysis, criminal investigative analysis, criminal personality profiling, criminological profiling, offender profiling, psychological profiling,* and *socio-psychological profiling.*

Not all types of crime are suitable for profiling. In general, crimes most suitable for profiling are (1) violent crimes, (2) crimes in which there were signs of psychopathology, (3) attacks on strangers, (4) crimes believed to be part of a series, and (5) contact crimes, crimes in which the offender engaged in long conversations and communications with the victim.[69] According to Holmes and Holmes, types of crimes most suitable for profiling include sadistic torture in sexual assaults, evisceration, postmortem slashing and cutting, motiveless fire setting, lust and mutilation murder, rape, satanic and ritualistic crime, and pedophilia.[70] Thus necrophilic acts—especially serial necrophilic acts—are very suitable for offender profiling.

Criticisms

Criminal profiling has faced severe criticisms. It has been alleged that instead of helping investigators, a criminal profiler may often send the investigators off track. This happened with the profile of **Gary Ridgway** (see Chapter 5).

Linkage Analysis

Linkage analysis is a method whereby the victimology, crime scene characteristics, behavioral patterns, wound patterns, and other aspects of two or more crimes committed at different crime scenes are examined in an attempt to ascertain whether the crimes were committed by one offender. **Robert Lee Yates** and **Gary Ridgway** (the Green River Killer), both necrophiles, killed during the same period and in roughly the same region (Washington State). While at the time of the murders nobody knew the identity of either, linkage analysis could say they were different people. **Gary Ridgway** operated in King County, Washington, between 1982 and 2001. He strangled his victims, mostly with his arm, but he would also use ligatures. Most of his victims were either prostitutes or teenage runaways picked up along Pacific Highway South (State Route 99). **Robert Lee Yates** operated in Spokane County, Washington, between 1996 and 1998. All of his victims were prostitutes. He did not strangle them; he shot them through the head, usually with a Raven .25-caliber handgun. This kind of analysis indicated that there were two different killers involved—not just one.

Geographic Profiling

Geographic profiling is an information management system and investigative methodology that evaluates the locations of connected serial crimes to determine the most probable area of offender residence (Table 6.2). It can be applied in cases of serial murder, homicidal necrophilic acts, rape, arson, robbery, and bombings.

Table 6.2 Geographic Profiling: A Brief Glossary

Term	Definition
Anchor point	Offender's search base for hunting. Usually the home, but may be workplace.
Circle strategy	A strategy often used by geographic profilers, that states that a serial offender's home will be located within a circle whose diameter is defined by the distance between the offender's two furthermost offenses.
Cognitive map	The concept of an offender regarding the safety of areas around him to commit an offense. This map is built up through his daily activities and social transactions, so he comes to realize what is possible, where. An offender's cognitive map influences his *spatial behavior*. Also known as *mental map*.
Crime hot spots	Areas of concentrated crime. Also known simply as *hot spots*.
Crime mapping	A system to map, visualize, and analyze crime incident patterns. It is a key component of crime analysis. Mapping crime, using *Geographic Information Systems* (GIS), allows crime analysts to identify *crime hot spots*, along with other trends and patterns.

Table 6.2 Geographic Profiling: A Brief Glossary (Continued)

Term	Definition
CrimeStat	A specialized geographical profiling software developed by Ned Levine.
Criminal Geographical Targeting (CGT)	A technique developed by Kim Rossmo that combines concepts from *environmental criminology* with a mathematical model, based on a *distance decay* function.
Distance Decay	A geographical term that states that the interaction between two locales declines as the distance between them increases. In criminology, it would refer to an *increased possibility of interaction* between a criminal and his potential victim if the distance between them were less, and vice versa. In other words, a criminal would be likely to select a victim near his home base. This is usually because the offender knows the environs closer to his home better. A similar term is *friction of distance*.
Dragnet	A specialized geographical profiling software developed by David Canter.
Environmental criminology	The study of crime, criminality, and victimization as they relate to particular places. It also includes the study of ways individuals shape their activities spatially, and in so doing are in turn influenced by place-based or spatial factors. The environmental criminology approach was developed in the 1980s by Paul and Patricia Brantingham.
Friction of distance	A concept that states that interactions between two locales will tend to take place more often over shorter distances; quantity of interaction will decline with distance. This is because it takes effort, time, and money to cover distances. This concept is similar to *distance decay*.
Geographic Information System (GIS)	An information system that captures, stores, analyzes, manages, and presents data that is linked to location. Typically, it includes mapping software. It allows users to create interactive queries (user-created searches), analyze spatial information, edit data and maps, and present the results of all these operations.
Geographic profiling systems	Specialized software used for geographic profiling. Major examples are *CrimeStat* by Ned Levine, *Dragnet* by David Canter, and *Rigel* by Kim Rossmo.
Home range	Geographical area around the home of an offender in which he travels regularly. This area is generally close to his home. Every individual—offender or nonoffender—has a home range.
Hot spots	Same as *crime hot spots*.
Least effort principle	When multiple destinations of equal desirability are available, all else being equal, the closest one will be chosen by the criminal to find his targets.
Mental map	Same as *cognitive map*.
Offender activity space	Area representing an offender's crime site locations. Some geographic profiling strategies assume that this space contains offender's residence.
Rigel	A specialized geographical profiling software developed by Kim Rossmo.
Spatial behavior	The behavior of an offender in relation to the space around him. His behavior is not the same in all kinds of spaces surrounding him. Only those spaces are chosen for offender activity, which the offender thinks (his *mental map* of the area) are safe, both geographically and psychologically.

SIDEBAR 6.8 Stationary, Territorial, and Nomadic Necrophiles

Necrophiles who kill in order to procure a dead body for sexual intercourse tend to fall into three broad categories. The rarest are **stationary necrophiles.** These tend to kill within a very narrow region, for example, near their homes or work area. The commonest are **territorial necrophiles,** who kill over a larger area but confined within a state. **Nomadic necrophiles** kill over very large areas spanning across states, or even nations.

There is now credible evidence that offense locations tend to have a systematic relationship to where the offender resides. In the case of individuals who carry out a number of killings over a period of time, mainly of strangers, this relationship between residence and offense sites may be of significance in helping to identify the locations of offenders' homes. A homicidal necrophile is more likely to select his victim near his home (*distance decay*).

References

1. Geberth VJ. *Sex-Related Homicide and Death Investigation—Practical and Clinical Perspectives*, 1st ed. CRC Press, Boca Raton, FL, 2003, p. 174.
2. Torre C, Varetto L. An exceptional case of necrophilia. *Am J Forensic Med Pathol.* 1987 Jun;**8(2)**:169–171.
3. Simpson K. *Forty Years of Murder*. Grafton Books, London, 1988, pp. 234–252.
4. Rebmann A, David E, Sorg MH. *Cadaver Dog Handbook: Forensic Training and Tactics for the Recovery of Human Remains*, 1st ed. CRC Press, Boca Raton, FL, 2000.
5. Jackson R. *Francis Camps—Famous Case Histories of the Celebrated Pathologist.* Panther Books, London, 1983, pp. 70–97.
6. Rule A. *The Stranger Beside Me—Ted Bundy, The Shocking Inside Story*. W.W. Norton, New York, 1980.
7. von Wurmb-Schwark N, Ringleb A, Gebühr M, Simeoni E. Genetic analysis of modern and historical burned human remains. *Anthropol Anz.* 2005 Mar;**63(1)**:1–12.
8. Sivolap Y, Krivda G, Kozhuhova N, Chebotar S, Benecke M. A homicide in the Ukraine: DNA-based identification of a boiled, skeletonized, and varnished human skull, and of bone fragments found in a fireplace. *Am J Forensic Med Pathol.* 2001 Dec;**22(4)**:412–414.
9. Theodore Harcke H, Monaghan T, Yee N, Finelli L. Forensic imaging-guided recovery of nuclear DNA from the spinal cord. *J Forensic Sci.* 2009 Sep;**54(5)**:1123–1126.
10. Wickenheiser RA. Trace DNA: a review, discussion of theory, and application of the transfer of trace quantities of DNA through skin contact. *J Forensic Sci.* 2002 May;**47(3)**:442–450.
11. van Oorschot RA, Jones MK. DNA fingerprints from fingerprints. *Nature.* 1997 Jun 19;**387(6635)**:767.
12. van Oorschot RA, Treadwell S, Beaurepaire J, Holding NL, Mitchell RJ. Beware of the possibility of fingerprinting techniques transferring DNA. *J Forensic Sci.* 2005 Nov;**50(6)**:1417–1422.

13. Pizzamiglio M, Mameli AD, My LG. Forensic identification of a murderer by LCN DNA collected from the inside of the victim's car. *Int. Congr. Ser.* 2004;**1261**:437–439.
14. Wiegand P, Kleiber M. DNA typing of epithelial cells after strangulation. *Int J Legal Med.* 1997;**110(4)**:181–183.
15. Rutty GN. An investigation into the transference and survivability of human DNA following simulated manual strangulation with consideration of the problem of third party contamination. *Int J Legal Med.* 2002 Jun;**116(3)**:170–173.
16. Horsman-Hall KM, Orihuela Y, Karczynski SL, Davis AL, Ban JD, Greenspoon SA. Development of STR profiles from firearms and fired cartridge cases. *Forensic Sci Int Genet.* 2009 Sep;**3(4)**:242–250.
17. Hochmeister MN, Budowle B, Jung J, Borer UV, Comey CT, Dirnhofer R. PCR-based typing of DNA extracted from cigarette butts. *Int J Legal Med.* 1991;**104(4)**:229–233.
18. Watanabe Y, Takayama T, Hirata K, Yamada S, Nagai A, Nakamura I, Bunai Y, Ohya I. DNA typing from cigarette butts. *Leg Med (Tokyo).* 2003 Mar;**5 Suppl 1**:S177–S179.
19. Lowe A, Murray C, Whitaker J, Tully G, Gill P. The propensity of individuals to deposit DNA and secondary transfer of low level DNA from individuals to inert surfaces. *Forensic Sci Int.* 2002 Sep 10;**129(1)**:25–34.
20. Bauer M, Tatschner T, Patzelt D. Digital imaging of the dissection and sexual abuse of a corpse—an exceptional case of necrophilia. *Leg Med (Tokyo).* 2007 May;**9(3)**:143–146.
21. Calloway AR, Jones PF, Siegel S, Stupian GW. Location of seminal stains by their phosphorescence and its use in determining the order of deposition of overlapping seminal and bloodstains. *J Forensic Sci Soc.* 1973 Jul;**13(3)**:223–230.
22. Montagna CP. The recovery of seminal components and DNA from the vagina of a homicide victim 34 days postmortem. *J Forensic Sci.* 1996 Jul;**41(4)**:700–702.
23. Kennedy L. *Ten Rillington Place.* Victor Gollancz, London, 1961.
24. Douglas J, Burgess AW, Burgess AG, Ressler RK. *Crime Classification Manual: A Standard System for Investigating and Classifying Violent Crimes*, 2nd ed. Jossey-Bass, San Francisco, CA, 2006, p. 238.
25. Jones EL. The identification of semen and other body fluids, in *Forensic Science Handbook*, Vol. II, 2nd ed. Ed., R Saferstein. Pearson Education, Upper Saddle River, NJ, 2005, Chap. 8.
26. Sweet D, Lorente M, Lorente JA, Valenzuela A, Villanueva E. An improved method to recover saliva from human skin: the double swab technique. *J Forensic Sci.* 1997;**42(2)**:320–322.
27. Sweet D, Lorente JA, Valenzuela A, Lorente M, Villanueva E. PCR-based DNA typing of saliva stains recovered from human skin. *J Forensic Sci.* 1997;**42(3)**:447–451.
28. Sweet D, Shutler GG. Analysis of salivary DNA evidence from a bite mark on a body submerged in water. *J Forensic Sci.* 1999;**44(5)**:1069–1072.
29. Lee S. Smile for new ID photos? Officials remain tight-lipped. *South China Morning Post*, July 6, 2003, p. 4.
30. Price DE. Necrophilia complicating a case of homicide. *Med Sci Law.* 1963 Apr;**3**:121–131.

31. Gray C. The detection and persistence of latent fingerprints on human skin: an assessment of the iodine-silver plate method. *J Forensic Sci Soc.* 1978 Jan–Apr;**18(1–2)**:47–52.
32. Nuckles DB, Herschaft EE, Whatmough LN. Forensic odontology in solving crimes: dental techniques and bite-mark evidence. *Gen Dent.* 1994 May–Jun;**42(3)**:210–214.
33. Silver WE, Souviron RR. *Dental Autopsy*, 1st ed. CRC Press, Boca Raton, FL, 2009.
34. Dorion RBJ. *Bitemark Evidence*, 1st ed. Marcel Dekker, New York, 2005, pp. 14–17.
35. Bowers CM. *Forensic Dental Evidence: An Investigator's Handbook*, 1st ed. Elsevier Academic Press, California, 2004.
36. *State v. Inman*, 350 A.2d 582 (Me. 1976).
37. *United States v. Moore*, 936 F.2d 1508.
38. *Yelder v. State*, 630 So.2d 92 (Ala.Cr.App. 1991).
39. Petersen LC. Lip Prints (thesis submitted to the National University, La Jolla, California, March 2006 for Master of Forensic Science). *Anil Aggrawal's Internet Journal of Forensic Medicine and Toxicology*, 2009;**10(1)**. http://www.geradts.com/anil/ij/vol_010_no_001/others/thesis/2/petersen_thesis.doc; Published: January 1, 2009. Accessed January 5, 2010.
40. Merkel H. Über den Glykogengehalt des Scheidenepithels, seine diagnostische Bedeutung und deren kritische Bewertung. [The glycogen content of the vaginal epithelium, its diagnostic significance and its critical evaluation] [In German]. *Dtsch. Z. ges. gericht. Med.* 1924;**4**:1–8.
41. Thomas F, Van Hecke W. The demonstration of recent sexual intercourse in the male by the lugol method. *Med Sci Law.* 1963 Apr;**3**:169–171.
42. Rothwell TJ, Harvey KJ. The limitations of the Lugol's iodine staining technique for the identification of vaginal epithelial cells. *J Forensic Sci Soc.* 1978 Jul–Oct;**18(3–4)**:181–184.
43. Hausmann R, Pregler C, Schellmann B. The value of the Lugol's iodine staining technique for the identification of vaginal epithelial cells. *Int J Legal Med.* 1994;**106(6)**:298–301.
44. Hausmann R, Schellmann B. Forensic value of the Lugol's staining method: further studies on glycogenated epithelium in the male urinary tract. *Int J Legal Med.* 1994;**107(3)**:147–151.
45. Wilson C, Pitman P. *Encyclopedia of Murder.* Pan Books, London, 1984, pp. 165–171.
46. Murray AD. The reclassification of extreme pornographic images. *Modern Law Review.* 2009 Jan;**72(1)**:73–90.
47. Farwell LA, Donchin E. The truth will out: interrogative polygraphy ("lie detection") with event-related brain potentials. *Psychophysiology.* 1991 Sep;**28(5)**:531–541.
48. Farwell LA, Smith SS. Using brain MERMER testing to detect knowledge despite efforts to conceal. *J Forensic Sci.* 2001 Jan;**46(1)**:135–143.
49. Noida killers undergo brain-mapping tests. January 07, 2007. Available at http://www.rediff.com/news/2007/jan/07noida.htm. Accessed March 11, 2010.
50. Klaf FS, Brown W. Necrophilia, brief review and case report. *Psychiatric Q.* 1958;**32(4)**:645–652.

51. Moreau P. *Des aberrations du sens génésique*. Asselin & Houzeau, Paris, 1884.
52. Butcher JN, Dahlstrom WG, Graham JR, Tellegen AM, Kreammer B. *The Minnesota Multiphasic Personality Inventory-2 (MMPI-2) Manual for Administration and Scoring*. University of Minneapolis Press, Minneapolis, MN, 1989.
53. Drayton M. The Minnesota Multiphasic Personality Inventory-2 (MMPI-2). *Occup Med (Lond)*. 2009 Mar;**59(2)**:135–136.
54. Taylor AJ, McLachlan DG. MMPI profiles of six transvestites. *J Clin Psychol*. 1963 Jul;**19**:330–332.
55. Blank L, Roth RH. Voyeurism and exhibitionism. *Percept Mot Skills*. 1967 Apr;**24(2)**:391–400.
56. Cutter F. Self-rejection distress: a new MMPI scale. *J Clin Psychol*. 1964 Jan;**20**:150–153.
57. Hartman BJ. Comparison of selected experimental MMPI profiles of sexual deviates and sociopaths without sexual deviation. *Psychol Rep*. 1967 Feb;**20(1)**:234.
58. Rosen AC. Brief report of MMPI characteristics of sexual deviation. *Psychol Rep*. 1974 Aug;**35(1)**:73–74. No abstract available.
59. Rader CM. MMPI profile types of exposers, rapists, and assaulters in a court services population. *J Consult Clin* Psychol. 1977 Feb;**45(1)**:61–69.
60. Armentrout JA, Hauer AL. MMPIs of rapists of adults, rapists of children, and non-rapist sex offenders. *J Clin Psychol*. 1978 Apr;**34(2)**:330–332.
61. Lanyon RI, Lutz RW. MMPI discrimination of defensive and nondefensive felony sex offenders. *J Consult Clin Psychol*. 1984 Oct;**52(5)**:841–843.
62. Hall GC, Maiuro RD, Vitaliano PP, Proctor WC. The utility of the MMPI with men who have sexually assaulted children. *J Consult Clin Psychol*. 1986 Aug;**54(4)**:493–496.
63. Kalichman SC. Affective and personality characteristics of MMPI profile subgroups of incarcerated rapists. *Arch Sex Behav*. 1990 Oct;**19(5)**:443–459.
64. Curnoe S, Langevin R. Personality and deviant sexual fantasies: an examination of the MMPIs of sex offenders. *J Clin Psychol*. 2002 Jul;**58(7)**:803–815.
65. Nichols DS. Tell me a story: MMPI responses and personal biography in the case of a serial killer. *J Pers Assess*. 2006 Jun;**86(3)**:242–262.
66. Aggrawal, A. *Forensic and Medico-legal Aspects of Sexual Crimes and Unusual Sexual Practices*. CRC Press, Boca Raton, FL, 2008, chap. 1.
67. Tichy P. Phalloplethysmography findings in pedophilia and exhibitionism offenders. *Cas Lek Cesk*, 1996;**135**:521–524.
68. Rapoport J. A case of necrophilia. *J Criminal Psychopathol*. 1942;**4**:277–289.
69. Ebisike N. *Offender Profiling in the Courtroom—The Use and Abuse of Expert Witness Testimony*, 1st ed. Praeger, Westport, CT, 2008.
70. Holmes RM, Holmes ST (Eds.). *Profiling Violent Crimes: An Investigative Tool*, 4th ed. Sage Publications, London, 2008.

Legal and Ethical Aspects of Necrophilia

7

You'd think a state which unfortunately has seen the likes of Ed Gein and Jeffery Dahmer would have addressed this issue (a comprehensive law against necrophilia) long ago.

Wisconsin State Senator Dale Schultz after Circuit Judge George S. Curry dismissed the charge of necrophilia against the Grunke twins and Dustin Radke, who attempted sexual intercourse with the dead body of Laura Tennesen in 2006, stating that there was no specific law against necrophilia in Wisconsin.

Legal Aspects of Necrophilia

In many nations and jurisdictions, there are no specific laws against sexual intercourse with a corpse. Thus any necrophiles who are caught have to be charged under related laws, such as "disturbing the peace of the dead," "defiling a dead body," "disturbing law and order," and "hurting sentiments of relatives." An interesting situation may arise if a fresh corpse is found in the possession of a necrophile and sexual intercourse is proved (e.g., by detection of offender's semen in the dead body). In such a case, the prosecution may try to prove that sexual intercourse was performed on the woman during life, and the woman was perhaps killed later. This would bring a more grave charge of rape and murder upon the offender. Since having intercourse with a dead woman is not rape, the defense would try proving it was a case of sexual intercourse *after* the woman's death, making it a case of necrophilia and attracting a far less severe sentence. From a medical standpoint, it is a matter of settling the question of antemortem or postmortem sexual intercourse. This is not an entirely hypothetical situation. Similar questions have been raised in Pandher and Koli's case recently. The cases are still under trial.

Laws relating to necrophilia in some major nations and jurisdictions are as below.

Australia

Western Australia

The Criminal Code of Western Australia does not mention the word *necrophilia* explicitly, but Section 214 of this code addresses the issue of "Misconduct with regard to corpses," which includes acts of necrophilia.

Necrophilia under this section is a misdemeanor, and the punishment is imprisonment for 2 years. It states,[1]

> Any person who, without lawful justification or excuse, the proof of which lies on him —
>
> (1) Neglects to perform any duty imposed upon him by law, or undertaken by him, whether for reward or otherwise, touching the burial or other disposition of a human body or human remains; or
> (2) Improperly or indecently interferes with, or offers any indignity to, any dead human body or human remains, whether buried or not;
>
> is guilty of a misdemeanor, and is liable to imprisonment for 2 years.
>
> Summary conviction penalty: Imprisonment for one year or a fine of $4,000.

Northern Territory

According to Section 140 ("Misconduct with regard to corpses") of the Criminal Code of Northern Territory, necrophilia is a crime and attracts a punishment of imprisonment up to 2 years. Section 140 states,

> Any person who, without authorization or excuse, the proof of which lies on him—
>
> (a) neglects to perform any duty imposed upon him by law or undertaken by him, whether for reward or otherwise, touching the burial or other disposition of a human body or human remains; or
> (b) improperly or indecently interferes with or offers any indignity to any dead human body or human remains whether buried or not, is guilty of a crime and is liable to imprisonment for 2 years.

New South Wales

The criminal law of New South Wales is governed by the *Crimes Act 1900*. While Division 10 of Part 3 of this act deals with most sexual offences, necrophilia is addressed by another division—Division 11, entitled "Misconduct with regard to corpses." It comprises just one section—section 81C. It states,

> Any person who:
>
> (a) indecently interferes with any dead human body, or
> (b) improperly interferes with, or offers any indignity to, any dead human body or human remains (whether buried or not),
>
> shall be liable to imprisonment for two years.

Tasmania

Necrophilia as such is not mentioned in the *Tasmanian Criminal Code Act 1924*. However, necrophilia is implicitly included in Section 139 ("Misconduct in respect of human remains") of this act, which is included in Chapter XIV, entitled "Crimes Against Morality." It states,[2]

> Any person who—
>
> (a) neglects to perform any duty, either imposed upon him by law or undertaken by him, with reference to the burial of any dead human body or human remains; or
> (b) improperly or indecently interferes with or offers any indignity to any dead human body or human remains, whether buried or not—
>   - is guilty of a crime.
>
> Charge:
>
> (a) Neglecting duty as to burial.
> (b) Interfering with human remains.

Any attempt at sexual intercourse with a dead body would be covered by clause (b) of the section (indecent interference or offering any indignity to any dead human body).

Victoria

According to Section 34B of the Crimes Act 1958 of Victoria, it is an offense to interfere with the corpse of a human being, either sexually or otherwise. Section 34 B states,[3]

> (1) A person must not intentionally—
>   (a) interfere sexually or commit an indecent act with a corpse of a human being; or
>   (b) unlawfully remove body parts from a corpse of a human being—
>
>   whether that corpse is in a public cemetery within the meaning of the Cemeteries and Crematoria Act 2003 or at any other place. Penalty: Level 6 (5 years maximum).
>
> (2) Subsection (1) does not apply to—
>   (a) any person who is engaged in the preparation of a corpse of a human being for the purposes of interment or cremation within the meaning of the Cemeteries and Crematoria Act 2003; or
>   (b) any other lawful interference with a corpse of a human being, including a lawful interference for the purposes of a medical, scientific or hygienic procedure.

Canada

The Criminal Code of Canada is a very comprehensive document containing 849 sections divided in 28 parts. Of these, **part V** (s 150–182) deals

Table 7.1 Necrophilia: Definition and Punishment under Section 182 of the Criminal Code of Canada

Dead body	182. Every one who (a) neglects, without lawful excuse, to perform any duty that is imposed on him by law or that he undertakes with reference to the burial of a dead human body or human remains, or (b) improperly or indecently interferes with or offers any indignity to a dead human body or human remains, whether buried or not, is guilty of an indictable offence and liable to imprisonment for a term not exceeding five years.

with sexual offenses, public morals, and disorderly conduct. According to **Section 182** of the **Criminal Code of Canada,**[4] necrophilia is an offense (Table 7.1).

France

In France, article L225-17 of French Penal Code makes necrophilia an offense. It allows the judge to punish necrophiles for "affect on the integrity of a corpse." The punishment is 1 year of prison and up to 15,000 euros.[5]

Germany

The German Criminal Code (Strafgesetzbuch, StGB) has ample provisions for punishment of necrophilia. The Code has 358 sections divided in 30 chapters. Chapter 11 (sections 166–168) deals with "crimes which relate to religion and philosophy of life." Section 168 entitled "Disturbing the Peace of the Dead" states,[6]

(1) Whoever, without authorization, takes away the body or parts of the body of a deceased person, a dead fetus or parts thereof or the ashes of a deceased person from the custody of the person entitled thereto, or whoever commits insulting mischief thereon, shall be punished with imprisonment for **not more than three years** or a **fine.**
(2) Whoever destroys or damages a place for lying-in-state, burial site or public place for remembering the dead, or whoever commits insulting mischief there, shall be similarly punished.
(3) An attempt shall be punishable.

This section has been used against necrophiles. Bauer and colleagues[7] describe the case of a 40-year-old, married civil engineer who was prosecuted under this section and given a sentence of 2 years and 3 months in prison. (For details, please see Chapter 6, "Medico-legal Investigation.")

A further section (section 211) appears aimed specifically at class IX necrophiles. It states,[8]

(1) The murderer shall be punished with imprisonment for life.
(2) A murderer is, whoever kills a human being out of murderous lust, to satisfy his sexual desires, from greed or otherwise base motives, treacherously or cruelly or with means dangerous to the public or in order to make another crime possible or cover it up.

Quite clearly it does not make much difference why the killing was done. A killing done for, for example, greed is as heinous as a killing done to satisfy sexual desires. But the specific mention of this phrase in German Penal Code is interesting.

India

In India, there is no explicit law, as in the United Kingdom, regarding necrophilia. However, section 297 of Indian Penal Code (IPC),[9] entitled "Trespassing on burial places, etc.," addresses this perversion to some extent. It states,

> Whoever, with the intention of wounding the feelings of any person, or of insulting the religion of any person, or with the knowledge that the feelings of any person are likely to be wounded, or that the religion of any person is likely to be insulted thereby, commits any trespass in any place of worship or on any place of sculpture, or any place set apart from the performance of funeral rites or as a depository for the remains of the dead, or offers any indignity to any human corpse, or causes disturbance to any persons assembled for the performance of funeral ceremonies, shall be punished with imprisonment of either description for a term which may extend to one year, or with fine, or with both.

Gravediggers and mortuary attendants, who are the professionals most often found practicing necrophilia, engage in this activity perhaps because of their loneliness, coupled with easy access to corpses. There have been several allegations by relatives of dead women that the dead bodies of their kin were defiled in the night by mortuary attendants, but none have been proved. The possibility of such an act taking place on a regular basis is not impossible to imagine. Medical students have also been found occasionally to have sex with corpses, for similar reasons.

This author has personally been involved as an autopsy expert in a case where a woman was alleged to have been raped and murdered and the autopsy surgeon failed to find any signs of rape. In such cases, the relatives have approached the authorities for a second postmortem (a phenomenon that is not uncommon in India). The second postmortem is invariably conducted at a different hospital, often necessitating that the body be deposited overnight at the mortuary of the second hospital. In cases where the second autopsy surgeon finds signs of rape, the defendants have been known to allege that the dead body was defiled by drunk mortuary attendants at night. None of such allegations has been proved in a court of law, however.

South Africa

According to the **Criminal Law (Sexual Offences and Related Matters) Amendment Act 2007** of the Republic of South Africa, sexual act with corpse is punishable under section 14. It states,[10]

> *A person who unlawfully and intentionally commits a sexual act with a human* corpse, is guilty of the offence of committing a sexual act with a corpse.

The meaning of sexual act is defined within the act.

United Kingdom

According to section 70 of the Sexual Offences Act 2003 of the United Kingdom,[11] sexual penetration of a corpse is an offense (Table 7.2).

Exposing a naked corpse in public is a public nuisance (*R v. Clark [1883] 15 Cox 171*).

Table 7.2 Necrophilia: Definition and Punishment under Section 70 of the Sexual Offences Act 2003 of the United Kingdom

70 Sexual penetration of a corpse
- (1) A person commits an offence if
  - (a) he intentionally performs an act of penetration with a part of his body or anything else,
  - (b) what is penetrated is a part of the body of a dead person,
  - (c) he knows that, or is reckless as to whether, that is what is penetrated, and
  - (d) the penetration is sexual.
- (2) A person guilty of an offence under this section is liable
  - (a) on summary conviction, to imprisonment for a term not exceeding 6 months or a fine not exceeding the statutory maximum or both;
  - (b) on conviction on indictment, to imprisonment for a term not exceeding 2 years.

When **Graham Coutts** committed his acts of necrophilia (in 2003), it was not an offense in the United Kingdom, so he could not be charged with necrophilia. (For details of his case, please see Chapter 5, "Case Studies.") However, his computer was found to contain a number of **violent pornographic images,** and his case signaled the beginning of a campaign to ban possession of violent images. On May 8, 2008, the efforts reached fruition, when **s.63** of the **Criminal Justice and Immigration Act 2008** was promulgated, which made possession of extreme pornographic images illegal. It was brought into force in January 2009 by Order of the Secretary of State.[12]

United States

In the United States, there are no federal laws regarding necrophilia.[13] Laws related to necrophilia have been left up to the individual states. Section 250.10 of the Model Penal Code (MPC), a statutory text developed by the American Law Institute (ALI) in 1962 to stimulate and assist legislatures in making an effort to update and standardize the penal law throughout the United States, makes it a misdemeanor to treat a corpse in a way that "would outrage ordinary family sensibilities."[14]

U.S. laws related to necrophilia have been discussed in great detail by Posner and Silbaugh.[13] They have included only those laws that specifically mention some kind of sexual conduct with a human corpse and have chosen not to mention any law that just prohibits derogatory and offensive treatment of human remains in general, without any explicit suggestion of sexual conduct with the corpse. It may be useful to have a look at necrophilia laws in some representative states.

Alabama

It is a misdemeanor to knowingly treat a human corpse in a way that would outrage ordinary family sensibilities.[15] Any person who willfully or maliciously desecrates, injures, defaces, removes, or destroys any tomb, monument, structure, or container of human remains, and invades or mutilates the human corpse or remains shall be guilty of a class C felony and upon conviction the person shall be punished as provided by law.[16] For a class C felony, the imprisonment is for more than 1 year and 1 day and less than 10 years.[17] The imprisonment includes hard labor. The fine is up to $15,000.[18]

Alaska

It is a class A misdemeanor to engage in sexual penetration of a corpse. Title 11 of Alaska Statutes describes the criminal law of Alaska. Chapter 61 under this Title describes "Offenses Against Public Order," and Section 130 of this chapter defines "Misconduct Involving a Corpse" as follows:[19]

> (a) A person commits the crime of misconduct involving a corpse if
> (1) except as authorized by law or in an emergency, the person intentionally disinters, removes, conceals, or mutilates a corpse;
> (2) the person engages in sexual penetration of a corpse; or
> (3) the person detains a corpse for a debt or demand or upon a lien or charge.
> (b) Misconduct involving a corpse is a class A misdemeanor.

Arizona

There is no specific statute against necrophilia in Arizona.

Arkansas

According to section 5-60-101 of the Code of Arkansas,[20] "Abuse of a corpse" is a class D felony. It states,

> (a) A person commits abuse of a corpse if, except as authorized by law, he or she knowingly:
> (1) Disinters, removes, dissects, or mutilates a corpse; or
> (2) Physically mistreats a corpse in a manner offensive to a person of reasonable sensibilities.
> (b) Abuse of a corpse is a Class D felony.

California

California did not have any specific law against necrophilia until 2004; therefore it was difficult to prosecute necrophiles. In a specific case, which evoked a great deal of controversy, a man charged with penetrating a dead 4-year-old girl in Southern California in 2003 could not be prosecuted. To prevent recurrence of such cases, on September 9, 2004, Governor **Arnold Schwarzenegger** made necrophilia officially illegal in California by amending **Section 7052** of the **Health and Safety Code,** relating to human remains. According to the amended Section 7052 of the Health and Safety Code of California (as amended in 2004) necrophilia is a felony. It states,[21]

> (a) Every person who willfully mutilates, disinters, removes from the place of interment, or commits an act of sexual penetration on, or has sexual contact with, any remains known to be human, without authority of law, is guilty of a **felony,** punishable by imprisonment in the state prison for three, six, or eight years. This section does not apply to any person

who, under authority of law, removes the remains for reinterment, or performs a cremation.

(b) For purposes of this section, the following definitions apply:
   (1) "**Sexual penetration**" means the unlawful penetration of the vagina or anus, however slight, by any part of a person's body or other object, or any act of sexual contact between the sex organs of a person and the mouth or anus of a dead body, or any oral copulation of a dead human body for the purpose of sexual arousal, gratification, or abuse.
   (2) "**Sexual contact**" means any willful touching by a person of an intimate part of a dead human body for the purpose of sexual arousal, gratification, or abuse.

Also according to Section 290 of the California Penal Code, a person convicted of specified sex offenses has to register his or her address with the law enforcement for life. The new amendment adds an act of sexual penetration on, or having sexual contact with, any remains known to be human to the list of specified sex offenses, the conviction for which requires registration as a sex offender with law enforcement.

Colorado

Section 18-13-101 ("Abuse of a corpse") of Colorado Revised Statute does not have a specific provision against sexual intercourse with the dead, but it does prohibit abuse of a corpse. Sexual intercourse with a corpse may outrage sensibilities of the family members and thus the act may attract the provisions of this section. It states,[22]

(1) A person commits abuse of a corpse if, without statutory or court-ordered authority, he or she:
   (a) Removes the body or remains of any person from a grave or other place of sepulcher without the consent of the person who has the right to dispose of the remains pursuant to section 15-19-106, C.R.S; or
   (b) Treats the body or remains of any person in a way that would outrage normal family sensibilities.

(2) Abuse of a corpse is a class 2 misdemeanor.

Connecticut

It is a misdemeanor to engage in sexual contact with a dead body. Section 53a-73a of the Connecticut Penal Code defines "Sexual assault in the fourth degree" (Class A misdemeanor or class D felony), which includes acts of necrophilia within its ambit. It states,[23]

(a) A person is guilty of sexual assault in the fourth degree when:
  (1) Such person intentionally subjects another person to sexual contact who is
    (A) under fifteen years of age, or
    (B) mentally defective or mentally incapacitated to the extent that such other person is unable to consent to such sexual contact, or
    (C) physically helpless, or
    (D) less than eighteen years old and the actor is such other person's guardian or otherwise responsible for the general supervision of such other person's welfare, or
    (E) in custody of law or detained in a hospital or other institution and the actor has supervisory or disciplinary authority over such other person; or
  (2) such person subjects another person to sexual contact without such other person's consent; or
  (3) such person engages in sexual contact with an animal or dead body; or
  (4) such person is a psychotherapist and subjects another person to sexual contact who is
    (A) a patient of the actor and the sexual contact occurs during the psychotherapy session, or
    (B) a patient or former patient of the actor and such patient or former patient is emotionally dependent upon the actor, or
    (C) a patient or former patient of the actor and the sexual contact occurs by means of therapeutic deception; or
  (5) such person subjects another person to sexual contact and accomplishes the sexual contact by means of false representation that the sexual contact is for a bona fide medical purpose by a health care professional; or
  (6) such person is a school employee and subjects another person to sexual contact who is a student enrolled in a school in which the actor works or a school under the jurisdiction of the local or regional board of education which employs the actor; or
  (7) such person is a coach in an athletic activity or a person who provides intensive, ongoing instruction and subjects another person to sexual contact who is a recipient of coaching or instruction from the actor and
    (A) is a secondary school student and receives such coaching or instruction in a secondary school setting, or
    (B) is under eighteen years of age.

(b) Sexual assault in the fourth degree is a class A misdemeanor or, if the victim of the offense is under sixteen years of age, a class D felony.

As can be seen, the scope of this section is very wide. It covers a number of sexual crimes and paraphilias within it, including not only necrophilia (subsection (a)(3)), but also bestiality (subsection (a)(3)).

Delaware

In Delaware law, there is no specific mention of sexual intercourse with a corpse, but abusing a corpse is a class A misdemeanor under Section 11-5-1332. It states,[24]

> A person is guilty of abusing a corpse when, except as authorized by law, the person treats a corpse in a way that a reasonable person knows would outrage ordinary family sensibilities.
>
> Abusing a corpse is a class A misdemeanor.

According to section 4206 of Delaware Code, the sentence for a class A misdemeanor may include up to 1 year incarceration at level V and such fine up to $2300, restitution, or other conditions as the court deems appropriate.[25]

Georgia

Necrophilia is a felony in the state of Georgia. Section 16-6-7 of the law states,[26]

> (a) A person commits the offense of necrophilia when he performs any sexual act with a dead human body involving the sex organs of the one and the mouth, anus, penis, or vagina of the other.
> (b) A person convicted of the offense of necrophilia shall be punished by imprisonment for not less than one nor more than ten years.

In 2006, 54-year-old Parker Ward of Georgia was sentenced to 4 years in prison to be followed by 4 years of probation for an act of necrophilia he performed on a 43-year-old woman who had died of accidental drug overdose in her camper on the night of December 27, 2005. Finding her motionless, her boyfriend had asked Ward to check on her. Ward tried to give her mouth-to-mouth respiration. When there was no response, Ward realized she was dead. He then had sex with the corpse and afterward called 911. It was later estimated that the victim had been dead for about 4 hours when Ward had sex with her. Her body was cold and rigor mortis had set in. Ward took the defense that he was drunk, as he had about six rum drinks on that night, but the plea was not entertained.

Hawaii

Chapter 711 of Hawaii Revised Statutes deals with "offenses against public order." Section 711-1108 within this chapter is entitled "Abuse of a corpse." It states,[27]

> (1) A person commits the offense of abuse of a corpse if, except as authorized by law, the person treats a human corpse in a way that the person knows would outrage ordinary family sensibilities.
> (2) Abuse of a corpse is a misdemeanor.

Commentary following this section states, "this section prohibits any sort of outrageous treatment of a human corpse, including sexual contact (necrophilia) and physical abuse. It does not, of course, relate to legally authorized activities of undertakers and physicians. Knowledge that ordinary family sensibilities would be outraged must be proved."

Iowa

In Iowa, necrophilia is a class D felony. Section 709.18 ("Abuse of a corpse") of Iowa code states,[28]

> A person commits abuse of a human corpse if the person knowingly and intentionally engages in a sex act, as defined in Section 702.17, with a human corpse. Abuse of a human corpse is a class "D" felony.

Section 702.17 defines the sex act as follows:

> The term "sex act" or "sexual activity" means any sexual contact between two or more persons by: penetration of the penis into the vagina or anus; contact between the mouth and genitalia or by contact between the genitalia of one person and the genitalia or anus of another person; contact between the finger or hand of one person and the genitalia or anus of another person, except in the course of examination or treatment by a person licensed pursuant to chapter 148, 148C, 150, 150A, 151, or 152; or by use of artificial sexual organs or substitutes therefore in contact with the genitalia or anus.

Thus even acts such as inserting a finger in the vagina of a corpse would be taken to mean as committing a sex act with the corpse, and would be punishable under Section 709.18 of the Iowa Code.

Indiana

Necrophilia is a class D felony in the state of Indiana. It is defined in Title 35, Article 45, Chapter 11, Sections 1 and 2 of Indiana Code. Chapter 11 is entitled "Abuse of a Corpse." Section 1 states,

> (a) This chapter does not apply to the use of a corpse for:
> (1) scientific;
> (2) medical;
> (3) organ transplantation;
> (4) historical;
> (5) forensic; or
> (6) investigative purposes.

(b) This chapter does not apply to:
    (1) a funeral director;
    (2) an embalmer; or
    (3) an employee of an individual described in subdivision (1) or (2); engaged in the individual's normal scope of practice and employment.

As added by P.L.249-1993, SEC.1.

Section 2 states:

A person who knowingly or intentionally:

(1) mutilates a corpse;
(2) has sexual intercourse or sexual deviate conduct with the corpse; or
(3) opens a casket with the intent to commit an act described in subdivision (1) or (2); commits abuse of a corpse, a Class D felony.

Kentucky

The state of Kentucky does not use the word *necrophilia* or "sex with a corpse" to outlaw necrophilia specifically. However, it does use the phrase "abuse of corpse." A corpse would be said to be abused whenever a person intentionally treats a corpse in a way that would outrage ordinary family sensibilities. Sex with a corpse would indeed outrage family sensibilities. Necrophilia is thus illegal in the state of Kentucky.

Section 525.120 ("Abuse of corpse") of Kentucky Revised Statutes (effective from July 15, 2002) states,[29]

(1) A person is guilty of abuse of a corpse when except as authorized by law he intentionally treats a corpse in a way that would outrage ordinary family sensibilities. A person shall also be guilty of abuse of a corpse if that person enters into a contract and accepts remuneration for the preparation of a corpse for burial or the burial or cremation of a corpse and then deliberately fails to prepare, bury, or cremate that corpse in accordance with that contract.
(2) Abuse of a corpse is a Class A misdemeanor, unless the act attempted or committed involved sexual intercourse or deviate sexual intercourse with the corpse or the deliberate failure to prepare, bury, or cremate a corpse after the acceptance of remuneration in accordance with any contract negotiated, in which case it is a Class D felony.

Michigan

Michigan does not have a specific law against necrophilia. However, if a person digs up a dead body (e.g., for intercourse), he may be charged under

Section 750.160 ("Disinterment, mutilation, defacement, or carrying away of human body; exception") of Michigan law. It states,[30]

> A person, not being lawfully authorized so to do, who shall willfully dig up, disinter, remove, or convey away a human body, or the remains thereof, from the place where the body may be interred or deposited, or who shall knowingly aid in such disinterment, removal, or conveying away, or who shall mutilate, deface, remove, or carry away a portion of the dead body of a person, whether in his charge for burial or otherwise, whenever the mutilation, defacement, removal, or carrying away is not necessary in any proper operation in embalming the body or for the purpose of a postmortem examination, and every person accessory thereto, either before or after the fact, shall be guilty of a felony, punishable by imprisonment for not more than 10 years, or by fine of not more than $5,000.00. This section shall not be construed to prohibit the digging up, disinterment, removal or carrying away for scientific purposes of the remains of prehistoric persons by representatives of established scientific institutions or societies, having the consent in writing of the owner of the land from which the remains may be disinterred, removed or carried away.

It is clear that under this law, carrying away of some body part as a trophy or as a possible masturbatory device (e.g., penis or breast) is prohibited as it would amount to mutilation and defacement of the dead body.

Ohio

Section 2927.01 of Ohio statute entitled "Abuse of a corpse" states,

> (A) No person, except as authorized by law, shall treat a human corpse in a way that the person knows would outrage reasonable family sensibilities.
> (B) No person, except as authorized by law, shall treat a human corpse in a way that would outrage reasonable community sensibilities.
> (C) Whoever violates division (A) of this section is guilty of abuse of a corpse, a misdemeanor of the second degree. Whoever violates division (B) of this section is guilty of gross abuse of a corpse, a felony of the fifth degree.

Pennsylvania

Section 5510 of Pennsylvania statute entitled "Abuse of a corpse" states,[31]

> Except as authorized by law, a person who treats a corpse in a way that he knows would outrage ordinary family sensibilities commits a misdemeanor.

Washington

Chapter 9A.44 of the Revised Code of Washington (RCW) deals with sex offenses. Section 9A.44.105 provides punishment for necrophilia ("Sexually violating human remains"). It states,

(1) Any person who has sexual intercourse or sexual contact with a dead human body is guilty of a class C felony.
(2) As used in this section:
(a) "Sexual intercourse" (i) has its ordinary meaning and occurs upon any penetration, however slight; and (ii) also means any penetration of the vagina or anus however slight, by an object, when committed on a dead human body, except when such penetration is accomplished as part of a procedure authorized or required under chapter 68.50 RCW or other law; and (iii) also means any act of sexual contact between the sex organs of a person and the mouth or anus of a dead human body.
(b) "Sexual contact" means any touching by a person of the sexual or other intimate parts of a dead human body done for the purpose of gratifying the sexual desire of the person.

Wisconsin

Section 940.225 of Wisconsin statute entitled "Sexual assault" mentions a number of sexual offenses including sexual assaults of four degrees, sexual contact including acts such as frotteurism. Subsection (7) of this section states,[32]

> (7) DEATH OF VICTIM. This section applies whether a victim is dead or alive at the time of the sexual contact or sexual intercourse.

This section quite clearly refers to necrophilia.[14] But in the famous Grunke case, the Grant County Circuit Court and the Wisconsin Court of Appeals ruled that it was not so (*State v. Grunke, 2007 WI App 198*). (Please see Chapter 5, "Case Studies.") In the Court of Appeals, the case was heard by justices Dykman, Vergeront, and Higginbotham. Judge Charles P. Dykman observed,

> The State asserts that the circuit court erred in concluding that § 940.225(7) allows prosecution for the sexual assault of a dead body only if the defendant committed the sexual assault in a series of acts including acts that caused the death of the victim. The State argues that § 940.225(7) unambiguously allows prosecution for the sexual assault of a dead body without limitation to the defendant's involvement in the death of the victim. We conclude that § 940.225(7) is ambiguous because it is subject to more than one reasonable interpretation. We conclude that the more reasonable interpretation is that § 940.225(7) was intended by the legislature to allow a sexual assault charge to succeed where a defendant sexually assaulted and caused the death of his victim and the sequence of events is unclear, rather than to criminalize necrophilia generally. Accordingly, we affirm. . . . We conclude that the legislature did not enact Wis. Stat. § 940.225(7) as a general necrophilia statute, which would criminalize Grunke's conduct.

Table 7.3 Comparison of Laws Relating to Necrophilia in Some Select Nations and Jurisdictions

Country/ Jurisdiction	Maximum Imprisonment	Maximum Fine	Relevant Law Regarding Necrophilia
Canada	Up to 5 years	—	Section 182 of the Criminal Code of Canada
France	1 year	15,000 euros	Article L225-17 of French Penal Code
Germany	3 years	Any amount	Section 168 of The German Criminal Code (Strafgesetzbuch, StGB)
India	1 year	Any amount	Section 297 of Indian Penal Code
UK	Up to 6 months on summary conviction and up to 2 years on conviction on indictment	Not exceeding the statutory maximum	Section 70 of the Sexual Offences Act 2003

Thus, for a time, it began to appear that Wisconsin had no specific statute against necrophilia. However, on July 9, 2008, the Wisconsin Supreme Court in a 5-2 decision ruled that the statute did refer to necrophilia.[33,34]

Comparing and Contrasting Various Laws Regarding Necrophilia

Table 7.3 compares and contrasts various laws related to necrophilia in different countries and jurisdictions.

Ethical Aspects of Necrophilia

Ethics, or **moral philosophy**, is a branch of philosophy that seeks to address questions about morality. Concepts such as *good* and *bad*, *right* and *wrong*, *justice*, and *virtue* are examined under this branch.

KEY POINT 7.1

Ethics may be studied under several sub-branches. The following questions typify what each major breach of **ethics** deals with:

Descriptive ethics: What is it that people think is right?
Prescriptive (normative) ethics: How should people act?
Applied ethics: How do we take moral knowledge and put it into practice?
Meta-ethics: What does *right* mean?

Not much has been written on the ethics of necrophilia. People who feel necrophilia is *ethically correct* are **pronecrophiles;** people who feel necrophilia is *ethically incorrect* or *wrong* are **antinecrophiles.** Both have their own set of arguments. One of the most detailed analyses on this issue has been done by McKearn.[35] She argues that *necrophilia is morally not wrong*. However, she is quick to add that she *does not encourage the practice,* because it is legally, socially, or hygienically not supported. Her argument for support is solely on ethical grounds.

McKearn[35] argues that once a person dies, his corpse loses **personhood** or **personal identity.** Necrophilia is held wrong by people who tend to associate the corpse with the person who once inhabited it. On this basis they claim that necrophilia violates the rights of said person.

However, this argument fails in light of the notion of personal identity. However one tries to understand personal identity, it is always lost after death. According to one view—that of **John Locke** (1632–1704) and **Thomas Reid** (1710–1796)—the body is simply a receptacle for the person, comparable to an airplane and its pilot, respectively. Naturally, the person is the more valued aspect as it determines one's identity, and the body is merely the flesh that contains it. The *person* evacuates the *physical body* upon biological death. This is comparable to the pilot of the plane ejecting himself from the cockpit and landing safely on the ground as his faithful vessel crashes and burns.

Another view of personal identity is that of **David Hume** (1711–1776) and **Derek Parfit** (1942–), who suggest that one's identity is composed of one's perceptions or psychology. According to this view, a person's death is comparable to the pilot dying within the plane as it careens into an unforgiving cliff face. Either way, the corpse contains no properties of the person after biological death. The body lying in the casket is merely a shell of the person who once occupied it.

According to yet another view, the following six characteristics are central to the concept of personhood:[36]

- **Sentience**—The capacity to have conscious experiences, usually including the capacity to experience pain and pleasure.
- **Emotionality**—The capacity to feel happy, angry, sad, loving, etc.
- **Reason**—The capacity to solve new and relatively complex problems.
- **Capacity to communicate**—By whatever means, messages of an indefinite variety of types.
- **Self-awareness**—Having a concept of oneself as an individual and/or as a member of a social group.
- **Moral agency**—The capacity to regulate one's own actions through moral principles or ideals.

An entity need not have *all* of these attributes to be a person. And none of them is absolutely necessary. Some people may be unemotional, some cannot communicate well, some lack self-awareness, and some are not moral agents. Many people would in fact not meet all the criteria of personhood. But if all six are missing (as in a fetus, according to the author), the entity cannot be called a person.

SIDEBAR 7.1 Mary Anne Warren's Concept of Person and Personhood—Are Fetuses and Corpses Persons?

Mary Anne Warren is an American writer and philosophy professor noted for her writings on the issue of *abortion*. In relation to fetuses, she argues convincingly that fetuses are *not persons* and thus can be aborted. Interestingly, the very same arguments could be applied to a dead person justifying necrophilia on moral grounds.

Warren starts by asking, "What does 'human' mean?"

Many would reply that "human" means "genetically human." Let us designate a human in that sense as human^G. Warren however takes a more "Kantian" view of "human"—human in the *moral* sense. Such a human may be designated as human^M. Being human^M implies (1) that one is a member of the moral community (i.e., one is bound by the commands of morality); and (2) that one possesses the rights and duties accompanying such membership. Warren argues that the word "person" should designate only human^M.

She further states that **human^M ≠ human^G.**

Some humans^G are not humans^M (e.g., infants, severely retarded people) and some humans^M are not humans^G (e.g., intelligent ETs, angels, etc., if they exist). None of this is controversial in philosophy.

Furthermore, an entity can have rights only if it has corresponding duties. One acquires a right as a consequence of the fact that one is capable of acting from duty, in other words, as a consequence of being a member of the moral community. *No duties mean no rights.*

Creatures with no possible duties have no rights. This is one reason why animals can be killed for food. **Since animals are thought to have no duties, they have no rights.**

According to Warren, fetuses are human^G only; they are not human^M. Because "person" means human^M, fetuses are not persons. Thus, according to Warren, they have no right to life and abortion is always permissible. One could extend the very same argument to corpses and assert that corpses are not human^M, and thus have no rights. Necrophilia thus—**at least ethically or morally**—is not wrong.

It is important to note that the author is trying to prove that a fetus is not a person (thus asserting that abortion is morally right). However, the same criteria may be applied to a corpse to state that *a corpse is not a person.*

Since a corpse has lost its personal identity (whichever way one looks at it), necrophiles are not disrespecting a person by having sex with a corpse (Table 7.4).

The Issue of Consent

Antinecrophiles would assert that necrophilia is wrong because the dead person would not have given consent for sexual intercourse, at least to a particular person during life. (The issue of a wife giving consent to postmortem sex to her husband is far from solved; please see Points to Ponder 7.2.) However, for several other activities in which a dead person's body or organs are intended to be used, a cover of **presumed consent** is often made. While many jurisdictions (e.g., the United States) operate under a system of

Table 7.4 Ethics of Necrophilia: A Brief Glossary

Term	Definition
Descriptive ethics (comparative ethics)	The study of people's beliefs about morality, e.g., determining **what proportion of people believe that necrophilia is wrong.** Of all categories of ethics, descriptive ethics is perhaps the easiest to understand—it simply involves **describing** how people behave and/or what sorts of moral standards they claim to follow. Descriptive ethics incorporates research from the fields of anthropology, psychology, sociology, and history as part of the process of understanding what people do or have believed about moral norms.
Ethical relativism	Also known as *moral relativism*. Concerned with the issue of differences in moral or ethical judgments between different people and cultures. For instance, *while necrophilia may be considered wrong by most cultures, it may be right for some other cultures.*
Ethics (moral philosophy)	A branch of philosophy that seeks to address questions about morality. It is concerned with concepts such as *good* and *bad*, *right* and *wrong*, *justice*, *virtue*, etc. **Ethics of necrophilia** is concerned with such questions as whether necrophilia is good or bad, right or wrong, justified, or not, and so on.
Prescriptive ethics (normative ethics, moral theory)	The study of ethical theories that prescribe how people *ought* to act. Concerned with **whether it is correct to hold the belief that necrophilia is wrong.**
Utilitarianism	An idea championed by the English jurist and philosopher **Jeremy Bentham** (1748–1832), and supported by **John Stuart Mill** (1806–1873). It asserts that the moral worth of an action is determined solely by its contribution to overall utility, i.e., its contribution to happiness or pleasure as summed among *all* people. The idea is often described by the phrase "the greatest good for the greatest number of people." According to utilitarianism, necrophilia is not correct, because although it might bring joy to one person (necrophile), it brings grief to several others (relatives of the victim, society). Since the grief of several people is far greater than the joy of one necrophile, necrophilia is not correct.

"expressed volunteerism," with consent received from donors and their families, other countries such as Spain, Belgium, and Austria use an "opt-out" policy frequently referred to as "presumed consent." Although the exact implementation varies, the general concept is that individuals opposed to donating their organs may list their objection on a national registry, rendering them ineligible to donate.

Adopting the rule of presumed consent, France revised its Bioethics Laws in 2004, whereby organ harvesting from cadaveric donors is permissible if the deceased did not make known his refusal during his lifetime.[37] This may be recorded in the national registry set up for this purpose.

Presumed Consent for Organ Donation and for Necrophilia—Are There Parallels?

When so many jurisdictions do not have any qualms about presumed consent in relation to organ donation, why are presumed consent and the so-called opt-out policy not applicable to necrophilic acts? The equivalent of opt-out policy in the present context would effectively imply that "if a person did not make known his refusal for sexual intercourse with his body after death, sexual intercourse would be permissible." What is the difference between the two?

A very simple answer is that while organ transplantation is being done for the larger good of the society, necrophilia does not serve any good purpose for the society. Presumed consent for organ donation is also justified by the **social contract theory,** which implies that the people give up some rights (the right not to donate organs, for instance) to a government or other authority in order to receive some benefits. The benefits received by people are maintenance of social order through the rule of law. Quite obviously the issue of the "larger good of the society" and "social contract theory" cannot be invoked by pronecrophiles to presume consent for sexual intercourse.

KEY POINT 7.2

Social contract theory assumes that organs and tissues belong to the State or to society rather than to individuals or families. **Presumed consent** thus can quite easily be justified for organ donation. This argument cannot easily be invoked for necrophilic activities.

Even for organ donation, presumed consent has been criticized on many grounds. It has been argued that presumed consent disregards autonomy, privacy, and the right to choose how one's body will be used after one's death. A "presumed consent" can also be considered analogous to the clearly unacceptable practice of taking the silence of a young woman as her consent to marry a 75-year-old groom.[38] In fact, the term sounds like an oxymoron along the lines of "honor killing" or "jumbo shrimp."[38]

Necrophilia from a Hedonistic Viewpoint

Necrophilic activities from a hedonistic point of view would be deemed correct. **Hedonism** is based on the **pleasure principle,** which states that pleasure (including the absence of pain) is the sole intrinsic good in life.[39] Since sexual intercourse with the dead gives pleasure to the necrophile, it must be the right action. Hedonists hold that, questions of morality aside, all persons inevitably do seek pleasure (**psychological hedonism**). Further they hold that, questions of psychology aside, morally one should seek pleasure (**ethical hedonism**) and that one inevitably does, and ought to, seek pleasure (ethical and psychological hedonism combined).

POINT TO PONDER 7.1

One of the greatest champions of hedonism, the Greek philosopher **Anniceris** (fl. c. 320–280 BC), would have probably thought that **necrophilia is ethically correct.** He subscribed to typical Cyrenaic hedonism, arguing that the end of each action should be one's own pleasure, since we can know nothing of others' experiences. In the case of the dead, the problem is even simpler, as the other person is dead and cannot have any experience whatsoever.

POINT TO PONDER 7.2

The issue of *ethics of necrophilia* is far from solved. Some burning issues that would likely be discussed endlessly are as follows:

- In many jurisdictions (e.g., India), the wife is presumed to have given unconditional consent for sexual intercourse to her husband at the time of marriage. Thus, marital rape is not possible in such jurisdictions. Sexual intercourse with an unconscious wife is thus legally permissible. Is it ethically permissible, too?
- A wife can clearly will her property to her husband after her death. Can she will her body to her husband for necrophilic sexual intercourse? Is her body not her property? She can certainly will her organs (e.g., her heart) to her husband, both legally and ethically. Suppose she wills that her vagina could be taken out and used by the husband for sex later? Is it ethically or legally correct?

Postmortem Sperm Procurement for Impregnation—Is It Necrophilia?

Postmortem sperm retrieval was first reported in 1980 by **Cappy Rothman,**[40] in a case involving a 30-year-old man who became brain dead following a motor vehicle accident and whose family requested sperm preservation. With the introduction of **intracytoplasmic sperm injection** (ICSI) in

1992,[41] floodgates of several confounding legal problems were opened, especially as many widows began requesting harvesting of seminal fluid of their dead husbands, so they could be impregnated. It has been argued that such impregnation may amount to necrophilia, especially as many legal statutes refer to necrophilia as "sexual contact with a dead body." However, having an erotic interest in a dead body and wanting to be impregnated by seminal fluid from a dead husband are two completely different activities. While the former is clearly necrophilia, the latter may not be termed necrophilia, as there is no erotic interest in the dead body.[42] The widow is merely interested in having a baby by being impregnated with the sperm of her recently deceased husband.

References

1. Criminal Code of Western Australia. Section 214 amended by No. 70 of 1988 s. 25; No. 51 of 1992 s. 16(2).
2. Section 139, Criminal Code Act 1924 (No. 69 of 1924).
3. Section 34B, Crimes Act 1958 (No. 6231 of 1958).
4. Section 182, Criminal Code of Canada (R.S., 1985, c. C-46).
5. *Nécrophilie* [in French]. Available from http://fr.wikipedia.org/wiki/N%C3%A9crophilie. Retrieved May 25, 2007.
6. Section 168, German Criminal Code (Strafgesetzbuch, StGB) as promulgated on November 13, 1998 (Federal Law Gazette I, p. 945, p. 3322).
7. Bauer M, Tatschner T, Patzelt D. Digital imaging of the dissection and sexual abuse of a corpse—an exceptional case of necrophilia. *Leg Med (Tokyo)*. 2007 May;**9(3)**:143–146.
8. Section 211, German Criminal Code (Strafgesetzbuch, StGB) as promulgated on November 13, 1998 (Federal Law Gazette I, p. 945, p. 3322).
9. The Indian Penal Code (Act No. 45 of 1860) [6th October, 1860].
10. Criminal Law (Sexual Offences and Related Matters) Amendment Act, 2007 (No. 32 of 2007), of the Republic of South Africa; effective December 16, 2007.
11. Sexual Offences Act 2003 of UK [November 20, 2003].
12. Murray AD. The reclassification of extreme pornographic images. *Modern Law Review*. 2009 Jan;**72(1)**:73–90.
13. Schwartz LB. Morals offenses and the Model Penal Code. *Columbia Law Review*. 1963;**63(4)**:669–686.
14. Posner RA, Silbaugh KB. *A Guide to America's Sex Laws*. The University of Chicago Press, Chicago, 1996, chap. 15.
15. ALA. CODE § 13A-11-13 (enacted 1977).
16. ALA. CODE § 13A-7-23.1 (enacted 1980).
17. ALA. CODE § 13A-5-6 (enacted 1977).
18. ALA. CODE § 13A-5-11 (enacted 1977).
19. ALASKA STAT. § 11.61.130 (enacted 1978).
20. ARK. CODE ANN. § 5-60-101 (enacted 1975).
21. California Codes: Health and Safety Code, § 7052.
22. Colo. Rev. Stat. § 18-13-101 (enacted 1971).

23. CONN. GEN. STAT. ANN. § 53A-73A (enacted 1975).
24. Del. Code Ann. Tit 11, ch. 5 § 1332 (enacted 1953).
25. Del. Code Ann. Tit 11, ch. 42 § 4206 (enacted 1953).
26. GA. CODE ANN. § 16.6.7 (enacted 1977).
27. Haw. Rev. Stat. §711-1108 (enacted 1972).
28. Iowa Code Ann. § 709.18 (enacted 1976).
29. Ky. Rev. Stat. Ann.. § 525.120 (Amended 2002 Ky. Acts ch. 276, sec. 8, effective July 15, 2002. Amended 2000 Ky. Acts ch. 490, sec. 1, effective July 14, 2000. Created 1974 Ky. Acts ch. 406, sec. 222, effective January 1, 1975.).
30. Mich Comp. Laws § 750.160 (enacted 1970).
31. 18 PA. Cons. Stat. Ann. § 5510 (enacted 1972).
32. Wis. Stat. Ann. § 940.225 (enacted 1987).
33. *State v. Grunke, 2008 WI 82, Wis. 2d, 752 N.W.2d 769.*
34. Foley RJ. Court: Wisconsin law bans sex with dead bodies. *The Associated Press State & Local Wire.* July 9, 2008, Wednesday.
35. McKearn S. Dead sexy: an essay on the ethics of necrophilia. *Anil Aggrawal's Internet Journal of Forensic Medicine and Toxicology* [serial online], 2008; Vol. 9, No. 2 (July–December 2008): [about 15 pp]. Available from http://www.geradts.com/anil/ij/vol_009_no_002/papers/paper002.html. Published July 1, 2008. Accessed January 11, 2010.
36. Warren MA. On the moral and legal status of abortion, in *Ethics in Practice: An Anthology*. Ed., H LaFollette. Blackwell, Malden, MA, 2002, p. 76.
37. Jousset N, Gaudin A, Mauillon D, Penneau M, Rougé-Maillart C. Organ donation in France: legislation, epidemiology and ethical comments. *Med Sci Law.* 2009 Jul;**49(3)**:191–199.
38. Jafarey AM, Moazam F. Presumed consent: a problematic concept. *Indian J Med Ethics.* 2009 Jul–Sep;**6(3)**:153–154.
39. Audi R (Ed.). *The Cambridge Dictionary of Philosophy*, 2nd ed. Cambridge University Press, Cambridge, 1999.
40. Rothman CM. A method for obtaining viable sperm in the postmortem state. *Fertil Steril.* 1980 Nov;**34(5)**:512.
41. Palermo G, Joris H, Devroey P, Van Steirteghem AC. Pregnancies after intracytoplasmic injection of single spermatozoon into an oocyte. *Lancet.* 1992 Jul 4;**340(8810)**:17–18.
42. Kerr SM. Post-mortem sperm procurement: is it legal? *DePaul Health Care Law.* 1999;**3**:39–77.

Expert Testimony in Necrophilia Cases

8

In cases of necrophilia, expert testimony of several specialists—pathologists, psychologists, psychiatrists, criminologists, scene-of-crime officers, forensic scientists who have examined trace evidence such as blood, hair, and fiber, DNA specialists, and so on—would be needed in courts for a successful prosecution. A very good investigation coupled with a fumbling testimony can spoil the case for the prosecution. Following some general principles can save a lot of unnecessary embarrassment for the expert.

It is important to realize that the expert witness provides knowledge and background to the judge, jurors, and advocates.

Who Is an Expert?

An expert is someone with specialized experience, training, or knowledge who is able to explain something to the jurors that they might not otherwise understand. **Rule 702 of the Federal Rules of Evidence** of the United States, says[1]

> If scientific, technical, or other specialized knowledge will assist the trier of fact to understand the evidence or to determine a fact in issue, a witness qualified as an expert by knowledge, skill, experience, training, or education may testify thereto in the form of an opinion or otherwise, if (1) the testimony is based upon sufficient facts or data, (2) the testimony is the product of reliable principles and methods, and (3) the witness has applied the principles and methods reliably to the facts of the case.

For instance, it may not be possible for a police officer to determine that the dead body that he recovered from the basement of the accused was really subjected to necrophilic activities. It is for the forensic pathologist to examine the body and see if there are any postmortem genital injuries. It is his specialized knowledge that assists the judge and jury to understand the nature of crime correctly, and come to the right conclusion.

Most other jurisdictions echo almost the same definition for an expert. Section 45 ("Opinion of experts") of the **Indian Evidence Act**[2] states,

> When the Court has to form an opinion upon a point of foreign law or of science or art, or as to identity of handwriting [or finger impressions], the

> opinions upon that point of persons specially skilled in such foreign law, science or art, [or in questions as to identity of handwriting] [or finger impressions] are relevant facts.
>
> Such persons are called experts.

Insanity Defense Taken by Necrophiles

Insanity defense, or NGRI (Not Guilty by Reason of Insanity), comes as a rather natural defense for necrophiles. It does not take much to convince a jury that a person who commits sexual intercourse with a dead body, perhaps mutilates it postmortem and eats its flesh, is insane. The psychologist's job in such cases is to explain to the jurors the limits of legal insanity, and why such a defense should not hold. As far as the offender is concerned, the following line of reasoning by him can very well prove that every offender is insane and thus entitled to an insanity defense. This rather specious line of reasoning is as follows:

> All sane persons must behave normally → If a person behaves abnormally (i.e., commits an offense), he is not normal → Implies he is not sane → He is insane → He is entitled to insanity defense.

When necrophile **John Christie**'s trial started on June 22, 1953, his lawyers thought that his only possible defense was insanity. The bodies of six females had been discovered in his flat at 10 Rillington Place, London, on March 24. It was decided that if they could prove Christie killed *more* females, he would appear more insane to the jury. Thus, paradoxically, their effort was to prove that Christie killed more females than the number of bodies found at his flat. When he was consulted about his opinion on this line of defense, he came out with his now famous quote: "the more, the merrier."[3] The plea was not successful.

The flaw in this reasoning is that it does not take into account the legal definition of sanity. Even if—by a great stretch of imagination—one may agree that all offenders are insane, all of them are not entitled to the insanity defense. It is the expert testimony of the psychiatrist that convinces the jury and the judge about the *extent* of insanity and whether it was of such a nature that (according to the law of most jurisdictions) the offender either did not know what he was doing or, if he did know the nature of his act, could not control his behavior *due to his insanity*. In other words, one cannot **put the cart before the horse** and allege insanity by taking into account the actions of the necrophile; instead, to be able to make a successful insanity defense, it must be proved that the necrophile committed the acts *because of his insanity*.

Some Basic Rules for Expert Witnesses

As Far as Possible, Use Lay Language

If the expert witness uses technical language, judges and juries may fail to understand the key aspects of the case. It is thus necessary for the expert to use lay language as much as possible instead of scientific terminology. It must be remembered that judges and jury are lay people, but are very intelligent. They are eager to understand what the expert is saying. They are able to understand the expert's statement better if it is expressed in lay language. For instance, while describing injuries to the neck, it might be a good idea to use the word *windpipe* rather than *trachea*. *Bruise* is a better word than *ecchymosis*. Instead of saying, "I found subconjunctival hemorrhages, which indicate asphyxiation," it might be better to say, "I found pinpoint bleeding spots in the eye, which indicate that the victim was suffocated to death."

Visual Display of Information

"A picture is worth a thousand words." As far as possible, the expert witness should try to use charts, diagrams, pictures, even multimedia if need be to drive a point home to judge and jury.

Do Not Venture into the Realm of Common Knowledge

In cases involving necrophilia, it may be very tempting for the expert to emotionalize the issue in order to impress the jurors. Emotionalizing may be easy given the highly bizarre acts performed by the necrophile, but the expert should refrain from this.

In one case in which the victim was tortured and bound before the offenders killed him (a situation that commonly occurs in necrophilia), the forensic pathologist **Dr. Isadore Mihalikis,** while commenting upon the amount of fear instilled in the victim upon binding, testified thus:[4]

> I have no doubt that fear is probably a mild term . . .to have gone through this kind of a confrontation, to have all these things on top of you, to have the binding . . .it is not fear, it is terror with a capital T.

Rejecting Dr. Mihalikis' testimony, the court observed,

> there certainly was no need for an expert to testify to the fear that Mr. Goodman [victim who was bound and killed] felt in his confrontation with Martin and King [offender couple acting in tandem]—the fact that a human being would experience fear and terror as he is brutalized and suffocated is so basic that expert opinion is unnecessary to assist the jury. Therefore, this is not a subject upon which expert testimony is admissible.

The lesson is that the expert should not venture into the realm of common knowledge—knowledge that the common man in the jury ordinarily understands. If the expert does that—perhaps to emotionalize the issue—not only will that part of his testimony not be admitted, but he can even cause doubt about the rest of his testimony, which may indeed be concerned with science.

Several court judgments have clarified that "Expert testimony is permitted as an aid to the jury when the subject matter is distinctly related to a science, skill, or occupation beyond the knowledge or experience of the average layman."[5] Where the issue involves a matter of common knowledge, expert testimony is inadmissible.[6] In yet another case, the court observed, "Expert testimony is inadmissible when the matter can be described to the jury and the condition evaluated by them without the assistance of one claiming to possess special knowledge upon the subject."[7]

The following two cases illustrate this principle very well, the second being very much akin to necrophilia, because it involves tying, suffocating, and killing the victim.

Collins v. Zediker, 218 A.2D 776 (PA, 1966)

The case concerned one **Mrs. Catharine Collins,** who was crossing an 18-foot-wide road from the western to the eastern side. She was about two-thirds of the way to her goal when an automobile traveling in a northward direction struck her.

The defense called an engineer, William P. Greenough, who testified that a person walking at a slow rate would take 6 seconds to advance 18 feet, 5 seconds at a moderate rate, and 4 seconds at a fast rate. He also testified that if the defendant's automobile was moving at 50 miles per hour, it would take 13.3 seconds to cover the unobstructed clear vision south of the plaintiff. Thus, clearly Mrs. Collins was at fault, as she could not clear the road even in 13.3 seconds, although even if she had moved with a slow pace, she would have taken only 6 seconds.

At first the argument sounds convincing, and indeed the trial court passed a judgment in favor of the defendants based on this testimony. However, on appeal, the appellate court rejected his testimony observing,

> No experience could be more ordinary and within the range of a jury's comprehension than the speed of a walker. Everybody walks. Every normal person has a pair of legs. Not every person, however, owns an automobile, and even if one does, he may not be able to calculate with accuracy the distance an automobile travels moving at a certain velocity. . . . Allowing expert testimony in the circumstances here related on the speed of walking was as much error as if the judge had allowed expert testimony on the speed with which the average person consumes a hamburger sandwich, wraps spaghetti around his fork or drinks a glass of California wine.

Clearly expert testimony does not work in areas of ordinary knowledge and understanding.

Commonwealth of Pennsylvania v. Carolyn Ann King (1998)

Parts of this case were mentioned at the beginning of this section. On September 15, 1993, **Bradley A. Martin,** who was serving a sentence at the Lebanon County Correctional Facility as the result of a parole violation, obtained a 2-hour visitation pass and left the prison. He met **Carolyn Ann King,** with whom he was romantically involved, and failed to return to prison as required. Instead, the two traveled to Palmyra, Pennsylvania, where they called upon **Guy Goodman,** 74, with whom Martin was acquainted. Mr. Goodman had written, telephoned, and visited Martin in prison, identifying himself as Martin's friend. Soon after their arrival at Goodman's home, Martin hit Goodman over the head with a vase (taken from the hallway). The couple then bound Goodman's wrists, ankles, and neck, wrapped a bathrobe around Goodman's head, placed a plastic bag over it, sealed the bag with duct tape, and wrapped a bedspread over the bag. Finally, they carried Goodman into the basement, tying him more securely. Goodman suffocated to death. The couple then stole Mr. Goodman's checkbook and credit card and drove away in his car. They used his checks and credit card to pay their expenses. They were ultimately apprehended in Arizona.

In this case forensic pathologist **Dr. Isadore Mihalikis** testified. His testimony encroached upon several areas that are commonly understood by a lay person and was thus excluded from the record. For example, Dr. Mihalikis stated that Goodman would have experienced terror because of the physical limitations and the resulting impossibility of freeing himself. On further questioning, Dr. Mihalikis went on to describe the physical sensations that Goodman would have experienced during suffocation, noting that there would have been a period of terror when he realized his impending death. In response to further questions concerning what Goodman experienced while he suffocated, Dr. Mihalikis reiterated that the altercation, the binding, and the wrappings were all "very, in fact extremely, terrorizing," and that Goodman experienced not so much actual pain, but terror because he was not getting enough oxygen and would eventually run out of air and die. Mihalikis stated further, "That's the kind of terror. He knows that if he doesn't get free, he's going to die."

Based on these statements, the jury in a lower court found both Carolyn King and Bradley Martin guilty of first-degree murder and related offenses. King and Martin appealed in the Supreme Court of Pennsylvania contending that the trial court erred in permitting the jury to allow Dr. Mihalikis's testimony concerning Mr. Goodman's emotional state at the time of the homicide, and that certain statements made by the pathologist were inflammatory and prejudicial.

On its part, the Commonwealth asserted that Dr. Mihalikis's testimony, if not admissible as expert testimony, could at least be admissible as lay opinion testimony. Rejecting this argument, the court said, "Dr. Mihalikis was presented by the Commonwealth as an expert witness. The Commonwealth obviously intended for the jury to view his testimony as being cloaked with the knowledge and skill possessed by persons in his areas of expertise."

The Commonwealth also asserted that if the admission of Dr. Mihalikis's testimony was error, such error was harmless for the very reason that the testimony was not properly admitted, namely, that the pathologist's commentary merely reflected the jury's existing, common understanding concerning Mr. Goodman's mental state at the time of the killing. However, the court rejected this argument, too, stating,

> improper expert testimony may place undue emphasis upon common inferences and explanations. Jurors are humans and are impressed by scientific talk even though, upon profound reflection, they could realize that in the particular field under discussion they are as much at home as the scientist. Here, particularly given the extensive focus of the district attorney upon Dr. Mihalikis' assessment concerning Goodman's mental state, we cannot conclude that the trial court's error in permitting the testimony was harmless to the jury's determination of the aggravating circumstance of torture. Accordingly, the trial court erred in permitting the jury to consider this aggravator in its penalty determination.

Proving Intent through Expert Testimony

In necrophilia testimonies, frequently the pathologist is faced with determining whether there was intent on the part of offender to kill his victim. Such a situation arose in the trial of **Graham Coutts.**[8] On **March 14, 2003,** Coutts killed a 31-year-old music teacher, **Jane Longhurst,** and kept her body in his possession for more than a month, presumably for necrophilic activities. (For details of his case, please see Chapter 5, "Case Studies.") At his trial the prosecution asserted that he had killed Longhurst for necrophilic activities, while Coutts in his defense maintained that he engaged in consensual asphyxial sex with Longhurst and that she died accidentally. The question was to prove whether he did in fact murder Longhurst or it was an accident.

During ordinary **strangulation** (not consensual asphyxial sex), the victim usually dies in a matter of 2–3 minutes. The death is by **stoppage of vascular supply to brain** or by **blockage of oxygen supply to lungs,** or both. In all cases, the victim dies in 2–3 minutes, and if there is another person around, he can usually administer help and also call for additional help.

However, during manipulation of the neck, as happens during "breath control play," carotid receptors may get stimulated, and the victim may die within 1–2 seconds by a completely different mechanism—**vagal inhibition.** If death occurs by vagal inhibition, even if a helping hand is around, nothing much can be done, simply because there is not enough time.

In Coutts case, if the defense could prove that death was caused by vagal inhibition, they could in effect prove that there was no *mens rea* on the part of Coutts, as death occurred immediately, and Coutts could not call for help. However, the prosecution's case was that the death occurred because of **stoppage of vascular supply to brain** or by **blockage of oxygen supply to lungs,** which causes death in 2–3 minutes. This in effect meant that the death was not an accident, and Coutts could certainly call for help during the time it took Longhurst to die. Forensic pathologists **Vesna Djurovic,** appearing for prosecution, and **Richard Shepherd,** appearing for the defense, agreed that the cause of the deceased's death was compression of her neck by the ligature. However, they disagreed on the most likely mechanism. **Djurovic** stated that vascular strangulation or respiratory strangulation was the most likely mechanism, and considered vagal inhibition to be less likely. This effectively meant that Coutts would have known something was wrong up to 2–3 minutes before Miss Longhurst died during the alleged breath control play. According to her, **Longhurst** could have been unconscious within 8 to 10 seconds and would probably have been bleeding from her nose and mouth and could also have made choking noises—signs enough to have alerted Coutts of impending danger, and he could have helped her or called for additional help.

Shepherd, however, thought that vagal inhibition was the most likely explanation, giving no time for Coutts to act. Both experts gave reasons for holding their opinions, which were fully explored in evidence before the jury. Table 8.1 summarizes both the prosecution and the defense positions.

Surviving Cross-Examination

The expert must keep in mind that most of the time the purpose of the opposing counsel is to prove that the expert is biased, dishonest, ignorant, or does not keep abreast of research. Thus, he should not say anything that appears to reflect any of these traits.

Dealing with Prior Statements

Ideally, the expert must submit his report only when *all* investigation reports have arrived, so that he can make an overall assessment of injuries, cause of death, and so on. Sometimes this is not possible, especially as toxicology reports take some time to be processed. In such cases, relevant opinions may be kept pending.

Table 8.1 Positions Adopted by the Prosecution and Defense in Graham Coutts' Trial

Side	Expert Pathologist Appearing for	Mechanism of Death Cited	Death Occurred in	Help Could Be Provided by Accused	*Mens Rea*
Prosecution	Vesna Djurovic	Stoppage of vascular supply to brain or by blockage of oxygen supply to lungs	2–3 minutes	Yes	Present. Help was not provided. Indicates the accused wanted to kill victim.
Defense	Richard Shepherd	Vagal inhibition	1–2 seconds	No	Absent. Help could not be provided in such a short time. Death was accidental.

If reports have been submitted for some reason without referring to all relevant reports, a tricky situation may arise if new facts emerge, in light of which the expert has to change his earlier stated position. The situation may be worse if the doctor has tendered the earlier opinion in writing and it has been submitted to the court. In such circumstances, if the earlier opinion favors the defense (or sometimes simply tries to impress upon the court that the expert is unreliable), it will always try to insist that the doctor was speaking a lie the second time (when he changed his earlier stated position).

Having made one mistake, many experts may like to stick to their earlier position, even if that is untenable in the light of new facts, as they may be afraid of uncomfortable consequences. This is likely to do more harm than good. Sticking to a wrong fact may spiral the expert into agreeing to more facts that he knows to be not true. The **best practice** is to **immediately state the new position** and also why this new position emerged. It must be remembered that while in science truth is absolute, in the court truth is merely absence of deceit. In the courtroom, a witness is perceived to lie only when he has the intent to deceive the court. In one case, the expert witness stated in his autopsy report that some bite marks on the breast were antemortem in nature. The pathologist had not referred to the histopathology reports. When the histopathology slides were examined, his earlier position became untenable, and he had to change his opinion (Testimony in Court 8.1).

TESTIMONY IN COURT 8.1
DEALING WITH PRIOR STATEMENTS

Q: Doctor, you stated in your report that the bite marks on the breasts were antemortem in nature, right?

A: Yes.

Q: Now you are stating in the court that the bite marks were postmortem in nature, and my client was in fact a necrophile, right?

A: Yes.

Q: So you are surely lying now?

A: No, I am not.

Q: How is it possible you are not lying now, when what you are stating now is exactly opposite to what you said earlier?

A: Because at the time I submitted my report, *I believed the bite marks were antemortem.*

Q: And, pray, what made you change your opinion now in the court?

A: After I submitted the report, I got access to histopathological slides of the bite marks. They did not show any vital reaction.

Q: What do you mean by that?

A: There are certain cells in the body called white blood cells, or WBCs or leukocytes. Their function is to look out for injuries and immediately reach out there to repair it. So if an injury is made during life, one would expect a concentration of leukocytes there. This is known as *leukocyte migration.* This can only be seen under a microscope. It took me some time to prepare histopathological slides because our machine was out of order. When I finally did get to look at the slides under the microscope, I discovered there was *no leukocytic migration.* Thus I am now of the opinion that the bite marks were postmortem in nature.

In this case, the expert demonstrates an awareness of courtroom standards for evaluating truth, and thus avoided the trap set up by the defense counsel.

SIDEBAR 8.1 When Donald Teare Changed His Opinion in a Case Involving Necrophilia

Donald Teare (1911–1979) was one of the most respectable forensic pathologists of Britain in his time. Teare, **Francis Camps,** and **Keith Simpson** were referred to by the police and the media as **The Three Musketeers**. He conducted the postmortem examination of the dead body of Beryl Evans, 19, wife of Timothy Evans. Her body had been discovered in December 1949 from the wash-house of 10 Rillington Place, London, where the Evans couple lived as tenants. She was 4 months pregnant at the time. In his autopsy, Teare noted two marks on the posterior wall of the vagina: an **old scar** and a **small bruise** near it. Teare testified at a magistrate's court that the bruise could have been caused by an attempt at forced intercourse or in a struggle.[3]

Later he learned that Mrs. Evans did not want the pregnancy. She already had a young daughter and the family income was not sufficient to sustain more children. Some evidence emerged indicating that she may have tried an abortion at home, which was unlawful in those days. Either she tried it herself, or **John Christie**, a co-tenant, helped her. In the light of new facts emerging, Donald Teare opined that the bruise could have been a self-inflicted injury caused by a syringe that Mrs. Evans tried to introduce in her vaginal canal in order to induce an abortion.[3]

Despite this changed opinion, there was no diminution in the respect he commanded, because each time he gave the opinion—although contrasting in nature—according to the evidence available at the time, Teare genuinely believed he was right. Ironically, later evidence emerged (discovery of six bodies from Christie's flat, more than 3 years later, on March 24, 1953) that indicated that the bruises could have been produced because of necrophilic activities of **John Christie**.

Corroborate Your Statements with Hard Scientific Facts

The opposing counsel or jury may not be intimidated or impressed merely by the weight of authority of the expert witness—however well respected in the field he may be. Thus, all statements made by the expert should be backed by scientific corroboration. In one case where the body of a victim was found in the basement of a necrophile, the cross-examination went as described in Testimony in Court 8.2.

TESTIMONY IN COURT 8.2
CORROBORATING STATEMENTS WITH SCIENCE

Q: Doctor, you stated in your report that the accused most likely engaged in postmortem sex with the victim. Is that correct?

A: Yes.

Q: How did you arrive at that conclusion?

A: Because I found spermatozoa in the vaginal canal.

Q: Doctor, if this person had engaged in consensual sex with this woman during life, would spermatozoa still be found in the vaginal canal?

A: Yes.

Q: Then how can you say that my client engaged in postmortem sex? Certainly this is your personal opinion.

A: No, the body was in an advanced stage of putrefaction, indicating the victim had been dead at least a week. I found motile spermatozoa in the vaginal canal. Spermatozoa remain motile in the vaginal canal for at most 24 hours. Thus, I arrived at the conclusion that the accused must have engaged in postmortem sex with the victim.

Don't Be Afraid of Countering Another Expert

If the expert witness knows that another expert has stated differently in the same case, and his own opinion is different, he should not be too anxious about it. As long as the expert can explain his own findings, it is the job of the other expert to explain his. Surprisingly, sometimes even both can be right! In **John Christie**'s case, the postmortem examination of **Mrs. Beryl Evans,** 19, and her 14-month-old daughter **Geraldine Evans** was done by **Donald Teare** in December 1949. He had found evidence of strangulation by ligature, but there was no mention of pink teeth.[9] When Christie was arrested in March 1953, it became necessary to exhume these bodies to find out if he really had committed their murders. (Another man, **Timothy Evans,** the husband of Beryl, had already been executed for the double crime on March 9, 1950. Christie wanted to take the insanity defense, and it was the opinion of his defense team that if more killings could be ascribed to Christie, his case of proving insanity could be that much simpler. Only an insane man would commit that many murders!)

The bodies of Mrs. Evans and Geraldine were exhumed on May 18, 1953 (after having been in the grave for more than 3 years), and the second postmortem was done jointly by Francis Camps, Donald Teare, and Keith Simpson. Simpson had been engaged by Christie's defense team and he discovered that the crowns of Mrs. Evans's teeth were cherry-pink. (Gassing by carbon monoxide was the usual *modus operandi* of Christie, and if CO poisoning could be proved, the defense's task would have been fulfilled.) Simpson knew that Donald Teare, who had conducted the postmortem examination earlier, had not mentioned pink teeth. He also knew that such pink teeth are a normal postmortem phenomenon, and the pinkness could have been a result of postmortem change, but since he was there *to prove* carbon monoxide poisoning (which also gives rise to pink teeth), he immediately took the teeth for analysis.[3] He also discovered that the anterior surfaces of both thighs of Mrs. Evans were cherry pink—this was not mentioned in Teare's earlier report—and he immediately told Camps, who was in charge of the autopsy, that he wanted specimens of the thigh tissue for carbon monoxide analysis.[3] **Donald Teare,** on his part, quite unflustered, told Simpson, "Yes, of course I'd like you to do that."[3]

Of course these discussions occurred in the postmortem room, but the same should be possible in the courtroom, too. As for the pink thigh tissue and pink teeth, none revealed carbon monoxide.[3]

If Serving as a Defense Witness

There may be occasions when the psychiatrist deposes on the side of the defense (i.e., defending the alleged necrophile). If the necrophilic acts have been proved beyond any doubt by the prosecution, the only good way to defend the necrophile is to try to **push the insanity defense.** Given the extraordinarily abnormal nature of necrophilic acts, the courts may not find it difficult to accept that a person who commits sexual acts with a dead body may indeed be insane. **Bartholomew and colleagues**[10] describe a case of homosexual necrophilia, where a 47-year-old necrophile (*R v. Isaacs*) killed a 9-year-old boy and had anal intercourse with his dead body. (For details of this case, please see Chapter 3, "Classification," under the heading "Anal Necrophilia.") In this case, the very act of killing a small and defenseless boy, burying his body, returning 15 hours later to the site of crime, and having anal intercourse with the dead body appeared so bizarre that one would not find it difficult to believe that the perpetrator was insane. Three psychiatrists and a clinical psychologist were called by the defense to prove the accused was insane. When asked about the likely mental state of a man capable of behaving in a necrophilic manner, the first psychiatrist answered,

> To carry out an act like that, and also in the circumstances which you have hinted at to me, indicates an extremely severe disintegration of control and the expression of very primitive impulses. It involves in essence, I suppose you could say, a break with reality. And the term *psychotic* might be used.

The second psychiatrist, when asked about the necrophilic behavior of the accused, answered,

> I think that such an action, by whatever standards you want to judge it, is evidence of a very great degree of mental derangement. I think that if it occurred within a short time of death of this boy, it would be very strong evidence of his psychotic state at the time of the killing. . . . I think the act occurring 12 hours or more later is indicative of even more disturbed behavior than it would have been if it had occurred immediately after death. On the other hand, it does not have the same compelling evidence in relationship in time of the patient's condition at the time of the killing, because it is 12 hours later.

The third psychiatrist opined,

> This sort of conduct or action supports me in my view that he is a psychotic person; that is, a person who is suffering from a mental disease or defect to such an extent that they could be considered to be insane. It is my experience and my knowledge—certainly from the literature—that this sort of thing occurs, fortunately very rarely; but I have never seen or known of this sort of act being performed by a person who could be considered to be sane. It is the act of, in lay terms, a mad person in my view—the act of having sexual congress with a dead body . . . I think that if it had occurred at any relevant time

> after the decease of the individual, I still hold to what I said, that my view is that this is the act of a psychotic or mad person.

These opinions tend to impress upon the court that the necrophilic act is so deranged that the very act of its having been committed by someone tends to prove the insanity of the perpetrator. In fact, this question was asked of the third psychiatrist after his testimony was over (Testimony in Court 8.3).

TESTIMONY IN COURT 8.3
DOES A NECROPHILIAC ACT BY ITSELF PROVE INSANITY OF THE PERPETRATOR?

Q: Every person who buggers a dead body—every necrophiliac in that sense—you say, is legally insane?

A: If you like to put it in those terms, yes. I think what I said was, I regard this as an act of a psychotic or, in lay terms, a mad person. My reading of the literature indicates that this is an opinion shared by others.

Q: Would you elaborate this further please?

A: Such persons (necrophiles) know what they are doing, but do not appreciate that such acts are wrong. I have heard of mortuary attendants indulging in such behavior. It is my view that they are all *legally insane* at the time of the relevant act.

These sound quite forceful arguments on the part of the defense. In any other case, they would have certainly affected the judge and the jury. Unfortunately, in this particular case, these failed to rescue the perpetrator, perhaps because the prosecution had proved intent beyond reasonable doubt.

Some Basic Rules for Lawyers

Proving Intent beyond Doubt

In the case of homicidal necrophilia (class IX necrophilia), prosecution would do well to frame questions in such a way that intent to kill is proved beyond any doubt. In the case described by Bartholomew and colleagues,[10] the defense had taken the plea of insanity, and the prosecution had to show a *definite intent* on the part of the accused. Testimony in Court 8.4 demonstrates how the examination by the prosecution went.

TESTIMONY IN COURT 8.4
PROVING INTENT BEYOND DOUBT

Q: When you struck the boy, did you do it on purpose?
A: Yes, of course, I did it to stop him.
Q: Did you intend to kill him?
A: I knew I had to stop him because if he got away and told someone, I would have been in awful trouble.
Q: I put it to you that when you took the boy into the hills you did so with the intention of killing him. Is this right?
A: Yes, I knew I couldn't let him go.
Q: I put it to you that even if he had not tried to escape that you would have killed him anyway. Is this correct?
A: Yes, I would have had to do something to him before daylight as I couldn't do it in daylight.
Q: What do you mean by that?
A: I would have had to kill him before daylight.
Q: Why would you have to kill him before daylight?
A: Because I could not do it in daylight because I would see how small and defenseless he was.

This examination by the prosecution made the task of the defense extremely difficult, even attempting a defense of insanity.

References

1. Rule 702. Testimony by Experts, Federal Rules of Evidence, U.S., enacted 1975.
2. The Indian Evidence Act, 1872 (1 of 1872) [15th March, 1872].
3. Simpson K. *Forty Years of Murder*. Grafton Books, London, 1988, pp. 234–252.
4. *Commonwealth of Pennsylvania, Appellee v. Carolyn Ann King, Appellant*, 105 Capital Appeal Docket, Appeal from the Judgment of Sentence entered on November 30, 1994 in the Court of Common Pleas of Lebanon County, Criminal 93-10898. Argued: February 2, 1998 and also *Commonwealth of Pennsylvania, Appellee v. Bradley A. Martin, Appellant*, 106 Capital Appeal Docket, Appeal from the Judgment of Sentence entered on November 30, 1994 in the Court of Common Pleas of Lebanon County, Criminal 93-10899. Argued: February 2, 1998.
5. Auker, 545 Pa. at 543, 681 A.2d at 1317 (citing *Commonwealth v. O'Searo*, 466 Pa. 224, 229, 352 A.2d 30, 32 (1976)).
6. O'Searo, 466 Pa. at 229, 352 A.2d at 32.
7. *Burton v. Horn and Hardart Baking Co.*, 371 Pa. 60, 88 A.2d 873, 63 A.R.S. 2d 731.

8. *R v. Coutts*, [2006] UKHL 39, [2006] 4 All ER 353, [2007] 1 Cr App Rep 60.
9. Beeley JA, Harvey W. Pink teeth appearing as a post-mortem phenomenon. *J Forensic Sci Soc.* 1973 Oct;**13(4)**:297–305.
10. Bartholomew AA, Milte KL, Galbally F. Homosexual necrophilia. *Med Sci Law.* 1978 Jan;**18(1)**:29–35.

Necrophilia and Abuse of Corpses—A Brief Chronology

Year	Event
5th century BC	Herodotus notes in *The Histories* that the practice of necrophilia among the Egyptians is prevalent, and that in order to discourage this practice, the dead bodies of women were made to putrefy before handing them over to the embalmers.
1827	A Frenchman named Leger mutilated the genitals of a young girl and drank her blood after necrophilia.
1847	Sergeant François Bertrand (1824–1850), a sergeant in the French army, digs up corpses from Montparnasse, a Paris cemetery, to have sex with them. His activities continue for a period of 2 years.
1849	Bertrand shot by the police at Montparnasse Cemetery (March 15). Trial starts (July). Pronounced guilty and convicted on 15 counts. Given a sentence of 1 year.
1850	Bertrand released from prison. Commits suicide soon afterward. In the wake of this case, the Belgian psychiatrist **Joseph Guislain** (1797–1860) gives a lecture during the winter of 1850 in which the word *necrophile* is used for the first time.
1852	Guislain publishes *Leçons Orales sur les Phrénopathies, ou Traité théorique et pratique des maladies mentales. Cours donné à la clinique des établissements d'aliénés à Gand,* in which he publishes a transcription of his 1850 lecture. The word *necrophilia* appears for the first time in print.
1860	Birth of notorious French necrophile **Henri Blot.**
1867	**Frederick Baker** (1838–1867), a clerk of a local solicitor in Alton, Hampshire, kills and mutilates 8-year-old **Fanny Adams.**
1872	Notorious French necrophile **Victor Ardisson** born (September 5).
1886	French necrophile Henri Blot arrested after he exhumed and fornicated with the dead body of a recently buried dancer (March 25).
1888	During a span of 71 days from August 31, 1888 to November 9, 1888, Jack the Ripper—a typical class IXa necrophile—kills and mutilates five prostitutes: Mary Ann "Polly" Nichols (August 31), Annie Chapman (September 8), Elizabeth Stride (September 30), Catherine Eddowes (September 30), and Mary Jane Kelly (November 9).
1900	First version of *International Classification of Diseases* (ICD) appears. Intended to classify only deadly somatic diseases. Behavioral problems such as sexual deviations do not find a place here. The first time that they find a place in ICD is in its 6th edition (ICD-6) in 1948.
1906	Necrophile Edward Theodore Gein born (August 27) in La Crosse, Wisconsin. He was the second child of George and Augusta Gein.

Year	Event
1924	Viennese psychotherapist Wilhelm Stekel coins the term *paraphilia,* from the Greek *para* ("beside") + *philos* ("loving"), which was first used in English in Stekel's translated works.
1927	In *State v. Schmidt,* 163 La 512, a criminal court rules that "sexual intercourse with a dead human body" is not a crime against nature and is permissible in Louisiana.
1946	Theodore Robert "Ted" Bundy, one of the most well known of all necrophiles, born (November 24). His period of activity was between 1973 and 1978.
1948	ICD-6 published by the World Health Organization. Sexual deviation as a general classification introduced for the first time. No subdivisions delineated yet.
1950	**Timothy Evans** hanged for the murders of his 19-year-old wife **Beryl** and his 14-month-old daughter **Geraldine** (March 9). It turned out later that the murders might have been committed by the necrophile **John Christie.** He also may have committed necrophilic acts on the dead body of Beryl.
1952	The first edition of *Diagnostic and Statistical Manual* (DSM-I) published.
1953	From **John Christie**'s house at 10 Rillington Place, Notting Hill, London, remains of six females discovered (March 24). It soon became apparent Christie had engaged in necrophilic activities with all of them.
	Bodies of **Beryl** and **Geraldine** exhumed on the request of Christie's defense team for a repeat postmortem (May 18).
	Christie's trial starts (June 22). Only 23 days later, executed (July 15).
1954	Mary Hogan, 51, disappears from the tavern she managed in Pine Grove, Wisconsin (December 8). Necrophile Ed Gein is a suspect but no charges filed. (Three years later, a shell casing found at the scene of the crime would be matched to a pistol found in Gein's home.)
1957	Necrophile Ed Gein arrested on suspicion of robbery charges relating to a theft at Worden's Hardware store in Plainfield, Wisconsin (November). Later the body of its owner, 58-year-old Bernice Worden, found hanging upside down in his shed.
1958	Ed Gein is brought to trial. However, the court rules him mentally unfit for trial, confining him to Central State Hospital for the Criminally Insane at Waupun, Wisconsin (January 16).
1960	American serial killer, sex offender, and necrophile **Jeffrey Lionel Dahmer** born (May 21).
1964	Winston Moseley (1935–) kills **Annie Mae Johnson** (February 28) and has sex with her dead body. Kills **Kitty Genovese** (March 13), and has sex with her, too, thinking she was dead. In reality she died a little later.
1965	ICD-8 published. Subdivisions of sexual deviation make their appearance for the first time.
1968	DSM-II published. Sexual deviations do not find a major mention. There is just one statement for the entire category, and then just a listing of each sexual deviation.
	Ed Gein trial starts (November 14). Lasts just 1 week. Gein found guilty of first degree murder, but because of his insanity spends the rest of his life in a mental asylum.
	Jerry Brudos strangles **Jan Whitney,** 23, with a postal strap, and has sexual intercourse with her dead body (November 26).

Year	Event
1977	ICD-9 published.
	The state of Georgia (U.S.) passes law to make necrophilia a crime.
1978	**Ted Bundy** enters the Florida State University Chi Omega sorority house at Tallahassee and kills two sleeping women, **Margaret Bowman,** 21, and **Lisa Levy,** 20, within a space of about 15 minutes (January 15). Levy is sexually assaulted, also—possibly after her death. Bundy leaves bite marks on her breast and buttock, making it possible for forensic odontologists to identify him positively.
	Dr. Richard Souviron, a forensic odontologist, states at a forensic seminar that Bundy's teeth matched the bite marks on Lisa's buttock (October 29).
1980	DSM-III published. Psychodynamic view of mental disorders is abandoned and the biomedical model becomes the primary approach, introducing a clear distinction between normal and abnormal. The word *paraphilia* used for the first time in DSM.
1982	**Kenneth Douglas** (1953–), a mortuary attendant at Hamilton County morgue, Ohio, from 1976 to 1992, performs sex act with the dead body of 19-year-old **Karen Range.** She was murdered by **David Joseph Steffen** and was brought to the morgue for autopsy. At autopsy, semen was found on the body of Range, and at the time it was believed that Steffen had raped and killed her. It was only after 26 years that Douglas was caught, because his DNA matched with that of sperm found on Range's body.
	Noted Hong Kong necrophile **Lam Kor-wan** (1955–), sometimes referred to as **The Hong Kong Butcher,** carries out his notorious necrophilic activities on four female victims.
1984	Necrophile **Ed Gein** dies in a mental asylum (July 26).
	Sir Alec Jeffreys discovers a new method to establish identity—DNA profiling (September 10). It became much easier to identify sexual predators if they leave semen on their victims' bodies.
1987	DSM-III-R (revised) published. The term *ego-dystonic homosexuality* dropped from it.
	Jeffreys' DNA profiling methods become commercialized.
1988	**Eli Ulayuk** (1968–), an Inuit from Igloolik, a small community in Nunavut, northern Canada, murders a 23-year-old female in Igloolik in order to have sexual intercourse with her dead body (August). At his trial, he maintains that he changed his mind after killing the victim and did not actually have sexual relations with her body.
1989	**Ted Bundy** executed by electric chair (January 24).
1991	**Jeffrey Dahmer** arrested after one of his would-be victims escaped from his apartment in west Milwaukee and ran outside, where he flagged down a police car (July 22).
1992	**Dahmer**'s trial starts (January 30).
	Eli Ulayuk given life sentence for his 1988 homicide.
1994	DSM-IV published.
	American serial killer, sex offender, and necrophile **Jeffrey Lionel Dahmer** beaten to death in Columbia Correctional Institution by a fellow inmate (November 28).

Year	Event
2000	DSM-IV-TR ("Text Revision" of the DSM-IV) published (July). It remains the most recent version of DSM.
2003	**Graham Coutts** murders school teacher **Jane Longhurst** (March 14). Commits necrophilic acts for 5 weeks before disposing of the body (April 19). Charged with murder (April 28).
2004	**Eli Ulayuk** kills again acting on his necrophilic urge. Kills parole officer **Louise Pargeter** with hammer and commits sexual intercourse with her dead body (October 6).
	Governor **Arnold Schwarzenegger** makes necrophilia officially illegal in California by amending Section 7052 of the Health and Safety Code.
	Graham Coutts convicted of murder (February 3) and sentenced to a life term serving a minimum of 30 years.
2005	14-year-old maid Rimpa Halder went to Moninder Singh Pandher's house (in **Nithari,** a small village on the outskirts of **Noida City,** in **Uttar Pradesh,** near New Delhi) and never returned (February 8). Later her body was found hacked. After this incident, several children started disappearing from the village. It later transpired that they were being killed by Pandher and Koli, who also possibly committed necrophilic acts on them. According to the prosecution, Koli was suffering from necrophilia, and had eaten body parts of his victims.
2006	ICD-9-CM (9th Revision, Clinical Modification), 6th Edition, issued for use beginning October 1, 2006.
	Twins Nicholas and Alexander Grunke, 20, and Dustin Radke, also 20, attempt to steal the dead body of Laura Tennesen, 20, from her grave in St. Charles Cemetery, in Cassville, Wisconsin, so Nicholas could engage in sexual intercourse with the corpse (September 2).
	Payal goes missing after she went to Moninder Singh Pandher's residence (Noida, India) (May 7).
	Pandher arrested by Indian police on the charges of murdering several children, and possibly committing acts of necrophilia on them (December 26). His cook and aide, Surendra Koli, is also arrested (December 27).
2008	In *State v. Grunke*, 2008 WI 82, Wis. 2d, 752 N.W.2d 769, the Wisconsin Supreme Court in a 5–2 decision ruled that § 940.225(7) of the Wisconsin statute does allow prosecution for the sexual assault of a dead body (July 9). Earlier, both the Grant County Circuit Court and the Wisconsin Court of Appeals had ruled that this section applied only when the victim died during the course of rape, and it was impossible to know whether rape was committed on a live or a dead body.
	Kenneth Douglas (1953–), a mortuary attendant at Hamilton County morgue, Ohio, from 1976 to 1992, convicted of Gross Abuse of a Corpse and sentenced to 18 months in prison (September 8).
2009	**Park,** a kitchen utensil installer and a **class V necrophile,** arrested for stealing the urn containing the ashes of South Korean actress **Choi Jin-sil** (1968–2008) (August 25).
2010	**Randy Uro Galvez,** 19, single, a resident of Barangay Boalan, Philippines, exhumes dead bodies of at least six females (including one of a 3-month-old girl) from the cemetery at Barangay Mercedes, Zamboanga, to have sex with them (between Feb and April).

Index

G

H

I

J

K

L

FSC
www.fsc.org
MIX
Papier | Fördert gute Waldnutzung
FSC® C083411

Zeitfracht Medien GmbH
Ferdinand-Jühlke-Straße 7
99095 Erfurt, Deutschland
produktsicherheit@kolibri360.de